How Curious a Land

Jonathan M. Bryant

The Fred W. Morrison Series in Southern Studies

The University of North Carolina Press

Chapel Hill and London

How Curious a Land

Conflict and Change in Greene County,

Georgia, 1850–1885

The paper in this book meets the guidelines for permanence
and durability of the Committee on Production Guidelines for
Book Longevity of the Council on Library Resources.

Library of Congress Cataloging-in-Publication Data

Bryant, Jonathan M.

How curious a land : conflict and change in Greene County,

Georgia, 1850–1885 / by Jonathan M. Bryant.

p.   cm.—(The Fred W. Morrison series in Southern studies)

Includes bibliographical references and index.

ISBN 0-8078-2257-4 (cloth : alk. paper)

1. Greene County (Ga.)—History.   2. Greene County (Ga.)—

Economic conditions.   3. Agriculture—Georgia—Greene

County—History—19th century.

I. Title.   II. Series.

F292.G7B79   1996   95-23506

975.8´612041—dc20   CIP

00 99 98 97 96   5 4 3 2 1

For Miriam, Naomi, Eleanor, and Alexander

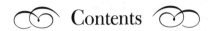 Contents

Acknowledgments

An author usually discusses debts in acknowledgments, and I certainly owe thanks to more people for helping me with this project than space permits me to express. Acknowledgments, however, should also include mention of friendship, the sharing of ideas, even the disputes between colleagues. Most important, acknowledgments should recognize the trust and the support given by others, for without them, these books cannot be written.

Throughout this project the most important support came from my family. Miriam Moore-Bryant inspired me with her understanding and her love. She knows a poorly written passage when she reads it, and her advice and ideas have greatly enriched this work. Naomi, Eleanor, and Alexander not only encouraged me to work on "the book," but also flattered me by writing and illustrating books of their own. My parents, Miriam's parents and her sisters, and many other kin by blood or marriage suspended disbelief and provided financial support, emotional shelter, and plenty of child care. Without my family, I could not have written this book.

Several organizations provided funds for this project. The Phelps-Stokes Fund, the Colonial Dames of Georgia, the University of Georgia, and the University of Baltimore all gave financial support. The Andrew W. Mellon Fellowship in Southern Studies at Emory University allowed me to live a charmed year while I revised this manuscript and did additional research.

Special thanks to Pat Smith and the Greene County Historical Society and Museum, who helped me more than they know. At the Greene County Courthouse Judge Laverne Ogletree, Cindi Christopher, Cindy Baugh, and Ray Marchman all guided me to important records. Marie Boswell, the clerk of court, went out of her way to find materials for me. Mrs. Willie Patience Brown guided me to information on Springfield Baptist Church that I feared was lost. John McMillan gave me access to what remains of Mercer University in Penfield, while Mary Ben Brown proved a jewel, and hospitable besides.

Eli Jackson, who has since died, spent several days guiding me around the county despite his aching eighty-year-old body. He opened doors to the black community I could never have found. A fascinating man, devoted to the cause of justice, Eli Jackson will be missed by me and by Greene County.

I cannot adequately describe the charged atmosphere of creativity and ideas that characterized the graduate program at Georgia in the late 1980s. The particular combination of graduate students and faculty there produced an exciting environment of debate and argument that sharpened all our work. Carolyn Bashaw, Andy Chancy, Stan Deaton, Russ Duncan, Beth Hale, Randy Patton, Chris Phillips, Mary Rollinson, Mark Schultz, Jenny Lund-Smith, Wally Warren, and Brian Wills all created a contentious yet supportive world in which our ideas grew. Glenn Eskew's home served as the locus for this group, while Glenn himself played the roles of facilitator, inquisitor, and social director. Of course, I graciously absolve all these persons of any errors in this book.

Mike Belknap, Jean Friedman, Eugene Genovese, Peter Hoffer, Will Holmes, John Inscoe, Claudia Knott, Lester Stephens, and Ben Wall at the University of Georgia represent the best of what faculty can be. At Emory, Dan Carter and Jim Roark shared their ideas and questions about the manuscript with me and gave me their friendship as well. Dan Crofts at Trenton State College gave me much needed advice and moral support. Lewis Bateman at the University of North Carolina Press has shown me that an editor can be a friend and an adviser, while I have just begun to appreciate the professionalism of Ron Maner and Mary Caviness as they helped prepare this book for publication. Finally, my colleagues at the University of Baltimore, especially Cathy Albrecht, John Mayfield, and Jeffrey Sawyer, have been very supportive of my work. My thanks to all.

Three exceptional people gave me gifts that significantly shaped this work. Bud Bartley awakened in me an enthusiasm for history that still drives me today. Emory Thomas gave me the courage to write in my own voice. Bill McFeely gave me his gentle guidance, through which I discovered the humane not just in me but also within an often brutal profession. These three mentors did the most difficult thing, they trusted me, and I hope the result is pleasing.

Ellicott City, Maryland
June 15, 1995

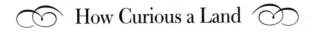 How Curious a Land

How curious a land is this—how full of untold story,
of tragedy and laughter, and the rich legacy of human life.
This is the Black Belt of Georgia.

W. E. B. Du Bois

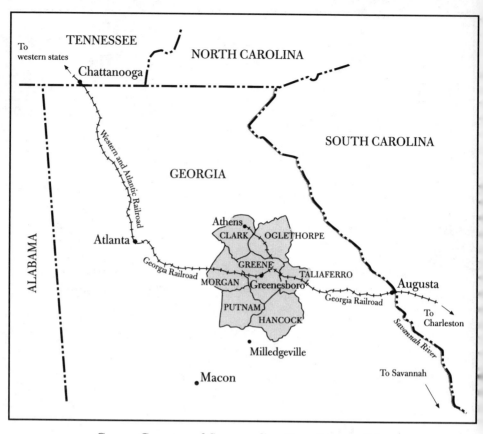

Greene County and Surrounding Counties, ca. 1860

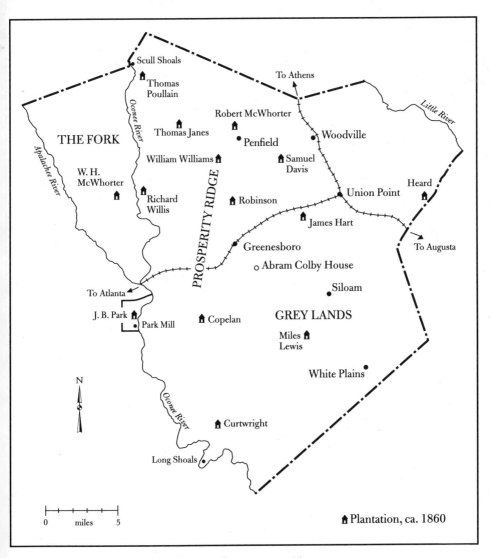

Greene County, ca. 1880

❦ Prologue ❧

Desolation. No other word adequately expresses the feeling of a drive through the redlands of northern Greene County. What once were fertile bottomlands and a rich plantation district known as Prosperity Ridge are now empty lands. Stunted second-growth timber covers most of the region. Occasionally, a pasture or a house trailer hidden in the trees breaks the monotony of the pine-covered landscape. Incredibly, not a single field of cotton appears in what was once one of the richest baronies of the cotton kingdom. The land has changed so that even knowledgeable visitors struggle to discern much of the old world, the world that existed before the people left the land and timber corporations or the U.S. Forest Service bought it.

The present owners are jealous of their rights, as indicated by nicely printed plastic squares posted on trees that detail the legal travails of trespassers. By risking corporate ire, however, an explorer can find many artifacts: rosebushes that once grew in a yard, old wells still full of sweet water, even the foundations of vanished mansions. On cold and cloudy days a sense of despair lingers in the tumbledown tenant cabins, and it can chill an explorer's heart.

Riding in a four-by-four truck down a rough dirt road through scrubby pines, we suddenly spy a small clearing on the left. A family graveyard occupies the clearing, the grass nicely mowed, with fresh flowers laid by one marker. These are the graves of poor people, five members of the Barrow family, the descendants of slaves once owned by David Crenshaw Barrow. Only one grave boasts a headstone; the rest are marked by embossed tin rectangles from the funeral home. The family no longer lives on the land, but they remember it and their ancestors who farmed it, honoring both with their care.

Farther down the road we turn left, cross a creek, and encounter another graveyard. Here there is a large cast-aluminum historical marker detailing the career of Thomas P. Janes. Janes, the son of one of Georgia's richest planters, received the finest education available in the schools of the Northeast, practiced medicine, and managed an enormous plantation with scores of slaves, where he implemented scientific agricultural techniques. After the Civil War Janes prospered as a politician and advocated combining the old plantation system of gang labor with scientific farming methods. From 1874 to 1879 he served as Georgia's first commissioner of agriculture. He died in 1885, a well-known and highly honored man.

The forest has reclaimed his graveyard. The heavy tombstones have been eroded by a century of rain and are tilted at crazy angles by the roots of trees. The granite slab that once covered Janes's own grave has fallen into the washed-out emptiness beneath. He and his world are gone.

The road to telling this story seemed longer and rougher than any I traveled in Greene County, Georgia. Now, however, I can look back and see that it was not as rough as I imagined. There may even have been some logical coherence to the journey. As an indifferent law student at Mercer University in the early 1980s, I had no idea the school itself connected me to Greene County and that one day I would wander through the ruins of Mercer's earlier incarnation at Penfield in Greene County. I knew only that law school was a disappointment and felt that there must be something more to law than torts, secured transactions, and the Internal Revenue Code. This idea that law was something larger gnawed at me, and two years after finishing law school, I entered graduate school, hoping through the study of history to understand more fully law's role in society.

At first, influenced by my legal training, I searched for individual appellate cases that "shaped" or failed to "shape" society in the American South. This approach, an attempt to discover and dissect "great" cases, proved futile. I realized that the paradigms of law school, of classical legal reasoning, offered limited help in understanding the role of law in social and economic change. Concluding that law was merely a reflection of society, I then launched a second project examining legislation enacted to change society, striving to discern why some acts were successful and others failed. This study led me away from a positivistic conception of law, but my socially based theory of "living law" soon seemed just as inadequate a tool for analysis. Far too many examples of law influencing society, of law redirecting peoples' lives, existed for me to feel comfortable with a "living law" approach. So, I turned in new directions.[1]

I wanted to see law in action, law in the midst of people, law shaping and being shaped by individuals and their communities. A focused community study seemed to offer a chance to do these things. Thus this project, based in the empirical paradigms of narrative history, was born. At first I knew only that I wanted to study a community in my native Georgia. I also decided to focus on a time of great social and economic upheaval, the era of Civil War and Reconstruction. Greene County was only

one of a number of counties I identified in my search for a suitable dissertation subject. Like more than a dozen others, Greene County offered
substantial original documents in the state archive, its courthouse had not
burned, and it had a good collection of newspapers from the nineteenth
century. In fact, several counties offered equal or superior resources to
those of Greene County for the project I envisioned—a study of the social, economic, and legal transformations of a cotton plantation community from before the Civil War to the New South.

Ultimately, however, a book led me to Greene County. Arthur Raper's
Tenants of the Almighty, published in 1943 after more than a decade of
work, is not a dispassionate or complete history of the community.
Though useful as a source for the history of nineteenth-century Greene
County, one must approach the book with care. Raper depended far too
much on the research and opinions of Thaddeus Brockett Rice, a local
historian who sometimes reported rumor or wishful thinking as fact. The
shortcomings of his sources, however, did not seem to bother Raper, for
he did not even include footnotes to guide other scholars. Instead, *Tenants* was a polemic written to boost New Deal programs in the South, and
Raper planned for it to reach a broad, popular audience.[2]

Raper, despite his weaknesses as a historian, knew the people of
Greene County. He genuinely cared about them, white and black, racist
and liberal, rich and poor. *Tenants* tells a story about people and the
shapes of their lives, recounted with a gentleness and an understanding
that drew me into the life of the county. "That's the place I want to study,"
I decided, "and those are the people I want to know." I chose Greene
County not because it was unique, or even the best subject available,
but because it "felt" right. So this project was born, the result of a vis-
ceral hunch rather than a cerebral choice. Thankfully, that hunch proved
fortunate.

Join me on some rutted red clay roads for a while, and we will travel
into an unknown country that is also not so far from home. The nar-
row places and the wide, the disappointments and the discoveries, the
muddled and the clear, all reveal the story of a community and its people
struggling with the forces of change. This is a tale about a place called
Greene County and a time not so long ago.

"How different were the planters of years ago," marveled Greenesboro attorney Edward Young in 1885:

> They were their own masters then. If money came rare with them, they had no need of it [for] there was no dread of impending misfortune, no horror of mortgages which lay heavy on their farms. We must contrast their happy lives with ours, and the contrast can not but make us regret we were not one of them.[1]

Although Young romanticized the life of the antebellum planter, he made a point that virtually every contemporary observer agreed with: the South had changed dramatically since the Civil War. In 1885 life moved at a faster pace and was more oriented toward commerce than in 1850, even in a small town like Greenesboro. Yet, despite all the business activity and commercial growth, in terms of per capita wealth and aggregate wealth, the farmers and workers of Greene County were poorer than ever before.

Before the Civil War the white people of Greene County generally enjoyed great prosperity. The average per capita wealth of Greene's free inhabitants in 1860 was about six times greater than the national average. More than 95 percent of Greene's white households in 1860 owned real or personal property. Black slaves, who made up two-thirds of Greene County's population, shared little of this prosperity, but their very persons constituted about 60 percent of the county's wealth. The high price of cotton and the relatively low cost of slave labor produced a half century of dramatic economic growth before 1860, and the white inhabitants flourished.[2]

Then, within a decade, the old ways and the institutions that had proved so profitable vanished. The stress and destruction of war, followed by the social and economic upheaval of emancipation seemed to abruptly end the county's prosperity. By 1870 the per capita wealth of white people in Greene County fell to one-eighth of 1860's level, and half the white households counted by the census that year owned no property at all. Most white inhabitants of the county had no choice but to agree with Henry Burns, editor of the *Greenesboro Herald*, who lamented in early 1871, "We are Poor!"[3]

Burns explained that he made this "mortifying confession" because "there has been no adequate realization of our true condition." In Greene County, Georgia, and across the South, he argued, many people refused to see the changes wrought by Civil War, emancipation, Reconstruction, and the resulting financial chaos. These events had swept away the pre-war prosperity, but most white southerners continued to think and act as if nothing had happened. "Our people are voyaging in bubbles," marveled Burns, "with all sail up and no ballast." He feared that unless white southerners responded quickly to their changed condition, disaster would sweep the South.[4]

Though Burns preferred not to notice, black southerners had responded quickly to their changing world. Emancipation and Reconstruction opened possibilities they could only dream of as slaves. The freedpeople of Greene County aggressively entered politics and against great resistance won control of local and state offices. Black workers in Greene County demanded and won new labor arrangements, which they hoped would afford them greater independence and a chance to accumulate wealth. An astonishingly united community of freedpeople sought to reshape their society so that black people could partake of what they saw as the American promise. In the process, they showed themselves willing to fight and die for their revolution.

Many white southerners fought as well, struggling to contain the changes sweeping their society. Greene County's white leaders willingly used lies, bribery, and terrorism to try to control the county's freedpeople. Over time, however, the county's conservative white leaders discovered that economic pressure and legal manipulation provided a much surer means of control over black workers. Laws and court decisions restructuring sharecropping, tenancy, landlords' liens, and property rights forced most black workers into new forms of dependency.

This legal instrumentalism, however, could not halt all the changes sweeping Greene County. Many of the changes sprang from an ongoing economic transformation that had begun even before the Civil War. This great transformation continued and even accelerated after the war, feeding on the poverty and growing economic dependency of Greene County. Between 1850 and 1885 Greene County changed from a largely self-sufficient agricultural community that produced a surplus for the market to a commercial agricultural society dominated by and dependent upon the larger world market economy. As a result, the people of Greene County underwent a commercialization of their everyday lives.

Not all white people in Greene County chose to voyage in bubbles, ignoring the economic and social changes reshaping their county. Some members of the county's planter families responded by becoming merchants, lawyers, and businessmen. They accomplished the conversion with little difficulty, for they had long participated in the market economy and had the means and the skills necessary for success. The changing economy, however, provided little opportunity for Greene County's small farmers. Market forces bore heavily on these households as the combination of debt and decreasing profit margins on cotton pushed many to the brink of failure. Some families fell over the edge, losing their land and their possessions—and perhaps even their dignity—in the process. Others survived but worried about their children's future as the plight of small farmers in Greene County only continued to worsen.

The freedpeople, meanwhile, struggled to remake their lives, and many hoped to become smallholding farmers independent of their former masters. Sadly, the very model of independent farming they chose became more and more tenuous in the new economy. Only a few succeeded, usually with the help of their former owners. The dream of landownership eluded most black farmers, who then had to settle for sharecropping arrangements or day labor.

Economic revolution also remade power relations in Greene County. During the 1850s planters unquestionably dominated community life. Social affairs and clubs revolved around the concerns of planters, as did financial and educational matters. Planters controlled local politics, and except in the town government of Greensboro, nearly all local officeholders were planters. The growing market economy in Greene County during the 1850s existed largely as an extension of the plantations, and the merchants and lawyers who directed the local market economy clearly deferred to the planters' needs. Smaller farmers in Greene County, some of whom were tenants, stood mostly on the sidelines and took little part in the market economy. Black slaves lay at the bottom of the social heap and usually participated in the market only as chattels.

By the 1880s merchants and lawyers led the community. Though many of these individuals owned large farms and may have come from planter families, they had a commercial orientation and made their living from commerce. Most resided in Greensboro or Union Point, leaving their farms to tenants and sharecroppers. Those planters who tried to continue operations with traditional methods as though nothing had changed usually failed financially and commonly became dependent upon their more progressive brothers or sons.

Meanwhile, small farmers, both white and black, faced tremendous environmental and financial problems. Most usable farmland in the county had been under continuous cultivation since the 1820s, and by the 1870s the soil's productivity in Greene County had declined dramatically. On many farms only heavy applications of fertilizer produced competitive crop yields, and most fertilizer had to be purchased in the market. Farmers also needed credit to rebuild their operations after the Civil War, which forced them to grow cotton. On small farms, growing cotton often meant that farmers displaced food crops, so they lost their traditional self-sufficiency. Small farmers became an integral part of the commercial market economy, producing cotton for the market and buying imported food and fertilizer. Increasingly dependent upon credit, faced with declining soil fertility and the costly necessity of fertilizer, and forced to buy food for their own subsistence, small farmers began to fall into debt and poverty.

By 1885 merchants dominated financial and social affairs in the county while businessmen and lawyers controlled local politics. Those who depended upon farming for their living no longer held the upper hand in Greene County. Some older observers bemoaned this shift of power, for it also entailed a paradigm shift from the antebellum culture of honor to a new, commercially oriented worldview. As Oliver A. McLaughlin of Union Point explained, "We have a new class of men, a new order of things." McLaughlin complained that men in the new order were no longer truthful and instead seemed focused only on making money. "That unwavering confidence between man and man, is sadly wanting," McLaughlin observed, and he found the decline of honor and the rise of a commercial consciousness quite confusing.[5]

McLaughlin remembered the world before the war, when white people enjoyed great prosperity and honor characterized the dealings between men. From that standpoint, he found the world of the 1870s incomprehensible. "Instead of that even, steady progress toward prosperity," McLaughlin worried, "we only see the fitful flashes of better times amid the dark, lowering clouds of adversity." As Greene County fell into increasing dependency on distant markets during the 1870s and 1880s, many observers, both white and black, surely agreed with McLaughlin that the "dark, lowering clouds" meant their society was in decline.[6]

No revolution completely transforms a society. No cultural, social, or economic force carries all before it. From one viewpoint, little changed in

Greene County between 1850 and 1885. In 1850 the community produced cotton in a dependency relationship with the world market. The same was true in 1885. At the level of human lives and experience, however, almost everything changed. The predominant labor relationship shifted from gangs of slaves directed by masters or overseers to families of tenants or sharecroppers directing their own day-to-day labor. Planters dominated politics, the economy, and social life in 1850, but by 1885 lawyers and merchants led the county. These and a host of other changes truly re-constructed Greene County.[7]

The study of a single community offers a consistent vantage point from which to explore these changes and their effects. This approach also emphasizes that the people of that time experienced events within the cultural, social, and economic context of their community. To ignore that context would only limit our comprehension. We also voyage in bubbles and may not be able to take these people on their own terms. We can, however, try to understand what those terms were. Though no more "typical" than any other county in the great plantation belt that stretched across the cotton South, the story of Greene County's transformation allows insight into experiences shared by several million white and black southerners. By trying to understand Greene County during this process of change, we may gain a greater appreciation of their lives and our own.

Land Fresh from the Hand of God

In March 1848 the Greene County Inferior Court accepted Atharates Atkinson's and David Demarest's plans for a new county courthouse. The plan called for the symmetrical Greek Revival building to measure seventy-six feet square. The first story would hold county offices, the second a large, high-ceilinged courtroom, and a third story would accommodate the local lodge of Masons. Four massive Doric columns would front the granite portico at the entrance. As the building rose on a large lot behind the old rock jail in the center of town, the effect became clear: Greene County was building a temple of justice.[1]

The new temple of justice was just one of many civic monuments built in Greene County during the late 1840s and early 1850s. The trend began in 1845, when Demarest built a huge brick Greek Revival chapel for Mercer University in Penfield. A new dormitory followed in 1848, a new science building in 1851, and finally, Mercer's Ciceronian Hall was built in 1852. In Greenesboro the newly established Female College constructed a large two-story classroom building that opened in January 1852. At its dedication the college took as its motto: "That our daughters may be as corner stones polished after the similitude of a palace." These brick monuments to education and justice were intended to last. They stood as symbols of the community that built them, demonstrating that Greene County's elite wished not just to commemorate their wealth, but also to permanently improve their society. Yet within little more than two decades every one of these buildings, save the courthouse, would stand abandoned or in ruins.[2]

Of course, no one could see the future when the people of Greene County gathered in 1849 for a barbecue celebrating the completion of the new courthouse. The party lasted all afternoon, and during it several distinguished lawyers spoke to the crowd about the meaning of the new temple of justice. That evening, despite a local church's recent expulsion of a member for dancing, many of the leading citizens of Greene County attended a ball. Perhaps to ensure things got off to the right start, Nancy Bickers, a woman of impeccable reputation, led the first dance. And well might the elite of Greene County dance, for in the summer of 1849 they were extraordinarily wealthy and secure. Some at the ball might have remembered the founding of the county less than six decades before, when it was undeveloped frontier at the edge of the Creek Nation. These older men and women surely saw in the courthouse confirmation of their community's rise from wilderness to civilization, from a dangerous frontier to a secure agricultural community, from poverty to wealth. Some may have even told their neighbors stories about the early days.[3]

Greene County lies between the Ogeechee and Oconee Rivers of northeast Georgia, part of a region of almost 3,000 square miles known in the eighteenth century as the Oconee lands. The Creek Indians valued this region highly; it served both as superb hunting grounds and as a thirty-mile-wide buffer zone between the homelands of the Lower Creeks to the west and the settlements of the Georgia Colony to the east. In 1782, as the Revolutionary War came to a close, the new State of Georgia summoned the leaders of all Indian tribes within its borders to a conference in Augusta. There, in October, the Cherokees of north Georgia agreed to cede more land to Georgia and to end all hostilities against settlers. The Creeks, however, proved more difficult to deal with. Large numbers of Creeks had sided with the British during the Revolution, and they continued to fight against the colonists. Perhaps more important, the Creeks thought of themselves as an independent nation, not subject in any way to the State of Georgia. Creek leaders simply ignored the summons to Augusta.[4]

In the spring of 1783 the Georgians again summoned the Indians and offered substantial presents to any Creek leaders who would come to Augusta. The leaders of only two of the more than 100 Creek towns responded. These two men enjoyed royal treatment and received many gifts. On May 31, 1783, they signed a treaty giving Georgia the Oconee lands. In response, a council of the entire Creek Nation assembled at Tuckabatchee to disavow the treaty. They also warned Georgians not to attempt to settle the land. The Georgia legislature ignored the protests and began organizing the new lands for settlement. Headright grants of between 200 and 1000 acres of free land drew hundreds of pioneers to the region between the rivers. This invasion set off a war with the Creeks that lasted fourteen years and cost scores of Indians and settlers their lives.[5]

In February 1786, as part an effort to organize the Oconee lands, the Georgia legislature created Greene County. Named for General Nathaniel

Greene, who owned a large plantation in coastal Georgia, the new county occupied almost 1,000 square miles in the heart of the Oconee lands. White settlers already occupied parts of the new county, and a string of private forts protected its western border. In May surveyors chose a well-watered site on Richland Creek near the center of the county and laid out the seat of Greensboro. Pioneer families built a log fort at Greensboro, and a log courthouse soon followed. By 1787 Greensboro had thirty houses, several businesses, and more than 100 inhabitants.[6]

The Creek war raged on as ever more settlers cleared land and planted corn in Greene County. Warriors raided across the Oconee, killing families, burning isolated cabins, and stealing slaves and horses. The settlers' militia retaliated in kind. In November 1787, the Indians struck at the core of the invaders' world. A large Creek war party attacked Greensboro; they killed thirty-one settlers, captured four prisoners, and trapped the rest of Greensboro's inhabitants, including twenty wounded, in the log fort. The Creeks then burned the village, took as many slaves and horses as they could gather, and fled across the Oconee. The settlers' militia pursued the raiders and attacked a small encampment of Creeks, killing twelve of them. Only after the battle did the militiamen learn they had attacked an innocent settlement, not the raiders they pursued.[7]

Similar small battles continued throughout the 1780s and 1790s, but despite the war, settlers continued to pour into the Oconee lands. Greene County's people rebuilt Greensboro, and by 1790, 5,405 white and black pioneers lived in the county. The region simply offered too much, and hundreds of families willingly took the risks of settling the new lands. As one early settler recalled, "those were the days when the land was fresh from the hand of God, the country covered with cane and magnificent forests, the rivers and creeks full of shad and other fish." Living in the midst of abundance, most white settlers farmed, growing food for their families and, if possible, a little tobacco for the market in Augusta. Occasionally, they owned a few black slaves, who helped clear and plant the new lands. On the whole these early settlers had few ties to the outside commercial market economy, maintaining rough self-sufficiency through farming, hunting, and fishing.[8]

In 1793 the Georgia legislature took about half of Greene County's area to create Hancock and Oglethorpe Counties. Despite this reduction in size, by 1800 the county's population reached almost 11,000, one-third of whom were slaves. Then the population began to level off, and in 1810 Greene County had about 12,000 inhabitants, a figure that would change only slightly over the following half century.[9]

The shape of the population, however, changed dramatically from 1800 to 1850. The number of white inhabitants declined rapidly, and the number of black slaves grew. Slaveowning became the key to wealth, as those who owned slaves profited not just from their workers' labor but also from their slaves' procreation. By 1810 almost 50 percent of Greene County's people lived in bondage, though individual slaveownership remained relatively small-scale. More than half the county's taxpayers that year owned slaves, but only 32 of 1,398 taxpayers owned 20 or more slaves. The largest-scale slaveowner held forty-nine people in bondage, the next largest, forty. The average slaveholder owned four slaves and probably worked alongside them on the farm. Ten years later, in the 1820 census, slaves made up a majority of the population. The growing number of slaves reflected the impact of the upland cotton revolution in Greene County. As cotton became more profitable to grow, many landowners purchased more slaves. Others seeking to profit from new land moved into the county along with their slaves. Through cotton the people of Greene County began to feel directly the influence of the larger national and international market system.[10]

Eli Whitney's cotton gin, first used on Nathaniel Greene's Mulberry Grove Plantation near Savannah, mirrored a far more important technological revolution taking place in Great Britain at the same time. Suddenly, great machines driven by water or steam could spin cotton thread and weave cotton cloth more cheaply than armies of individual workers. Cotton cloth, no longer an expensive luxury, began to clothe people, cover tables, and as sails even propelled the great ships bringing more cotton to the factories. The world market demanded more cotton, prices soared, and farmers in Georgia responded. As a staple crop, cotton held great promise. Unlike tobacco it did not require a skilled labor force for gathering, drying, and packing. The quality of the cotton grown in east Georgia equaled that grown anywhere, while the quality of local tobacco remained substandard compared to Virginia's crop. Further, while the market for tobacco remained relatively static, improving industrial methods for the manufacture of cotton cloth meant that the demand for the fiber seemed to grow insatiably. Farmers discovered that enormous profits lay in the white bolls, and they turned to its production in droves. The successful invested their profits in ever more land and more slave laborers. By the 1830s slaves made up almost two-thirds of Greene County's population and produced around 12,000 bales of cotton each year.[11]

The cotton boom made many in Greene County wealthy, and a few men grew enormously rich. Planters Absalom Janes and Dr. Thomas N. Poullain were reputedly two of Georgia's first three cotton millionaires. Most planters understandably used their profits to buy more slaves, and so the growing number of unfree laborers in Greene County represented much of the capital accumulation resulting from cotton production. A few individuals, however, found other ways to invest their profits.

In 1836 Thomas Poullain's cotton mill at Scull Shoals in northwest Greene County began operation. The factory employed about 200 workers and consumed 4,000 bales of cotton each year. John Curtwright and Greene Moore opened a larger factory in the southwest corner of the county at Long Shoals in the late 1830s. They hoped to offset the effects of declining cotton prices following the Panic of 1837 by manufacturing their own and other planters' crops into cloth. The Curtwright factory served as the center of a complete mill-owned community, including both a school and a church connected to the factory building for the edification of the workers. In Greenesboro a group of planters and merchants financed a third, smaller mill that began operation in 1845. This mill, the Greenesboro Manufacturing Company, used steam power so that it could be next to the railroad in Greenesboro, simplifying shipment to market. All three cotton mills used a mix of slave and white laborers and potentially could process about half of Greene County's annual cotton crop. Yarns and cloth from the mills were sold locally and in Augusta, Savannah, Philadelphia, and New York. Although these mills were important and employed several hundred workers in Greene County, their economic impact was small compared to another technological development financed by cotton profits.[12]

In 1833 and 1834 the newly chartered Georgia Railroad began raising capital to lay track from Augusta into Georgia's cotton-producing heartland. Excitement swept through east Georgia, and local offerings of railroad stock in Athens, Eatonton, Greenesboro, and Augusta sold out. Not everyone, however, welcomed this sort of economic development. In Greene County, Gwynn Allison refused to give the railroad a right-of-way across his plantation. When chief engineer J. Edgar Thompson arrived with a survey crew, Allison drove them off his land at gunpoint. Eventually, Allison spent time in jail for contempt while the railroad surveyed his property, but for the rest of his life he refused to touch the railroad's payment for the right-of-way. Allison may have understood the railroad's potential more clearly than his neighbors, for ultimately the railroad transformed Greene County and increased its people's dependency on the world cotton market.[13]

Before the railroad arrived, every fall long wagon trains loaded with cotton inched eastward over truly dismal roads to Augusta. There, rafts or steamboats carried the cotton down the river to factors' warehouses in Savannah. The factors then found buyers for the cotton and eventually shipped it to mills in the northeast or in Europe. Meanwhile, the farmers' wagons returned home loaded with supplies purchased from merchants in Augusta. These supplies were generally luxuries, for virtually every farm or plantation in Greene County produced its own food and other necessities. The cost and difficulty of transporting cotton under these conditions limited production, thus limiting Augusta's business as well.[14]

The Georgia Railroad changed all this. Not only did it prove a great business success, producing substantial profits for its shareholders, it also put control of east Georgia's cotton crop firmly into the hands of Augusta's merchants and factors. In 1838, the year it reached Greenesboro, the railroad carried its first significant shipments of cotton. The 8,000 bales of cotton that traveled to Augusta that year were only a beginning. Cotton planters discovered that they could save much time and expense if they shipped by rail, so the wagon trains began to travel only short distances to depots in Greenesboro, Union Point, or Crawfordville. Each year the railroad carried ever-larger amounts of cotton. In 1849 it transported more than 150,000 bales of cotton to Augusta, and in 1855 shipments topped 200,000 bales. In 1860 Augusta received more than 285,000 bales of cotton worth more than $12 million, though 63,000 bales were through shipments to Charleston and Savannah. About 80 percent of the cotton shipped by the Georgia Railroad passed through factors and merchants in Augusta, and their businesses blossomed.[15]

The railroad also brought new opportunities to Greene County. Many farmers along the route added to their incomes by cutting wood for the locomotives. The new community of Woodville in Greene County took its name from the enormous piles of fuel gathered there for the railroad. More ambitious entrepreneurs made construction contracts with the railroad, and these contracts became the basis for at least two Greene County fortunes. The railroad also gave Greenesboro's merchants the ability to obtain large stocks of goods at very low cost. Local merchants' selection and prices were suddenly very competitive with those of Augusta, and their businesses flourished. As a result, by the 1850s a class of prosperous businessmen dominated the town of Greenesboro.[16]

Most important, the railroad encouraged Greene County's farmers and planters to rely increasingly on cotton production, reinforcing the community's economic dependence on Augusta and the larger world cotton market. Before the railroad existed, the people of Greene County had to feed themselves. Roads were so bad that only a small amount of food could be brought into the county, and a failure to grow sufficient food meant hunger. Some farmers and planters continued to maintain virtual self-sufficiency in food production after the railroad came. A few, like David Terrell and his two sisters, took self-sufficiency to the point of obsession. Emeline Stepney, one of the Terrells' seventy-five slaves, recalled that the plantation was completely self-sustaining. The master and his sisters went so far as to wear only the same plantation-made homespun as the slaves.[17]

In theory, each farm or plantation in Greene County could produce sufficient food for its inhabitants' own use and would then market only surplus production. As late as 1849 the county's farmers produced a considerable surplus of food crops, but during the 1850s that changed. Food production per capita fell by more than 40 percent between 1849 and 1859, and in 1859 Greene County's total food production barely equaled the subsistence needs of the inhabitants of the county. Food production dropped across east Georgia during the same period, and in 1859 more than one-quarter of the region's farms and plantations produced insufficient provisions for their own needs.[18]

Small farms in east Georgia showed the most dramatic change. Over half of those who farmed less than fifty improved acres did not grow enough food for home consumption in 1859. Yet, the same small farmers grew ever-larger cotton crops. The reason was quite simple: cotton, if successful, gave a much greater financial return per acre than corn. The railroad, by facilitating access to market and reducing the problems and cost of transportation, made growing cotton a preferable alternative to growing corn for many farmers. The cash from a cotton crop allowed farmers to obtain things they could never dream of making at home, and for smaller farmers this promise of extra income seemed a chance to get ahead.[19]

Even as the railroad encouraged ever-greater cotton production at the expense of food crops, other factors began to support the change. Year after year farmers planted the same fields with the same crops, and after decades of abuse the fertility of Greene County's soil declined dramatically. The "land fresh from the hand of God" became worn, and farmers struggled to maintain its productiveness. Corn requires more nutrients and nitrogen than cotton, so successive corn crops exhausted the soil more quickly than cotton. Cotton yields on old fields could continue at acceptable levels longer than corn, something Greene County's farmers discovered through experience. The rub lay in farmers' need to grow enough food for subsistence.[20]

The railroad soon provided a ready solution to the farmer's dilemma over growing cotton or corn. During the late 1840s, the Georgia Railroad began to bring cheap food supplies into the cotton belt of east Georgia. Before 1846 the railroad carried negligible shipments of grain into the counties along its route, but as the new Western and Atlantic Railroad tapped the grain-growing regions of northwest Georgia and Tennessee, the Georgia Railroad's shipments of grain increased dramatically. By 1848 the Georgia Railroad carried more than 250,000 bushels of grain into eastern Georgia, and in 1856 shipments surpassed a million bushels. As the Augusta *Daily Chronicle and Sentinel* explained in 1849, the railroad was a "new source of supply" for everyone along its route. Food or animals raised west of the Blue Ridge could be brought directly to markets east of the mountains. Thus, farmers along the railroad's route could earn money by growing cotton and with that money could buy inexpensive imported provisions.[21]

This growing dependence on distant food sources and the increasing acreage devoted to growing cotton worried some in Greene County. Reformers began to call for change in Greene County's methods of agriculture. Rowan H. Ward told the Greene County Agricultural Society in November 1850 that the present system of agriculture threatened to leave only exhausted fields and hungry people. The remedy, he argued, was not in moving west but in a diversification of crops and the production of more food in the county. The following year Judge Garnett Andrews spoke of "the fearful destruction of our soil" and farmers' growing dependency on food from outside of Georgia. He too called on the farmers to protect and nourish the soil, to diversify their crops, and to grow more food for home consumption. These reformers, while devoted to the expansion of the commercial market economy in Greene County, also struggled to ameliorate the effects of that economy on their community. Their program, however, spoke mostly to large farmers and planters, who had the land and the labor available to raise sufficient food. Small farmers could not afford to follow the reformers' methods of diversification and soil conservation and so grew ever more dependent on cotton production.[22]

In 1852, predicting a good corn crop, the editor of the Penfield *Temperance Banner* warned that "our Tennessee friends, who calculate so confidently upon keeping Georgia poor and dependent upon them, had better get rid of their notions and surplus produce at an early day." Bad weather, however, later destroyed that year's corn crop in Greene County, and the *Banner* reported that farmers purchased more corn than ever before from Tennessee. Between 1849 and 1859 the county's corn and hog production declined significantly as farmers focused on growing more cotton and struggled with the declining fertility of the soil. Greene County's increasing dependency on cotton production and imported foodstuffs, especially among smaller farmers, did not bode well for the future.[23]

The transformation of Greene County's local subsistence economy into part of a larger commercial market economy took time. Although the process began with the cotton boom in the early nineteenth century, the greatest changes occurred between 1850 and 1880. By the 1880s the commercial market system dominated Greene County's economy, and the vast majority of Greene County's people supplied their basic needs through commercial exchange rather than subsistence activities. As Adam Smith explained, when "every man thus lives by exchanging; . . . the society itself grows to be what is properly a commercial society."[24]

This process of becoming a commercial society accelerated dramatically in Greene County during the 1850s as farmers produced more cotton to sell for cash and increasingly bought food from sources outside of Greene County. The Civil War slowed this process, not just by creating an attempted return to subsistence agriculture, but by providing a forum for criticism of the market economy. Emancipation and the rise of sharecropping and tenancy, however, gave Greene County the final impetus to produce a fully commercial market society. Examining Greene County's agricultural economy before and after the Civil War reveals a sweeping process of change as the commercial market economy transformed the community and its economy.[25]

During the first half of the nineteenth century, Greene County witnessed other developments as well. At the time the most fertile and prosperous areas of Greene County were the rich bottomlands along the Oconee River and the redlands in the northwestern third of the county. Using money donated by Josiah Penfield, in 1832 the Georgia Baptist Convention bought a plantation in the heart of Greene County's redlands and there began to build Mercer Institute. Mercer operated as an academy until 1837, when a state charter created Mercer University. In 1839 the university and an associated female seminary began operations. The Baptists also created a new town on land owned by the university and named it Penfield. The university and the female seminary soon attracted more than 100 students, and the population of Penfield quickly surpassed 500. The town developed a thriving business district, and two important Georgia newspapers, the *Banner* and the Baptist's *Christian Index*, as well as a literary magazine called *Orion*, were published there. Penfield became the center of Greene County's wealthiest plantation district, and it soon rivaled Greensboro for social dominance in the county.[26]

Greensboro, however, could not be ignored. By 1860 the town had more than 1,000 inhabitants and was one of the most important shipping points for cotton on the Georgia Railroad. The volume of traffic on the railroad increased steadily through the 1840s and 1850s as the railroad's western terminus, Atlanta, grew in importance and connected the Georgia Railroad to lines from other parts of the country. Greene County also benefited from a spur line that ran north, connecting the city of Athens in Clarke County to Union Point in Greene County. The construction of six fine new brick stores along Main Street in 1859 and 1860 reflected the prosperity the railroad brought to Greensboro's merchants. Charles A. Davis and William S. Davis, perhaps the most successful merchants in town, built an enormous edifice in 1860. Two stories tall, 65 feet across the front and 105 feet deep, the Davis Brothers store had more than 12,000 square feet of floor space. Soon nicknamed the "big store," it was the largest mercantile establishment between Augusta and Atlanta. In 1860 clock makers, gunsmiths, coach builders, jewelers, wine makers, tavern keepers, printers, and a variety of other service people, including Hope Mattox and her "disorderly house," could be found in Greensboro.[27]

Determined to become more than a market and shipping center, Greensboro's leaders convinced the Presbyterian Synod of Georgia to build a college for girls in their town. The Greensboro Female College began operation in 1852 with teachers mostly from the Northeast. The college offered courses in deportment, music, art, and the traditional academic disciplines of rhetoric, logic, natural science, mathematics, astronomy, English, and French. Despite the demanding courses available, Dr. Joseph R. Wilson, the father of the future president, Woodrow Wilson, clearly expressed the college's viewpoint in his 1858 commencement address: "Let your women keep silent in church." A correspondent of the *Temperance Crusader* characterized the elite women of the college as "educated two ways—both for parlor and kitchen. They meet the world with superiority, and can smile you out of your heart." Unable to contain himself, the writer then gushed, "Talk about good wives!"[28]

By 1860 the per capita wealth of Greene County's free inhabitants exceeded $2,200, about twice that of the average free Georgian. Interestingly, the average wealth of each of Greene County's free people was three times greater than the per capita wealth of Massachusetts and four times that of Ohio. Less than 5 percent of Greene County's households in 1860 reported no property holdings, and 50 percent of households had $2,500 or more of wealth. Good farmland at the same time advertised for sale at between $5 and $8 an acre, and the average value per acre in the 1860 census was $6.58 in Greene County. The increasing pace of industrialization in Europe and the United States during the 1850s kept cotton prices high, and the resulting prosperity seemed to benefit most of Greene County's white households. This prosperity, however, was not without cost. The people of Greene County lived in an increasingly dependent economy, producing a single crop for a market almost completely outside of their community, a market they could not control.[29]

Slaves were the central element of that production, and in 1860 they made up two-thirds of the county's 12,652 people. The average assessed taxable value of a Greene County slave in 1860 was $650; thus, Greene County's 8,398 slaves constituted about 60 percent of all wealth in the county. Slaveholding was fairly widespread; of the 798 households recorded in the 1860 census, 56 percent owned one or more slaves. More than 18 percent of households owned twenty or more slaves, and about 4 percent owned more than fifty. Only six heads of households controlled over 100 slaves. Thomas Poullain owned 134 slaves, the largest number held by any individual residing in Greene County. Among the slaveowning households, about half owned less than twelve slaves, 25 percent had five or fewer slaves, and 10 percent owned only one slave. Thus, fairly small slaveholdings typified most slaveowners' experience in Greene County, but those slaves were the key to wealth.[30]

As agriculture dominated the economy of Greene County, so farms dominated the landscape. A bit more than half of all household heads in 1860 reported their occupation as that of planter or farmer, while another 10 percent worked as overseers, meaning almost two-thirds of heads of free households engaged directly in agriculture for a living. In 1850 Greene County's farms averaged just under 500 acres in size. By 1860 the number of farms had declined 20 percent, while the average farm size grew to almost 700 acres. During the same period Greene County's white population declined more than 10 percent. Advertisements in local papers told the story: "the subscriber, desirous of moving west, offers for sale his valuable plantation in Greene County," or "the undersigned, having determined to move west, offer their land for sale." Between 1850 and 1860 more than 100 white families left Greene County, many of them moving west to seek new land and a chance to get rich. Some of those who remained in Greene County bought up the emigrants' land and consolidated ever-larger farms. Others stayed because they could not afford to leave.[31]

Though most of those who left Greene County were small farmers, in 1860 many small farmers still lived in Greene County. About 15 percent of all heads of households who farmed in 1860 owned no slaves and less than $1,000 worth of real estate. Another 20 percent of all farmers listed in the 1860 census owned no land at all, and many of these farmed as tenants or sharecroppers. Thus, small farmers and tenants made up about a third of all farm operators in Greene County. Some still farmed for subsistence and may have fit the mold of the plain folk yeomen, but increasing numbers of small farms between 1850 and 1860 grew cotton for the market. Rising cotton prices through the 1850s increased the attractiveness of growing the fiber, while the railroad and imported foodstuffs freed farmers from the necessity of growing their own food. By 1860, Greene County was no longer a self-sufficient social and economic island but a community on the verge of integration into the commercial market economy.[32]

In 1860 both Greensboro and Penfield offered cultural advantages seldom found in rural Georgia. Seven professors taught more than 140 students at Mercer University, which also offered a library of over 10,000 volumes and active music, debating, and literary societies. Four professors taught fifty-two students at the Greenesboro Female College, and the town organized a public lyceum that invited speakers from across the state to discuss topics such as the deterrence value of public execution or whether phrenology was a science. In addition to the specialized periodicals published at Penfield, Greenesboro's own weekly newspaper had a circulation of 800 copies. Known as the *Weekly Gazette* prior to March 1860, the editors then changed its name to the more lyrical and appropriate *Planters' Weekly*. This paper became the chronicle of Greene County's material and cultural success.[33]

Because of the railroad, during the 1850s Greene County functioned less and less as an island community and became increasingly part of a prosperous regional economy. Even the poor had opportunities in Greene County not usually found in rural areas, for they could try to find work with the railroad or in one of the county's cotton mills. For one-third of its population Greene County offered opportunity and prosperity; the white elite could enjoy music and benefit from good educations and intellectual debate. The other two-thirds of Greene County's people, however, lived in bondage. While witnesses to and an integral cause of the county's prosperity, these slaves inhabited another world.

Slaves Sho' Did Fare Common
in Dem Days

In about 1800 John Colby and his wife, Abigail, settled in Greene County. Though illiterate, Colby proved himself a shrewd man of business over the next few years. As the cotton boom swept Greene County, he rode it to prosperity, accumulating land and slaves, eventually becoming one of the county's wealthiest planters and slave traders. Sometime after his wife Abigail's death in 1808, Colby began a sexual relationship with a teenage slave named Mary. Mary ultimately bore him several children, including a son named Abram, who was born in about 1820. John Colby raised Abram in his own house, and the boy grew to be a large, powerful man, though virtually illiterate like his father.[1]

In June 1850 John Colby died. He left all of his real property, 2,665 acres of farmland, to his legitimate daughter by his white wife. He also left her most of his 106 slaves, but not Mary or her children. By 1850 Georgia law made it almost impossible to manumit slaves, so John Colby sought another way to reward Mary and her children. Colby's will explained, "knowing the laws of Georgia are opposed to and entirely forbid any wish I might indulge toward liberating a fraction of my slaves, I do here give to William L. Strain the following negroes, requesting and trusting that he will treat them with kindness and humanity." The will then named Mary and her seven children, including Abram. Strain, a lawyer and the postmaster of Greenesboro, took his friend John Colby's charge to heart. From that day on Mary and her children lived as free people in their own home, working at their own trades, though they remained slaves at law.[2]

After 1850 Abram Colby lived a relatively independent life, working in Greenesboro as a barber. He married and fathered four children, the oldest a son named William, born in October 1850. Colby considered himself free and later in life insisted that his father had indeed freed him. Beyond this, little information about his life—like that of most slaves—exists. Slavery functioned largely on a private and personal level, and except in rare cases, information about an individual slave's life was not recorded. Even census enumerators merely noted the age and sex of each slave, not the name. One can only speculate that as a barber Abram Colby held elite status among Greene County's slaves and certainly lived well compared to his peers. More interestingly, barbering acquainted him with several leading men of the county and allowed him to listen to discussions of business and politics.[3]

Dosia Harris also experienced slavery in Greene County. Dosia was born in the mid-1850s on Samuel Davis's plantation outside of Penfield. Her mother died soon after Dosia's birth, so Dosia grew up with her grandparents. Grandfather Joe served as the plantation carpenter, though he also worked in the fields and helped care for the livestock. Dosia's grandmother, Cretia, had been bought by Samuel Davis's father, Kelsey, "soon after she was brung over to dis country from the homeland of de black folks." Cretia still remembered Africa and "never did larn to talk dis language right plain." The children often listened with fascination to Cretia's stories about her childhood in Africa.[4]

Daily life on the Davis plantation was quite simple; most of the slaves worked in the fields from before sunup to after sundown. "All I knowed Niggers to do at night atter dey come in from de fields," explained Dosia, "was to eat supper and fling deirselfs on the beds and go right off to sleep." Dosia also remembered the violence that accompanied slavery. The overseer often beat slaves brutally; "sometimes it seemed lak he jus' beat on 'em to hear 'em holler." On Sundays slaves could go to church, but since they could not read, they devised their own understanding "'bout de Lord from deir heads." Other than a few entertainments at Christmas or corn-shucking time, the slaves led a monotonous life of hard labor and poverty. As Dosia explained, "all dey ever give slaves was a belly full of somepin t'eat, de clo'se dey wore, and de orders to keep on wukin'."[5]

Abram Colby and Dosia Harris both lived as slaves in Greene County not more than six miles apart. The same legal structures and cultural context surrounded both individuals, yet they led very different lives. The different lives of these two and the more than 8,000 slaves in the county, caution against absolute pronouncements concerning the slave experience. There were, however, commonalities of experience in the testimony of both white and black people who lived through slavery that make possible an impressionistic portrait of the lives of slaves.

In the 1850s the Jefferson Agricultural Society of Penfield calculated that each slave worker in Greene County generated between $300 and

$500 worth of marketable product a year. If slave families resembled free families in composition, then each two adult workers producing between $600 and $1,000 worth of product a year supported three nonworkers. To make a meaningful profit each year the slaveowner had to keep the cost of feeding, housing, and clothing slaves as low as possible. In 1860 the average cost of room and board for a laborer in Greene County exceeded $100 a year. Clearly, to make a profit while paying for seed, draft animals, equipment, and land, the annual cost of caring for a slave had to be the same or lower than the cost of paying a poor white laborer. Slaveholders managed to do much better than that and kept the yearly maintenance cost for a slave somewhere between $30 and $50. Slaves may have had enough food to eat, clothing, and a roof over their heads, but they lived a very hard life with few comforts. As William McWhorter, a slave of Joseph H. McWhorter, explained, "I'se tellin' you, slaves sho' did fare common in dem days." [6]

Frederick Douglass characterized each plantation as "a little nation of its own, having its own rules, regulations, and customs." Slaves did not experience a uniform system of bondage; instead, slave experience varied due to both structural differences between regions and the varieties of human personality. For the slave, after the basic fact of what crops would be produced, perhaps the most important variable was the master. Isaiah Greene, who lived on Richard Willis's Dover plantation in Greene County, explained that "yo' actual treatment depended on de' kind o' marster you had." The master's financial situation, the number of slaves she or he owned, the master's conception of slavery, and the master's personality were crucial factors shaping the lives of slaves. [7]

"Dem houses slaves had to live in, dey warn't much . . . jus' one-room log cabins with dirt and stick chimblies," remembered William McWhorter. Most slaves in Greene County seem to have lived in similar small log cabins, though on Richard Willis's plantation the slaves lived in two-room cabins. These cabins and rooms were usually crowded, with adults sleeping on beds nailed to the walls and children sleeping on the floor. Some planters divided cabins or rooms by families, recognizing the existence of slave marriages. On Joseph McWhorter's plantation, however, "dey crowded jus' as many Niggers into each cabin as could sleep in one room, and marriage never meant a thing when dey was 'ranging sleepin' quarters." [8]

Slaves generally had sufficient food, though they ate less meat than free people. Mahala Jewel recalled that on James H. McWhorter's plantation in the Forks district the slaves ate at long tables next to the kitchen. On other plantations and farms slaves cooked and ate in their cabins or took food to the fields. Some slaves had permission to keep dogs for hunting. Rabbit, squirrel, and especially the fatty opossum were considered delicacies by the slaves. Slaves often worked garden plots for themselves, and Richard Willis allowed his slaves to sell their produce and keep the money. Bill Austin's father, a carpenter and bricklayer, sometimes worked for wages on other plantations when not needed by his master. Another slave, Jack Terrell, worked as a traveling blacksmith, moving around the county from place to place as his services were needed. On Christmas day each year Terrell settled with his master for hiring his own time and apparently made a decent living besides. Not all slaveowners were so lenient. Some, fearing the effects of a black market among the slaves, forbade them to earn or keep any money at all.[9]

Slaves traveled around Greene County to a remarkable extent, especially in light of the patrol laws, which required that slaves off their plantations and not in the company of a white person have written passes. The patrol laws called for two companies of ten men to constantly patrol each of Greene's sixteen militia districts, apprehending and punishing wayward slaves and visiting and examining the slave quarters on every plantation twice each month. In reality, however, patrols seldom maintained this level of vigilance. Slaves often traveled around at will, though they always risked being caught and whipped. Three-quarters of Greene's slaves lived on farms or plantations with fewer than fifty slaves; thus most farms were too small to have self-sufficient slave communities. Only through interaction between these farms could slaves create community, a need that usually outweighed the possible results of being caught.[10]

In November 1853 the Greene County grand jury deplored "the laxity and supineness evidenced in our regulations . . . so as to render our patrol laws a dead letter." They called for enforcement of the patrol requirements, but at the next term, in March 1854, the grand jury complained that "the patrol laws are but partially executed in this county" and again called for more "regular and efficient patrols." Such vigilance, however, seemed unnecessarily burdensome to most citizens, and throughout the 1850s the patrol laws were generally unenforced. Even after John Brown's Harpers Ferry raid, when many in the South feared slave insurrection, most citizens in Greene County still ignored the patrol laws. The September 1860 grand jury observed that "the patrol law is very loosely enforced in our county," and in that same term Superior Court Judge Iverson Harris felt compelled to lecture the community at length about the patrol requirements. "The great object that should be kept in view," he argued, "is to keep the slaves in subordination." Slaves who moved about at will, continued Harris, would become insubordinate and threatened the very fabric of society. The editor of the Greensboro *Planters' Weekly* agreed that the patrol laws should be enforced but not so much to control the slaves as to protect them from "suspicious white men." Greene County's slaveholders did not fear their slaves as much as they feared outsiders' influence on their slaves.[11]

Slaves traveled around legally as well. Masters loaned slaves back and forth, hired slaves out, even allowed slaves to travel several miles to visit families. Minnie Davis's father was hired out to the Georgia Railroad and traveled on trains across eastern Georgia selling food to passengers. Emeline Stepney's parents belonged to different masters, and her father had standing permission to walk the five miles to visit his family on Wednesday and Saturday nights. On Sundays many slaves traveled to church, sitting in balconies or outside on the grass with fellow slaves. Other community events such as frolics, holidays, corn shuckings, and barn raisings also brought together slaves from different farms. This constant movement of slaves—their continual contacts with each other through work, church, and even forbidden nighttime forays—laid the basis of a slave community that transcended property lines.[12]

After 1830 the Greensboro Baptist Church had more slave members than white members, though it required permission from the owner for a slave to join the church. Some Baptists, believing salvation came from God and not man, questioned this requirement. At Penfield the Baptist Church rejected any permission requirement, treating prospective slave members the same as prospective white members. This religious egalitarianism did not, however, lead to closer relations between white and black members. Some of the Penfield church's members may have felt uncomfortable about worshiping with their black sisters and brothers, and other members sincerely believed that a separate church would better serve the slave members' needs. Billington M. Sanders, the pastor, thought that the slaves would develop fuller and more complete Christian lives if they could direct their own worship. For these reasons, in 1848 the Penfield Baptist Church organized a completely separate church called Penfield African Church, which usually had only nominal white supervision.[13]

Within the churches some slaves found an opportunity to escape the oppressive anonymity of their lives. The churches also gave slaves a legitimate focus for community, a place they could make their own. The African church at Penfield raised money for missions, called its own black minister and deacons, and exercised discipline over its members. At Shiloh Baptist Church, midway between Greenesboro and Penfield, Willis Williams built a life of his own separate from his life with his master. Willis served on church committees, preached to the black members, and eventually met his wife, Lucretia, within the church community. Though slaves, Willis and Lucretia created viable identities through their church.[14]

The churches, however, also acted to reinforce the social structure of slavery. The Bethesda Baptist Church in eastern Greene County regularly excluded slave members who violated the boundaries of slavery. Brother Buck, a slave of William Daniels, ran away twice in one year and was excluded from the church. Cyrus Thornton, a slave preacher, confessed that he knowingly ate stolen meat. For this, the church conference revoked Cyrus's privilege of preaching. Church conferences acted to enforce Christian conduct among all members, white and black, but for slaves, acceptable conduct included good behavior as slaves. Many slaves found, however, that the promise of salvation outweighed any additional restraint on their liberty and gladly participated in religious organizations. The slave community in Greene County largely crystallized around the various churches, laying the foundation for the centrality of churches in the black community after emancipation.[15]

But work, more than any other factor, structured and shaped life in the slave community. "Dere warn't never no let-up when it come to wuk," recalled William McWhorter of his life as a slave. Most slaves worked in the fields from sunrise to sunset and then often had other tasks to perform after dark. On some farms work for the slaves ended at noon on Saturday, but on others slaves toiled six full days each week. On Sundays they could till their own garden plots and attend to personal matters. The vast majority of slaves performed agricultural labor, typically in gangs assigned to specific functions. Plow gangs usually consisted of strong young men (and occasionally women) who could handle the heavy equipment, while older men and women made up the hoe gangs. Most planters found gangs the most productive and secure way to manage slaves. A few privileged slaves were artisans, working as blacksmiths, carpenters, masons, and as other skilled tradesmen. These slave artisans were often among the best at their trade in a community, and many took great pride in their work. When fire swept Greenesboro in March of 1860 the architect of the new Presbyterian church hurried to his building, fearing the worst. There he found his slave carpenter, Alex, already on the roof with buckets of water, prepared to save the church he had worked so hard to build.[16]

Slaves who failed to meet their owner's standards of hard work were punished, though many slaves blamed the harshness of the punishment on overseers, not masters. Richard Willis's plantation of 2,000 acres along the Oconee River required two overseers, one white, the other a slave. Slaves whose work failed to satisfy Colonel Willis received between twenty-five and fifty lashes as punishment, often given by the black overseer. Willis, however, adamantly insisted that the skin not be cut by the blows, for such scars could lower the value of a slave. On Joseph McWhorter's plantation, marveled William McWhorter, "de overseer sho' did drive dem slaves," and when asked how the overseer made the slaves work so hard, he explained that "dey almost beat de life out of the Niggers to make 'em behave." [17]

Such beatings, however, could have unintended consequences. "Some of 'em run off after a bad beatin'," continued McWhorter, "but dey jus' went to de woods. . . . None of our Niggers never knowed enough 'bout de North to run off up dar." Dosia Harris agreed, stating, "slaves didn't run off to no North dat I ever knowed of." When a slave ran away from Joseph McWhorter's plantation, one of the older slave women, Aunt Sookie, would go to the spring to wash clothes and leave behind clothing for the runaway. Usually slaves who ran to the woods returned soon after, but one Greene County slave reportedly lived in a cave for more than seven years, emerging only after emancipation. Occasionally slave patrols caught these runaways. In December 1858 William F. Luckey advertised a $40 reward for the return of two runaway slaves. Both were about thirty years old, dark complected, and "slow spoken." In May of 1859 neighbors captured one of the slaves and returned him to Luckey. When Luckey tried to take the slave indoors to punish him, the slave grabbed a knife and stabbed Luckey fifteen times, killing him. The slave then fled to the woods, and searchers never found him. [18]

Beatings were not the only horror slaves suffered. Isaiah Greene, the last of eleven children, never knew his father, who was sold when Isaiah was just two years old. Mary Craddock served as a wet nurse for her owner's baby Lucy. If Mary fed her own baby and Lucy began to cry, "Marse John would snatch the baby up by the legs and spank him, and tell Aunt Mary to go and nuss his baby fust." Trapped, Mary often cried "til de tears met under her chin." William McWhorter's mother also served as a wet nurse, and once she accidentally made her master's baby cry. In a rage, Joseph McWhorter beat her head with a stick. "Ma never did seem right atter dat, and when she died she still had a big old knot on her head," lamented her son. [19]

In 1860, 8,398 of Greene County's 12,652 inhabitants were slaves. Though central to the world of plantations, railroads, cotton mills, and colleges, these slaves lived on the fringe of the public sphere. As a group, slaves were a crucial part of public political discourse, and the experience and nature of slavery greatly shaped the worldviews of white and black southerners. Individual slaves, however, entered the public sphere only on rare occasions, usually as unwilling participants in the legal system. Most commonly the cases involved commercial or estate litigation, within which the slave's role remained that of an asset, a *thing*.[20]

Being a thing meant more than being swapped around for debts or having one's family divided among several heirs. In 1859 Elizabeth Moody's overseer hired a slave named Kit from Jasper Haynes and put Kit to work cleaning out a well. A rope broke, and a bucket full of mud fell on Kit's head, killing him. Haynes hired Thomas R. R. Cobb, a famous Athens lawyer, to sue Moody, and he eventually recovered $1,200 for the death of his slave. Kit's family, of course, recovered nothing. In another case, Joseph Parker grew angry with Eaton Mapp's slave Washington, so he shot Washington in the legs with a shotgun, disabling him. Washington was the plantation blacksmith, a very valuable slave, and Mapp sued for $1,000 in damages to his property. But Washington, a man crippled for life, had no right to recover for his injuries. He, after all, was only a thing.[21]

In a commonly noted contradiction, criminal law treated slave defendants as a class of person and even gave slaves specific and apparently real rights. But in cases where slaves were not defendants, they could not testify or bring charges, even if they were the victims. In 1860 Thompson Malone, a wealthy farmer from the Scull Shoals district, faced charges of cruelty to his twenty-seven slaves. Witnesses related stories of excessive and unnecessary whippings, of absurdly demanding labor requirements, of Malone's allowing slaves to suffer in cold weather with no clothing, and of his even starving slaves as punishment. The white witnesses, however, could give only hearsay evidence, while those who actually suffered under Malone's terror could not testify at all. The jury found Malone not guilty.[22]

Of 240 cases before the Greene County Superior Court from the March term of 1859 through the September term of 1861, 42 were criminal cases, of which only two involved slave defendants. During the same period the inferior court recorded no criminal cases involving slaves. Clearly, most criminal acts by slaves never made it to court and were instead handled within the private sphere. In January 1860 the Penfield African Church excluded Caesar Northen from fellowship because of his "most aggravated violence to his master." No court record of Caesar facing charges exists, so presumably Caesar suffered punishment only at the hands of his master and his church. In a more serious case, Mit Carlton killed a fellow slave named Nat in a fight. Under cover of darkness Mit went to his wife's master and told him what had happened. Arrangements were made among the slaveowners, and Mit suffered whippings and a branding, but no criminal charges.[23]

A more horrifying example of extralegal punishment of a slave occurred in 1860 just over the Greene County line in Oglethorpe County. William Smith and his slaves were threshing wheat on Friday afternoon, and just as it grew dark, Smith ordered his slave Jim to help put away the straw. Perhaps feeling the workday was over, Jim refused, and an argument broke out between him and his master. As Smith tried to pick up a stick to hit Jim, the slave took out a knife and stabbed his master to death. Jim then fled to the woods, but searchers captured him Sunday morning. After some debate, the captors decided to punish Jim immediately rather than wait for the justice system. The next morning, in front of a large crowd, Jim was burned at the stake.[24]

The two criminal cases from Greene County involving slave defendants do not fully represent the society's concept of "justice" for slaves. Further, though these cases give some insight into the slave experience, they must be used carefully, for one slave's experience was not always that of other slaves. Interestingly, of the variety of crimes that surely must have occurred among more than 8,000 slaves over a three-year period, the only cases to reach the superior court during this period consisted of slave-on-slave crime. Both cases involved charges of murder.[25]

Soon after Christmas 1859 an argument broke out in Greensboro between two slaves, Tom Cartright and Wash Wagnon. Whatever the cause of the dispute, it soon grew violent when Tom Cartright picked up a heavy hickory stick and swung at his antagonist's head three times. The stick hit Wash Wagnon above the left ear, smashing his skull and leaving a four-inch-deep depression. The town marshal arrested Tom and put him in jail. Wash lingered for two days and then died. At the next term of superior court, in March 1860, the grand jury indicted Tom for murder.[26]

Tom's master, John Cartright, was one of Greene County's richest men. He controlled the Long Shoals Cotton Mill, owned 2,400 acres of land, and held sixty slaves. Cartright hired Greensboro's leading attorneys, Yelverton P. King and Miles W. Lewis, to represent his slave. Cart-right may have truly cared about Tom's fate, but he also must have been aware that a twenty-seven-year-old male slave sold for $1,310 in Greenes-boro the previous week. John Cartright had to protect his investment.[27]

The prosecution seemed to have a simple case, for several witnesses saw Tom pick up the stick and strike Wash. The prosecutor argued that a reasonable man knew such a blow with a heavy stick would kill and that in taking the time to pick up the stick and then strike his opponent, Tom showed sufficient malice aforethought for the act to be murder. King and Lewis wisely did not dispute the witnesses' accounts of the blow; instead, they questioned the charge of murder. An angry man, they argued, might on the spur of the moment grab a nearby stick and strike out. Such an act required no malice aforethought, and surely no one could say with cer-tainty that Tom intended the blow to kill. At most, they argued, Tom committed manslaughter.[28]

The jury agreed with the defense and found Tom guilty of involuntary manslaughter. As punishment, the court ordered that Tom be branded on his cheek with the letter "M" and be given twenty-five lashes a day for four continuous days before being sent back to his master. King and Lewis had accomplished their goal—they saved Tom's life and his mas-ter's investment. Interestingly, when both the prosecution and the de-fense referred to reasonable-man standards or asked the jurors to imagine Tom's state of mind, they asked the white men on the jury to assume that they thought and felt the same as a slave. This sort of reasoning implied that Tom was the equal of the jurors, something they no doubt would have vehemently denied.[29]

The next term brought another case of murder before the court. James Lankford and his family lived near Penfield in northern Greene County. Lankford made a good living trading livestock and by 1860 had accumu-lated more than $5,000 worth of property, including three adult slaves. One slave, twenty-six-year-old Becky, had three children and so was es-pecially valuable. In March 1860 Lankford's wife, Caroline, threatened Becky with severe punishment for stealing dough from the kitchen. Ap-parently this threat upset Becky enormously, perhaps because she knew of the rumor that another Greene County slaveowner had his slave Sookie's mouth sewn shut to prevent her from stealing food.[30]

Early the next morning Lankford's daughter Mary went to the well to draw some water. Strangely, the well rope hung down inside the sixty-five-foot pit, and when Mary looked in for the bucket, she saw someone at the bottom. Mary called her father, and Lankford quickly climbed into the well to attempt a rescue. Becky was at the bottom, clinging to the rope to keep her head above water. When Lankford reached her, either from terror or in an attempt to drown her master, Becky almost pulled him into the water. As he pulled her out, Lankford discovered that Becky's three children lay beneath her. All three children had drowned.[31]

A coroner's jury assembled at the Lankford place to investigate the deaths. By that afternoon they found sufficient evidence to believe that the children were murdered. Becky was taken to Greenesboro and locked in one of the jail's dungeonlike cells to await the September term of superior court. Almost six months passed before Becky's trial, and during that time different stories about the incident began to emerge. One version held that Becky threw her children into the well and then climbed in herself to make certain they drowned. When asked why, Becky allegedly confessed she sought revenge against her mistress for threatening her with punishment. Another account explained that Becky, depressed and "tired of life," had tried to commit suicide. She threw her children into the well first because she "didn't want to leave any children behind her." When she jumped in herself, their bodies prevented her from drowning.[32]

The case against Becky had other complications as well. James Lankford had a reputation for drinking and telling incredible lies. Just a couple of weeks before the death of Becky's children, Lankford participated in an elaborate hoax. He claimed to have found an enormous cave on his farm full of geological wonders and the fossils of prehistoric animals. A letter to the *Christian Index* from Professor Henry H. Tucker of Mercer University confirmed "Brother" Lankford's find, described the wonders of the cave, and theorized as to the origins of the fossils. This letter and comments by Lankford appeared in newspapers across Georgia and excited a great deal of interest. The fun, however, did not last long. Professor Tucker vigorously denied writing the letter, and there proved to be no such cave on Lankford's property. As the *Planter's Weekly* observed a week later, "Lankford is a 'Brother' of the drinking persuasion, and about the only cave he has ever explored has been some well that needed cleaning out." If Lankford could take part in such a hoax, what of his tale concerning Becky's children?[33]

Lankford also faced a dilemma. As a slaveowner he had lost a substantial investment when the three children died, but if Becky hanged as a murderess, he would lose far more money. A young female slave of childbearing age could easily bring more than $1,000 at auction, which meant

Becky represented a substantial portion of James Lankford's wealth. Lankford hired George O. Dawson, a respected Greenesboro attorney and a former state representative from Greene County, to handle the case. In September 1860 the Greene County grand jury assembled and indicted Becky for murder, charging her with killing a "female negro child named Violet, the property of said James M. Lankford and about one year old." Nothing in the indictment mentioned that Violet was Becky's daughter, nor did the indictment name the other two children who died in the well. Perhaps Solicitor James Lofton thought it would be easier and sufficient to convict Becky of murdering the youngest child rather than seeking to prove she murdered all three.[34]

What had once seemed an easy, open-and-shut case, where Becky would "no doubt be hung," had by September become something else. Solicitor Lofton probably had only a passing acquaintance with the case before he and the other circuit riders arrived in Greene County for court week. George Dawson, by contrast, had weeks to prepare his case. Further, the prosecution's central witnesses, the Lankfords, had good reason to give lukewarm testimony, and James Lankford himself had a questionable reputation. At trial the jury listened to the prosecution's case, the evidence of the coroner's jury, and the testimony of the Lankfords. Then, the defense presented a different story. Dawson told of a woman, a slave, depressed, confused, and suicidal, who, struck by a fit of momentary insanity, decided to take her children with her to a better world. After a brief recess, the jury found Becky not guilty.[35]

As others have observed, most slaves who came before the legal system received all the procedural fairness a white defendant would enjoy. Becky had an attorney to represent her, and had her master not hired Dawson, the court would have appointed counsel. The jury heard Becky's story and apparently accepted her version of events. Through this trial Becky moved out of the legal role of a thing and took on the role of a person. Courts offered slaves full procedural rights and legal personality for two reasons. First, to maintain legitimacy as a venue of "justice," courts had to offer all participants the appearances of fairness. If courts failed to do so, their authority would diminish greatly in the community. Second, giving slave defendants full procedural rights served the interests of slaveholders. Slaves such as Becky or Tom represented substantial investments, and slaveowners needed the courts to help them protect their investments. Thus, as criminal defendants, slaves would receive all the fairness and protection the court could offer.[36]

Becky, however, certainly would have preferred to avoid this sort of participation in the public sphere. Even her victory revealed the horrible contradictions of the slave's situation. For all the fairness of the court and all the rights given her at trial, when discharged, Becky did not win her freedom. Instead, she returned to bondage and a potentially angry, drunken master.[37]

In the Hands of a Lawyer

In 1810 Hugh McWhorter married Helen Ligon, the daughter of a prosperous Watkinsville, Georgia, miller. The couple moved to McWhorter's small farm in southern Oglethorpe County, and over the next fifteen years Helen bore five children, four of whom survived. In 1825 Hugh McWhorter died, leaving Helen and his children only the seventy-acre farm. During the next few years the family struggled to stay out of poverty. Fourteen-year-old James, the eldest child, left school to manage the farm. Mary Ann worked beside her mother in the home and the garden. The two youngest children, ten-year-old William and six-year-old Robert, alternated years working on the farm and attending school. After much effort, the family began to escape its modest circumstances. James married Eliza Penn, and together they purchased a small farm in Greene County. Mary Ann married William Tuggle, the wealthy son of a Greene County planter. William moved to Alabama, where he gained admission to the bar and began practicing law. Even their mother Helen escaped through marriage. In 1835 she married David Geer and moved to his plantation in northern Greene County.[1]

Living on the Geer plantation allowed the youngest child, Robert Ligon McWhorter, to finish his secondary schooling at nearby Mercer Institute. After completing school he worked for his stepfather while awaiting an opportunity to make his own way. The chance came when Mercer began operations as a university in 1839. That year Absalom Janes, one of Georgia's wealthiest planters and a trustee of the university, moved to the new town of Penfield, which had sprung up next to Mercer. Janes built a fine house on Main Street and enrolled his son Thomas in the university. He also opened a mercantile establishment in the growing community and hired twenty-year-old Robert L. McWhorter to clerk in the store. This was the chance McWhorter had waited for, and his performance so impressed Janes that within three years he became a partner in the firm. A big, hearty man, who enjoyed telling a joke, McWhorter also impressed Janes's daughter Winifred. In November 1843 the couple married, and as a wedding gift Absalom Janes sold McWhorter the mercantile business at a bargain price.[2]

Robert McWhorter's fortunate marriage, however, brought him both wealth and tragedy. His business thrived, and he grew influential enough to serve as Penfield's justice of the peace. He also bought some land and purchased his first slaves. Through his own hard work and his father-in-law's aid, McWhorter soon became a wealthy man. Winifred bore a son, Robert Ligon Jr., and soon became pregnant again. Then disaster struck. In 1847 Winifred lost the second child and died soon after. Absalom Janes, who had taken on the roles of McWhorter's father and sponsor, also grew ill and died that year. Suddenly, Robert McWhorter had his business and farm, but little else.[3]

A year and a half later, in December 1848, sixteen-year-old Nancy Pope Thurmond visited a cousin in Penfield. An orphan, Nancy Thurmond was the ward of her uncle David A. Vason, one of southwest Georgia's richest planters. Among the people she met in Penfield was the twenty-nine-year-old Robert McWhorter. Fifty years later Nancy remembered him as a "young man engaged in merchandising and farming ... a man of magnificent physique, brilliant in conversation, and masterful of purpose." A whirlwind romance followed, and two months later Nancy and Robert married. McWhorter then bought a large plantation north of Penfield, and "uniting farming with his mercantile affairs, he was successful in both vocations."[4]

Having entered the ranks of Greene County's planters, Robert McWhorter began to take a greater interest in politics. He had been involved locally, serving one term as Penfield's justice of the peace and then as the town's postmaster. He also joined the local Whig Party, for, as he later explained, the party represented the better sort of people. "I could smell a Democrat across a ten acre field," he once joked. McWhorter served on several party committees and as a delegate to county and state conventions. After the Whig Party's demise he joined the American Party and then in 1860 the Constitutional Union Party. Electoral success finally came in 1857, when he won election as an "opposition candidate" to the Georgia House. In 1859 Greene County's voters returned him for a second term. In 1860 McWhorter reported to the census that he owned $50,000 worth of property and fifty-five slaves. He was a well-known and influential man in state politics and one of the most powerful men in Greene County.[5]

Robert McWhorter rose from his modest background to a position of wealth and power through a combination of fortunate marriages and good business sense. The other members of his family also did well. James H. McWhorter, Robert's oldest brother, made a modest living as a small farmer until the Georgia Railroad began construction through Greene County. James carried out several lucrative clearing and grading contracts for the railroad and opened a small but profitable store in the new railroad town of Woodville. From these two sources he accumulated enough money to buy several large parcels of land adjacent to the old family farm in Oglethorpe County and there began "to plant on an extensive scale." William H. McWhorter, Robert's other brother, practiced law in Alabama until he made enough money to buy a plantation. In 1859 William returned to Greene County, purchased a large plantation in the Forks district, and entered county politics. These three ambitious men focused on their goals of wealth and power and would not have chosen planting had it not offered the best route to their goals. Once established as planters, the McWhorter brothers built an economic and political dynasty that dominated Greene and Oglethorpe Counties for more than fifty years.[6]

Each McWhorter had followed a different path to success, but they all shared the same goal of owning a successful plantation and exercising political power. And although they owned plantations, none of the brothers abandoned his previous calling. Robert and James McWhorter both maintained significant mercantile interests, while William practiced law. Like the McWhorters, late antebellum leaders in Greene County were usually both planters and men of business. The terms "merchant" or "planter" could often be applied to the same man, though when asked, such men almost always identified themselves as planters. Successful merchants typically bought farms and slaves, while successful planters typically invested in mercantile businesses. Little economic conflict occurred between the two callings; what economic conflict there was within the elite usually occurred between families. Family relationships provided the structure for most extensive business and planting enterprises in the county, and the members of each leading family usually engaged in a variety of occupations. These successful families tended to dominate politics in Greene County.[7]

Individuals or groups with power have the "capacity to produce intended and foreseen effects upon others." Slaveowners obviously had power over their slaves, and to a lesser extent, fathers had power over their wives and children. Fewer than 100 men, however, had the economic or political power to influence the lives of the more than 12,000 people in Greene County. This relatively small oligarchy of merchants and planters may have disagreed at times over their means, but they clearly agreed on their ends. Political power, they believed, should serve the needs of planters by seeking to increase the profitability of growing cotton for the world market.[8]

Who were these men, and how did they exercise their power? A variety of approaches exist for understanding power in human society. Some scholars have assumed that wealth equals power and so search for a ruling class identified by its wealth. Others focus on politics and elections, seeking to discover who really turns the wheels and why. Drawing upon work in anthropology, some historians have investigated the cultural components of power, looking at elements of status, family, occupation, and education to find the basis of power. Many scholars have rejected all such approaches, arguing that power rises out of language and is diffused throughout society within a variety of human relationships. A few, perhaps frustrated with the process, have abandoned all efforts to rationally understand power in human society. Society and events within it are random, they argue, and no one can pretend to comprehend the exercise of power amid chance events. At best, one can hope to write a detailed chronology of events.[9]

These approaches may offer some help in grasping the variety and means of power, but the key to understanding power lies within the conception of society. If human events result only from the random choices and interactions of individuals, like the collisions of atoms in a formless gas, then a society per se does not exist, and any attempts to understand events are illusory. Societies, however, do exist, both in day-to-day experience and in historical perspective. Societies consist of patterns and structures that shape the roles and relationships of individuals and give meaning to events. These structures are not immutable; rather, change usually occurs so slowly that societies maintain a substantial continuity. Understanding something of the structures that shape a society makes some understanding of that society possible. The number and variety of patterns and structures within a society can be enormous, but the most important include the physical environment, economic structures, labor relationships, governmental structures, political systems, kinship systems, belief systems, cultural patterns, and language structures. Sorting through these and other structures can be daunting, and no paradigm for understanding them can be complete, but by focusing on these structures and how they work, one can learn much about a society and the people within it.[10]

A society's structures do not exist apart from its people. They result from and are dependent on the aggregate of human activity in the society, and this activity is not random; once established, the various structures of a society produce an interrelated pattern of "reality" that influences the members of that society to act in ways that reproduce and reinforce the existing structures. The structures do not determine the actions of individuals, but they do create enormous social, cultural, economic, and legal pressures for individuals to conform to existing norms. People make their personal choices within "envelopes" of possibilities and seldom stray outside those boundaries. Those who do vary from the norms are considered odd, dangerous, or even insane, depending on the nature of the variation. Change embraced by large numbers of people, an event usually called a revolution, however, can reshape a society's structures.[11]

Power in a society must reflect and utilize the existing structures in order to have lasting effect. Thus, the structures themselves make the exercise of power possible and help identify those who hold power. Governmental and legal institutions offer ready identification of many powerful individuals, as do the leadership structures of political parties. Those whose power depends on other structures require a bit more work for identification. Throughout most of the nineteenth century, for example, Greene County's economy revolved around producing cotton for the world market. Individuals who facilitated the transactions necessary for cotton production, by financing it, for example, potentially would have had significant power in the community. A merchant, for example, who extended credit to farmers and planters so that they could obtain necessary supplies may have had substantial power. This sort of analysis can extend to all aspects of society in Greene County. The problem, however, is determining which of all the people identified really did have meaningful power. The testimony of contemporaries in a society and an investigation of the course of events can help resolve this problem.[12]

Greene County's citizens took great pride in having given Georgia two U.S. senators, Howell Cobb and William C. Dawson, but men in less lofty positions exercised far more power in the community. The most important local officials were the justices of the inferior court. These five men, elected by the county at large for two-year terms, handled some minor cases at their biannual terms of court. Much more important, however, they performed functions similar to modern county commissions. The inferior court contracted for roads and bridges, kept public property in good repair, issued bonds, determined local tax rates, appointed slave patrol captains, appointed road commissioners, and oversaw the local justice courts of each militia district. In fact, most local matters came under their scrutiny. Further, serving as inferior court justice rarely became a stepping stone to a political career. Instead, many members of the elite felt it their republican duty to serve on the court, but only for a limited time. Most justices did not run for reelection. Across Georgia during the 1850s about three-quarters of inferior court justices held their office for only one term. In Greene County sixteen different men held the five seats between 1851 and 1861, most serving only one or two terms.[13]

Despite the rapid turnover of justices, the inferior courts remained firmly in the hands of the planters and, to a lesser extent, the merchants. Statewide, three out of every four justices farmed or planted, while merchants filled another 10 percent of places on the inferior courts. Lawyers made up only 2 percent of all justices in the state. These men were also very wealthy. Among Georgia's inferior court justices in 1860 the median property value reported to the census was about $12,000. Across the state more than 95 percent of Georgia's inferior court justices in 1860 owned real property, and more than half owned slaves.[14]

In Greene County between 1851 and 1861, of fifteen men who served on the inferior court two-thirds were farmers or planters. Three merchants also won election to the court during the same period. Greenesboro's magistrate, who was a successful businessman, and the clerk of the superior court also won seats on the inferior court. Perhaps most interestingly, no lawyers at all served on the court throughout the decade. These fifteen men who did serve each held an average of more than $26,000 worth of property in 1860, about twelve times the average per capita wealth of Greene County's free people. All but one of Greene County's justices owned real property, and all but two owned slaves. Together, the fifteen justices owned a total of 328 slaves, or an average of almost 22 slaves each. Greene County's inferior court truly belonged to the community's wealthy planters and merchants, while lawyers lacked sufficient influence to gain a seat on the court.[15]

Other important local officials included the sheriff, the ordinary, the tax collector, and the tax receiver. For much of the 1850s Charles C. Norton, who had been a farmer and a grocer, served as Greene County's sheriff. In 1860 Sheriff Norton owned $13,000 worth of property, including nineteen slaves. The county ordinary court handled probate matters, and in 1860 the ordinary, Eugenius L. King, reported no wealth to the census.

Though thirty-two years old, King still lived at home with his father, Yelverton P. King. Yelverton King and his law partner, Miles W. Lewis, were probably the most respected lawyers in Greene County. Eugenius King, however, despite the sometimes complicated probate matters before his court, was not a member of the bar.[16]

The office of tax collector required travel throughout the county, and the collector made personal contact with most of its leading citizens. Many saw this office as a stepping stone to a political career. Benjamin Alfriend, the tax collector in 1860, though wealthy himself, was also the son of the wealthiest planter of the White Plains area. Of all the local officials, only Greene County's tax receiver, Garrett Woodham, lived in modest circumstances. Though from a farming family in the Long Shoals area, since 1852 the tax receiver's office had become Woodham's sinecure, for he lived off its modest salary. Thus, as a group Greene County's local officials in 1860 were virtually all wealthy, involved in agriculture or merchandising for their livelihood, and belonged to many of the county's leading planter families. None was a member of the bar, and only Eugenius King had significant family connections to the practice of law.[17]

After 1851 each Georgia county sent one senator and, depending on population, one or two representatives to the General Assembly. These legislators not only exercised power by passing special acts, corporate charters, and general laws, but they also had greater opportunities to exercise influence within their own political parties. In 1860 the median wealth of state representatives reached $13,000, and that of state senators topped $21,000. More than 70 percent of the legislators owned slaves, and almost 30 percent owned twenty or more slaves. Two-thirds of the legislators farmed, and about 18 percent practiced law.[18]

Greene County's legislators in 1860 surely felt at home in this group. Senator Rowan Ward managed a large plantation along the Oconee River and also served as president of the Greene County Agricultural Society. Farmers across the state knew of Ward's eager support for scientific agriculture and soil conservation. Assemblyman Robert L. McWhorter made his first fortune as a merchant and then bought a large plantation north of Penfield and entered politics. Miles W. Lewis, Greene County's other assemblyman, ran a plantation near White Plains and practiced law in Greensboro. In 1860 these three men each owned an average of $35,000 worth of property and held an average of forty slaves. During the 1850s four planters, two lawyers, and one farmer/lawyer represented Greene County in the General Assembly. All were wealthy men, and all had large investments in slaves and agriculture.[19]

One group of public officials showed significant variation from this trend, but their exception proved the rule. As an incorporated city, Greensboro had a government separate from the county and so elected its own mayor and four aldermen each year. In 1860 three aldermen were merchants, while the remaining alderman and the mayor practiced law. In a commercial town, merchants and lawyers understandably dominated local leadership, but their power did not yet extend to county or state offices. Town leaders tended to be younger than county leaders, and they each owned an average of only seven slaves, though the average wealth of each was almost $15,000. Their positions reflected the power of men who facilitated business transactions in the cotton economy. Greensboro's political leadership in 1860 also provided a glimpse of Greene County's future, for these were men whose success hinged on the community's participation in the world market. Though local in orientation, Greensboro's leaders depended directly on and served a larger world market, which extended to New York, London, and beyond. As Greene County became ever more closely tied to that market, these men would gain ever-greater power in their community.[20]

Greene County's business leaders engaged in a variety of pursuits, though most also owned plantations and slaves. Dr. Thomas N. Poullain owned both a large plantation and a successful cotton mill at Scull Shoals on the Oconee. Twenty miles downstream, Dr. John Curtwright operated a similar mill near his plantation at Long Shoals. In 1860 each mill employed about 100 hands, producing rough cloth that most buyers used to clothe slaves. Another important businessman was James B. Hart, an Augusta merchant who spent most of his time at Oak Grove, his plantation near Union Point. Hart had such influence with the Georgia Railroad that trains made unscheduled stops at Oak Grove to pick up or drop off members of his family. Planter and businessman James B. Park inherited a large grist mill, tavern, and a toll bridge across the Oconee River on the road from Greensboro to Eatonton, as well as a large plantation in Greene County. These planter/businessmen all exercised enormous economic power in the community and were probably more powerful than any of Greene County's local politicians.[21]

The growing commercial market economy gave those engaged in commerce more power as well. Greensboro's merchants did much more than simply run stores. All sold supplies on credit to local farmers and then collected when the farmers sold their cotton in late fall. A few merchants also bought cotton from local farmers and planters, and when they had accumulated sufficient amounts, resold it through factors in Augusta.

Greene County's most successful merchants, Charles A. and William S. Davis, dealt in such large amounts of cotton that they bypassed the Augusta factors and sold directly to New York. John F. Zimmerman, another successful merchant, owned a small tinware factory, where his slaves hammered out pots and pans for use on local plantations. Josiah Davis, a retired merchant, controlled the clockmaking firm of Davis and Barber. By 1860 the firm had ceased manufacture of its own clocks and sold clocks assembled by slaves in its Greensboro factory from parts made in Connecticut. These clocks were then distributed successfully across Georgia and Alabama.[22]

In the late 1830s a group of merchants and planters had financed the Greensboro Manufacturing Company, which operated a steam-run mill weaving cotton cloth. The company struggled and ultimately had to borrow substantial sums from banks in Savannah. Burdened by heavy debts, the firm failed during the Panic of 1857. A similar group of investors backed the Bank of Greensboro, and it too failed in 1857, though the cashier fled north with the plates for the bank's notes and continued to print money for his own use. In 1860 only Phillip Clayton carried on banking activities in Greensboro. The Clayton Bank, a private institution, financed some of the local planters who chose not to deal with factors in Augusta, Savannah, or Charleston. Phillip Clayton himself spent much of his time outside of Greene County, serving as assistant secretary of the treasury for the Buchanan administration.[23]

Many of Greene County's most influential men belonged to Greensboro's Masonic Lodge. Greensboro lawyer Yelverton P. King served as master of the lodge, and through this organization he gained influence and recognition throughout the county. Perhaps because of his success moderating the lodge's meetings, community leaders often called on King to chair public functions. Other organizational leaders included planters Thomas Stocks and James A. Davidson. Stocks, a former justice of Greene County's inferior court, served for several years as president of the Southern Central Agricultural Society, and both Stocks and Davidson served on the society's executive committee. Both men won great respect in the community through their marked success in farming and through their support of scientific agriculture. The most important organizational leaders in Greene County, however, controlled the local political parties.[24]

Through the 1840s and into the 1850s the Whig Party dominated politics in Greene County, and the demise of the party did not shake the former Whigs' hold on the community. Calling themselves first the American

Party and then the Opposition Party, these men joined the Constitutional Union Party in the summer of 1860. The leadership of these parties remained relatively the same. In 1860 the most powerful local party leaders were Robert L. McWhorter and Miles W. Lewis, Greene County's representatives. State senator Rowan Ward, Greenesboro merchant John F. Zimmerman, and planter Thomas P. Janes also held great power within the Opposition Party. These men viewed themselves as progressives, and though strongly wedded to the cotton economy, they called for the scientific improvement of agriculture and the expansion of commerce. Essentially, these former Whigs represented the planter/businessmen and merchants who benefited from and favored the ongoing process of commodification as Greene County became more tied to the commercial market system. Greene County's Democrats were more cautious and generally represented the more conservative planters and small farmers who distrusted the growing forces of the market. The Democratic Executive Committee in 1859 consisted of five wealthy planters, including Richard Willis and James R. Sanders, two of the county's richest men. In 1860, like the national party, Greene County's Democrats split into factions supporting two different presidential candidates. This split further limited the Democrats' influence in the community.[25]

Grand juries had an important role in county government and in the administration of criminal justice, so the selection criteria for grand jurors were strict. From a list of county property owners, the justices of the inferior court chose "able and discrete . . . free white males" who were "fit and proper persons to serve as grand jurors." The list of grand jurors, then, gives us a contemporary assessment by Greene County's elite of who mattered in the community. Grand jurors were local status leaders, and the list of who served as grand jurors reveals the characteristics of those leaders.[26]

In 1860 forty-five men served on Greene County's grand juries, forty-one of whom appeared in the 1860 census. Some of the grand jurors were local business and political leaders, but most were men who owned successful plantations. Only one juror, a teacher and, at twenty-five, the youngest man to serve, reported no slaves. The rest of the grand jurors, including the teacher's father, owned slaves, and two-thirds owned twenty or more slaves. About 60 percent of the heads of households in Greene County farmed or planted for a living, but almost 90 percent of the grand jurors engaged in agriculture. Together, the forty-one grand jurors reported more than $1,104,000 in property to the census. These men, making up less than 1 percent of Greene County's free population, owned

more than 12 percent of all wealth in the county. Not all of the grand jurors were rich, but among them only Greenesboro's bookseller reported
less than $4,000 worth of property, and the average wealth of each grand
juror exceeded $27,000.[27]

Excepting Greenesboro's town government, Greene County's leaders
generally came from the community's upper quartile of wealth; most
owned slaves, and most farmed. Merchants and lawyers possessed a bit
more influence in the community than was typical statewide, probably
due to the greater and more sustained impact of the railroad and market
forces on the county. Yet, despite the accelerating processes of dependency and commodification, Greene County's merchants and lawyers
still played second fiddle to the county's planter leaders. In fact, lawyers
held a surprisingly modest place in the local hierarchy of power, but they,
more than any other group, stood to gain from the commercial market
transformation of Greene County.[28]

C. Vann Woodward once characterized the economy of the "New
South" as a vast pawnshop. If it was a pawnshop, it certainly had a fine tradition to build on. The antebellum cotton economy functioned almost entirely on credit. Planters and farmers relied on credit from factors, banks,
merchants, and even each other to buy their supplies and equipment each
year. They used their anticipated crop or, more commonly, their slaves as
security. Factors dominated this financial system, benefiting from the lack
of a developed commercial market economy in rural areas.[29]

Factors had the expertise and the connections to find buyers for cotton, something most planters in small interior towns could not do. During the year, factors advanced money and supplies to their clients, transactions that were usually unsecured by specific liens or contracts. After
harvest producers shipped the cotton to their factors. Factors did not buy
the cotton; instead, they functioned like brokers, finding buyers for the
cotton in New York or Europe. After selling the crop the factor sub-
tracted his fee for the transaction as well as the principal and interest on
advances made to the client. The factor either held the remainder as a
credit, forwarded it to the client's bank account, or, rarely, paid cash to the
client himself. Most planters' and many farmers' operations were highly
leveraged this way, and even if self-sufficient in food, they depended on
credit, which ultimately came from New York or Europe. Of course, farming on credit meant that debtors had to produce enough crops for market
to pay off each year's debt, and cotton offered the greatest return.[30]

Sometimes debtors would not or could not pay these debts. If their
financial failure resulted from a bad year and the debtor still seemed

sound, factors, merchants, or neighbors might carry the debt over to the following year. An astonishing number of people, however, delayed or even refused to pay their debts, even when fully able to pay. As one South Carolina planter explained, "a gaming debt is a debt of honor, but a debt due a tradesman is not." Many planters saw debts as simply one aspect of their relationship with another person, not the core of that relationship. Though producing for a market economy, many cotton growers still acted on beliefs developed in a cooperative subsistence economy. Given such attitudes, creditors had little choice but to seek help in collecting. As an 1855 notice from the McWhorter's Penfield mercantile firm explained, all due "notes and accounts will be found in J. H. McWhorter's hands until the first of June, after which time they will be found in the hands of a lawyer."[31]

In the 1860 census of Greene County, ten men reported their occupation as lawyer, which translated to one lawyer for every 425 free people in the county. Five lawyers headed households, while the other five boarded in various Greensboro homes. As their living arrangements suggest, young men dominated the local bar. Half the lawyers in 1860 were under thirty years of age. These young men, however, tended to be prosperous, their median net worth of $8,100 placing them firmly in Greene County's second quartile of wealth. Most owned at least one slave, with about four slaves the median holding. Three lawyers owned no slaves, but all three came from prosperous slaveowning families.[32]

Not all attorneys came from wealthy families. A few individuals from modest backgrounds rose to positions of wealth and power in nineteenth-century America through the practice of law. The careers of Abraham Lincoln or Alexander Stephens, for example, emphasized the possibilities open to men from modest backgrounds who took up the law. Even the very structures for becoming a lawyer seemed to make the profession open to any truly motivated man. Since 1806, applicants for membership in Georgia's bar only had to be a citizen of the state, possess a reputation of "moral rectitude," and submit to a public examination before one of Georgia's superior courts. Theoretically, any man with enough education to read Blackstone, Kent, and a few other standard works and who had a decent reputation in the community could stand for the bar examination.[33]

Most Georgia lawyers in the mid-nineteenth century, however, were not "self-made" men, and the legal profession did not welcome all comers. Even if a poor man managed to obtain the necessary basic education to competently read the law, he still faced the examination. Alexander

Stephens successfully read law alone with a library he purchased for $25. His achievement, however, only demonstrated his exceptional ability and application, not the openness of the profession. Most applicants read law for six months to a year under the guidance of a mentor, usually a respected local attorney. Men from poor families might find securing such a mentor difficult, especially since most charged about $100 for the privilege of reading law in their office. At the applicant's examination the mentor attested to the applicant's ability and knowledge; a man with no mentor had much more to prove in his examination. Thus, intentionally or unintentionally, the very process that seemed so open actually limited admission to the bar.[34]

All of the attorneys practicing in Greene County in 1860 came from "good" families, meaning families with some property and reputation. Miles W. Lewis had a fairly typical background for a successful lawyer in Greene County. His father, Walker Lewis, settled in Greene County in the early 1790s and in 1854 owned a substantial farm and twenty-two slaves. Miles Lewis graduated from Emory College in 1842 and read law under one of Greenesboro's most successful lawyers, Augustus Baldwin Longstreet. In 1843, after less than a year working under Longstreet, Lewis gained admission to the bar. A successful career in both law and politics ensued. Philip B. Robinson followed a similar course. After graduating from Mercer University in 1854, he read law with Judge Francis Cone in Greenesboro before passing his bar exam in 1855 and beginning his legal career. Both of these men read law with highly respected local attorneys, and their mentors' reputations probably helped them during their examination by the court.[35]

Despite occasional murder trials or personal injury lawsuits, the bread and butter of Greene County's lawyers was the collection of debts. Of 240 cases before the superior court from March 1859 through September 1861, 198 cases involved civil matters. One hundred and fifty-seven of these 198 cases, or about 80 percent, were suits to collect debts. The defendants seldom faced financial hardship; on the contrary they were usually prosperous members of the community. Attorney James L. Brown's experience during the September 1861 term of court was fairly typical. The Greenesboro mercantile firm of Davis and Johnson hired him to collect their overdue accounts. Brown filed seven complaints against debtors of the firm. The average wealth of each defendant exceeded $11,500 dollars, while the average amount due was only $189.10. In two cases the defendants might have found paying the debt difficult, but the other five cases involved some of Greene County's wealthiest citizens. In every case the defendants had simple goals: avoid payment until the last possible moment. It was only when their case came before the court that the defendants would acknowledge the debt. After judgment they seemed to have no problem finding the money to pay. In most cases the actions in court were not really one of conflict resolution; rather, the process seemed to have provided a ritualistic affirmation of the debt relationship between the parties.[36]

Besides the seven cases for Davis and Johnson, James Brown's other business during that term of court included acting as an arbiter in deciding the value of Jasper Haynes's slave Kit, who died when a bucket fell on him while he was working in a well. He also defended two clients against claims for debt. In both the debtor cases, Brown delayed payment as long as possible and then finally confessed judgment for his clients. Thus, Brown played both sides of the debt game at the same term of court. The actions of most defense lawyers in delaying payment as long as possible seem to have reflected the wishes of debtors, not a cynical attempt by lawyers to generate larger fees. In January 1860, for example, three Greene County planters gave notice in the *Planters' Weekly* that they refused to pay a note for more than $1,600 they had given to the Davant brothers of Penfield. It seems that after concluding their business with the Davants, these planters became dissatisfied with the deal and decided not to pay their debt. "We are determined not to pay it," they explained, "unless compelled by law."[37]

This resistance to paying debts did not necessarily injure the debtors' reputations. Garrett Woodham, the county's tax receiver, was one of the men sued for debts by Davis and Johnson in September 1861 for refusing to pay debts he clearly owed; he finally paid under court order. That same fall, Woodham won reelection as tax collector. These men and many others in Greene County saw debts as something more than the result of singular, completed business transactions. Debts represented an ongoing relationship, the conditions of which changed over time. These views reflected the ideological perspective of people living in an undeveloped economy not yet completely shaped by the market, a society that had not yet fully experienced the "great transformation" to a commercial market economy.[38]

Lawyers' work let them meet and socialize with their community's leaders, affording ambitious men the opportunity to make business and political connections. Court gave lawyers a chance to perform for their community, to gain a reputation, and to project a particular persona through word and deed. Court also allowed these men to display their speaking abilities, and in a society that valued skilled oratory, such demonstrations could lay the foundation for professional and political success.[39]

Although most of Greene County's attorneys did not seek political office, the practice of law offered them another form of power in the community. The key to this power was the language of the law, and lawyers' understanding and control of this language system gave them a potent tool. Legal issues centered on language, and the process of applying legal words to actions or events often determined the outcome of a case. The process began with the rituals of pleading, a struggle between lawyers over the language used to describe the cause of action and the defense in a case. The conflict over language then continued in court, as lawyers argued other language questions before judges or juries. In a murder case, for example, lawyers on both sides would try to define the word "murder" and show how it did or did not apply to the defendant's actions. The most successful lawyers had the skill to make these arguments both within the language of the law and in a form convincing to jurors. Unskilled lawyers attempting this could end up looking like fools, but good lawyers would appear very learned and clever as they wove a path through a demanding, complicated, and almost mystical language system. Thus, in the relationships and social mechanisms defined and controlled by the law rather than by community practices, lawyers and judges possessed significant power.[40]

Despite their almost undisputed power in the courtroom, Greene County's lawyers in the years before the Civil War held only modest power in the community. For all their activity and reputation, lawyers had only a peripheral role in the county's central business of growing and selling cotton. Lawyers had no real influence on the labor relationships, the financing, or the marketing components of cotton production. Local lawyers did not even directly facilitate the working of the system; that role was left to factors and lawyers in the port cities of Savannah, Charleston, Baltimore, and New York. Greene County's lawyers served merely to tidy up local problems, particularly the collection of debts.

Contract law appeared and waxed quickly dominant as an essential part of the growing commercial market economy of nineteenth-century America. Contracts provided much of the organizing structure necessary for a modern commercial system, and through contract law, lawyers gained a central role in America's developing economy. Lawyers in Greene County before the Civil War, however, rarely drew up or dealt with contracts. From March 1859 through September 1861 only two contract cases reached Greene County's superior court. The assumptions of a precommercial economy still dominated business relationships, and when local merchants or planters conducted business, they relied on oral agreements and the relationships between the parties. Only on occasion, in large or risky transactions, did one of the parties draw up a promissory note. Though their conduct in these transactions created a "contract" at law, this legal fiction was vastly different from a document largely negotiated and written by lawyers that defined the business relationship of the parties. The idea of asking lawyers as "experts" to draw up contracts for commercial transactions would have astonished most of Greene County's citizens.[41]

In an undeveloped, precommercial society, lawyers acting through the criminal justice system and civil law simply buttressed the orderly functioning of society. This began to change as the growing international industrial market and its technological manifestations such as steamships, railroads, and telegraphs transformed many precommercial societies during the nineteenth century. Some societies, such as the cotton South, found that this process drew them more tightly than ever into potentially exploitative market relations with the industrializing regions. In Greene County, this process began with the rise of cotton culture and accelerated after the arrival of the railroad. Though perhaps gaining some influence as the market began to transform the region, lawyers still occupied a peripheral role in Greene County. Only as the county "developed" into full participation in the market system and adopted its business practices and legal structures would lawyers gain substantial local power. Even if someone in Greene County had understood the ongoing commercial revolution, they would have expected this transformation to continue at a very slow pace, as it had for more than a decade. In 1860 no one foresaw that war and the destruction of Greene County's plantation economy would throw the community into the maelstrom of rapid and uncontrolled change.

Until Our Country Is Free

The fun began in a Greenesboro tavern. In March 1855 a New Englander named Webster visited town to sell embossed plates for marking clothes. One evening he stopped in a tavern for a drink and while there unwisely expressed his abolitionist sentiments. Several tavern patrons warned him to leave town, but he refused. A mob of young men began to gather, and suddenly realizing the danger he was in, Webster fled. Cheered on by an excited crowd of townspeople, the young men pursued Webster through the streets of Greenesboro. He almost gave them the slip but then was discovered hiding on top of a large wardrobe in Mrs. Colt's house. The mob dragged their prisoner to the Greenesboro Female College at the edge of town and asked the students for judgment. "Tar and feathers," decreed the girls, so the mob rode Webster back to the center of town on a fence rail and there blacked him with tar. A slave joined in the celebration, calling the abolitionist "brother" and giving him several lashes with a strap, saying it was "all in fun between us equals." Then the mob rode Webster down the hill to the depot and put him on the train, "resembling slavery very much." [1]

Modern readers might find in this event confirmation of many popular assumptions about the irrational and violent South. Paranoid, xenophobic, plagued by guilt over slavery, another southern mob struck at an imagined threat. Only their failure to lynch Webster makes this tale surprising. But such popular images are misleading. Human communities have often engaged in ritual acts of disorder, from cat massacres to cockfights to tearing down goalposts after a football game. From the cultural perspective of the participants such actions are anything but irrational; they may seem naughty, daring, funny, or even necessary, but not irrational. A particularly popular form of ritual disorder in both Europe and the United States has been the charivari, the ritual humiliation of a victim in order to reaffirm community values. During the charivari the community's young men mocked the victim by symbolically transforming him into a lesser being. For different reasons, Webster could have suffered a similar fate in Illinois, New Hampshire, or Bavaria.[2]

Many of Greenesboro's people joined in this symbolic humiliation of an abolitionist, having great fun while protecting their community, proving its solidarity, and punishing Webster for his claims to moral superiority. Though Webster certainly did not enjoy this experience and may even have been injured while riding the rail, the community found it amusing, reassuring, and proper. Secure in their own values, the people of Greenesboro saw abolitionist values as irrational, silly, laughable, and even tasteless. As for the slave, his master may have ordered him to join the fun, or as part of a community shaped by the prevailing ideology of slavery, he may have joined in on his own. Even the editor of the Penfield *Temperance Banner*, who seldom missed an opportunity to paint taverns as the source of disorder and dissipation in society, approved of the action taken by Greenesboro's young men. Saying nothing about drink or the role of the tavern, he praised the young men and then observed that "this doesn't prove that a man hasn't a right to his own opinions, but he should be very particular as to how and where he expresses them."[3]

Four years later, in November 1859, a similar situation arose, but it had quite a different ending. Thomas Miller got off the evening train at the Greenesboro depot and struggled up the hill with his heavy trunk and sample case to his hotel. He registered as a silver polish salesman from Cleveland, Ohio, and retired to his room. The next morning, Sunday, Miller wandered around town, admiring the fine homes and the growing business district. He stopped to chat with several townspeople, asking many questions about the town and repeatedly inquiring how many slaves lived in Greenesboro and Greene County. As the morning passed, some citizens grew suspicious. Why, they wondered, would a northern salesman be so interested in the layout of the town and the number of nearby slaves? After the midday meal, a group of concerned citizens decided that Miller was a threat and took action.[4]

Several men approached Miller and explained that a train would depart Greenesboro at half past two. They suggested that he catch it. Miller refused to leave. Moments later a group of vigilantes appeared and escorted Miller and his belongings down the hill to the depot. The grave seriousness of the men must have impressed Miller, for he did not resist. There was no celebration, no riding on rails, no tar or symbolic humiliation. At the depot, several of the men questioned Miller about his activities while others searched his trunk for incriminating evidence and tried out samples of his silver polish. Though they discovered nothing to suggest he intended to do anything but sell polish, the vigilantes loaded Miller aboard the train and told him never to return.[5]

The dreadful earnestness of Miller's inquisitors was very different from the joyful charivari surrounding Webster's humiliation. The vigilantes did not engage in ritual symbolism or make appeals to pure womanhood for judgment. Instead, they treated Miller much as they would have treated someone suspected of carrying smallpox. The charivari celebrated and reaffirmed community values, while the vigilantes simply gave Miller a "bum's rush," hustling him out of town before they even knew for certain that he was a threat. Their hair-trigger response to Miller's curiosity shows that something had changed, that the community no longer felt so secure in its assumptions about slavery and politics. The crisis of fear had begun.[6]

Though outnumbered two to one, Greene County's white population seldom feared the slaves. As Edmund Ruffin observed, a similar lack of fear manifested itself across the South in a "general neglect of all police regulations and means for defense against possible violence." The planters in particular, with their assumptions of racial superiority and personal honor, rarely questioned the safety of living surrounded by slaves. Their day to day experience of power over slaves, the way in which "reality" complemented their prevailing beliefs about slaves and slavery, made any such fear unlikely. The same ideological assumptions affected the slaves as well. The culture of slavery, its customs and structures combined with the virtual impossibility of organized revolt, turned most slaves' resistance into nonviolent efforts. The crisis of fear did not grow out of a deep-seated foreboding about the slaves, nor did it rise out of some haunting psychological guilt over slavery. Instead, it resulted from the growing political and ideological conflict between North and South, a conflict that seemed to have become a threat to southern life, society, and future prosperity.[7]

Only a month before the vigilantes ran Thomas Miller out of Greensboro, John Brown led his raid on Harpers Ferry, Virginia. Brown expected his raid to set off a general slave revolt and made vague plans to help it spread across the South. The slaves, however, proved more prudent than Brown imagined, for they understood the vast forces that could be used to suppress them. While Brown's raid failed, its impact echoed across the South. Southern slaveholders may not have feared their slaves, but they did fear the potential influence of outsiders on the slaves. Believing most slaves to be simpleminded souls accustomed to obeying commands, worried slaveowners feared that slaves could be misled by abolitionist agitators. Worse, John Brown finally confirmed the true colors of abolitionism. A correspondent to the Greenesboro *Weekly Gazette* commented on Brown's raid as no little boy crying wolf, for "the monster [of abolitionism] has been actually seen and captured in his ravages." Abolitionists meant not just to free the slaves but to encourage slaves to slaughter their masters. Thus, for many southerners, John Brown's raid only exacerbated the growing conflict between North and South.[8]

As fear swept Greene County following John Brown's raid, some tried to profit from the events. "Prepare for the Insurrection" read one local advertisement announcing that "all those who anticipate danger from the insurrectionists should come immediately to Wm. C. Smith's and equip themselves with a fine double barrel shot gun." Even within this ad, "insurrectionists," not slaves, were the potential threat. The editor of the *Weekly Gazette* called for a local committee to monitor the activities of strangers and to ship any threatening individuals to the "other side of Mason and Dixon's line." Even nine months after Brown's raid the Greene County grand jury worried that "there are at this time quite a number of suspicious white men straggling about the county, visiting negro quarters and conversing with negroes." The grand jury continued that "in view of the political excitement of our country, we recommend proper vigilance throughout the county in the enforcement of the law in bringing all such characters to judgement."[9]

Commenting on the number of suspected abolitionists driven out of communities around Augusta in the weeks following Brown's raid, the editor of the Augusta *Dispatch* explained, "We state it as our cool opinion that it is right to visit with the most summary penalties of lynch law the Abolitionist intruders from the North." Though many believed the threat came only from a few "emissaries of Northern fanaticism," others took a larger view of events. During the first week of November 1859, Greene County organized a new military company, "ready for any emergency." These emergencies included not just abolitionist agitation but also "defending the state from hostile invasion." Clearly, the invaders would come from the North. The editor of the *Weekly Gazette* agreed, calling for the creation of an arms foundry in Augusta so that the state could have the means of defense in case of war with the North. One month later a correspondent to the paper called for a general mobilization across the South to prepare for when "the fanatics of the North invade our soil." He also called for complete economic separation from the North, worrying that the South's dependency siphoned off "wealth that ought to be kept at home" and that would be used by the North against the South.[10]

The fear resulting from John Brown's raid fed into the ongoing ideological conflict with the North, creating an enormously heightened perception of crisis among southerners. Such crises had occurred before and ultimately died down, but this time the fear merged with southern concern over the 1860 campaign for president of the United States. Abraham Lincoln, a powerful spokesman for the North's free-labor ideology, clearly intended to restrict the westward expansion of slavery. He also seemed to have little concern about the number of organizations and state governments that prevented enforcement of the fugitive slave laws, which were openly violating federal law, the U.S. Constitution, and the decisions of the Supreme Court. Meanwhile, the national Democratic Party fell apart over these same issues, its split making Lincoln's election a virtual certainty. Thus, the crisis of fear spread to the political sphere, and for many southerners, the election of 1860 served as a bellwether for the future.[11]

Professor Shelton P. Sanford of Mercer University was a meticulous and careful man, as befitted a middle-aged mathematician. His diaries reflected his personality, for he filled them with detailed weather observations, gardening notes, and astronomical sightings. In October 1860, however, he took up new concerns. "Very much worried," he wrote, "about the Presidential election. Trust and pray the Good Lord will prevent the election of Lincoln." Several days later, on November 6, Sanford voted for John Bell and Edward Everett of the Constitutional Union Party. Then, like many others, he waited for the results, "curious to hear the news yet almost afraid to hear." Two days later, on Thursday evening, word came of Lincoln's victory. "Felt exceedingly depressed and gloomy on hearing the sad news," wrote Sanford. "May the Good Lord protect us and guide us in this time of peril to our country."[12]

Most of Greene County's voters shared Sanford's concerns. Bell and Everett received 528 of 781 votes, 68 percent of the popular vote in the county. Clearly, a majority of the county's citizens hoped for compromise with the North through the Constitutional Unionists. By contrast, Breckenridge and Lane, the Democratic splinter ticket favored by secessionists, won only 108 votes. Greene County's citizens viewed Lincoln's election as a threat but apparently were not yet ready to leave the Union.[13]

In response to Lincoln's election, local leaders called a public meeting at the courthouse in Greensboro of all citizens, and on November 16 a considerable crowd gathered there. Some observers believed it was the largest political meeting in county history. Yelverton P. King, a leading lawyer, slaveowner, and a supporter of Bell and Everett, chaired the meeting. Thomas Stocks and Dr. Thomas N. Poullain, two of Greene County's wealthiest planters and ardent secessionists, joined King as vice presidents of the meeting. Professor Sanford served as secretary. The assembly was not, however, one of fire-eaters. Mercer professor Henry H. Tucker had set the tone of the gathering when he reminded the crowd of Georgia's state motto: "Wisdom, Justice, and Moderation." As Sanford marveled later that evening, "everything was conducted with order, gravity, and solomenity [*sic*]." [14]

In the usual pattern of such "mass meetings," the organizers had prepared resolutions and chosen speakers before the meeting assembled. After a few comments by King, Professor Tucker moved for the creation of a resolution committee. Seven "leading citizens," who had a vested interest in a total of 348 slaves, received a voice vote of approval from the gathered citizens to "draw up" resolutions. After the committee withdrew, the show of herrenvolk democracy continued with a brief speech by Mercer University president Nathaniel M. Crawford. He called for "constitutional resistance to Northern aggression" and argued that only if such resistance failed should the South take up arms. The Greenesboro *Planters' Weekly* reported that the speech commanded "profound respect and breathless attention." [15]

Having complied with the necessary ritual, the committee returned with ten lengthy resolutions. These condemned Lincoln's election, called for enforcement of the fugitive slave laws, and concluded that only if the North refused to respect the constitutional rights of southern states should secession be considered. Finally, the resolutions pointed out that months of organizing would be needed before dissolving the Union could be considered an option. Anticipating Herschel V. Johnson's platform at the Georgia Secession Convention, the resolutions were strongly cooperationist, asserting that the southern states should not secede individually but as an organized group and only after all attempts to compromise with the North had failed. Shelton Sanford probably expressed the feelings of many when he wrote, "The resolutions adopted were dignified and conservative, yet firm and strong. May the Good Lord make them instrumental of good to our common country." [16]

Not all of Greene County's citizens were so moderate. Expecting conflict, Greensboro organized a company of "minute men" under the command of two well-known attorneys, Frederick C. Fuller and Philip B. Robinson. Taking the name Greene Rifles, the members pledged themselves to "defend the rights of their Sunny South." Some even suggested each militia district organize vigilance committees to help the county prepare for war. The division between those who sought compromise and those who sought immediate secession became clear when the state legislature authorized an election of delegates to a convention on the issue. One faction, led by attorney Yelverton King and merchant John Zimmerman, called for cooperation with the other southern states. Apparently, they wanted to slow down events in hope of finding a route to sectional reconciliation, as had happened in 1850. The other faction followed the lead of seventy-five-year-old Thomas Stocks, a wealthy planter and one of the few surviving original settlers of the county, demanding immediate secession. These two groups stood at loggerheads, and an ugly struggle for the election of delegates loomed.[17]

The crisis of fear had reached its peak, and Greene County's slaveowners had very real reasons for concern. A multitude of psychological, political, and cultural factors influenced the secession movement, but the most potent factors by far were economic and ideological. In the larger sense southerners were worried about northern control of the growing market economy and northern political control of the federal government. In Greene County the students of Mercer University addressed this issue in March 1860, decrying increasing northern political and economic influence and pledging to buy "no more apparel of Northern manufacture . . . [and] to appear on the rostrum at our next Annual commencement in Southern-made clothing." Others were concerned about the possible prohibition of slavery in the western territories. As Robert Toombs argued, "we must expand or perish." Expansion, many believed, was essential to the continued viability of southern civilization. These concerns were shared across the South, but there were also pressing local concerns in Greene County.[18]

During the 1850s agricultural production in Greene County began to decline. Wheat production increased during the decade, but it could not replace precipitous declines in corn and oat production. The value of farmland in Greene County also declined or, at best, remained stagnant during the decade. Most important, because of bad weather and eroding soil, Greene County produced almost one-third less cotton in 1859 than it had in 1849, moving Greene from eighth to thirty-first among Georgia's cotton-producing counties.[19]

Despite these declines in agricultural production and farm values, many of Greene County's citizens felt wealthier in 1860 than ever before. Of the almost $9 million worth of property reported to the 1860 census, only 20 percent represented the value of farms. Fully 60 percent of all wealth in the county lay in the value of slaves. Throughout the 1850s slave prices had soared, rising approximately 100 percent, and slaveowners enjoyed enormous capital gains.[20]

In Greene County the average taxable value of slaves increased from $498 per slave in 1858 to $650 per slave in 1860, an increase of 30 percent in just two years. As more than half the households in Greene County owned slaves, most of the county's citizens probably saw their personal wealth increase dramatically during the 1850s as the value of slaves increased. The Greenesboro newspapers reported the ever-higher prices of slaves with unconcealed delight. In December of 1859 the editor of the *Weekly Gazette* observed, "There were a large number of negroes sold in the city yesterday, at good figures. Some of them—young negroes—ran as high as $1,400 to $1,450." In March 1860 a twenty-seven-year-old male slave sold for $1,310, and a twenty-seven-year-old female sold for $1,360. In April the *Planters' Weekly* commented on even higher prices paid for slaves in a neighboring town. In this environment of ever-higher prices even investors with no land could make a good return, as Professor Henry H. Tucker did by simply leasing his family's slaves to farm owners while he watched their capital value grow.[21]

Slave values, however, depended on a vast regional market stretching from Delaware to Texas. Although a variety of cultural and economic factors could shape slave values, potential purchasers largely operated within market constraints, weighing the returns anticipated from the labor and fertility of individual slaves as well as the expected viability and security of the investment. Most Greene County planters had no direct interest in westward expansion, but limits on the future spread of slavery could reduce the value of their slaves. Similarly, few if any slaves escaped from Greene County to the free states of the North, but lax enforcement of fugitive slave laws directly affected the value of Greene County's slaves. A small minority of active abolitionists in the North stood little chance of overthrowing the constitutional protection of property in slaves, but their activities could reduce the prices investors would pay for slaves. If Greene County slaveowners wished to preserve their prosperity based on the capital appreciation of their slaves, then they somehow had to limit the impact of such threats.[22]

Greene County's slaveowners clearly understood these threats and could even joke about them. The *Planters' Weekly* reported that a famous New York medium had spoken to John Brown's spirit and that the repentant Brown confessed that he had been wrong: God did not oppose slavery. "The price of slaves will doubtless go up as soon as this pronouncement becomes generally known," quipped the paper's editor. On a more serious note, the newspaper summarized southerners' demands in December 1860 as including enforcement of the fugitive slave laws, an end to antislavery agitation, and federal action to protect southerners' property. In the same issue a correspondent stated the case more bluntly. "If the South submits to the administration of the Federal Government," worried the writer, "the reduction in the valuation of slaves will be on each one hundred dollars." [23]

Perhaps more important, many saw Lincoln's election as the final step in an ideological and political attack on slavery. A correspondent to the *Planters' Weekly* argued that the free states "have in the election of Lincoln made an overwhelming decision that slavery must be extinguished." Slavery shaped and literally colored the economic, social, and cultural structures that defined southern society. An attack on slavery threatened not just the linchpin of Greene County's economy but also the key element in the inhabitants' comprehension of their world. A world without slavery would for them be a world without pattern or form. Black and white, male and female, slave and free, all used slavery as a central reference point of their identity. The southern white elite, for example, constructed an elaborate code of honor around the system of slavery that defined individual roles and relationships within the slave society. Slaveownership within that code conferred more than mere wealth and power; it gave the slaveowner very real duties, privileges, prestige, and responsibility. The master or mistress, as much as the slave, was shaped by his or her role within the slave society. [24]

An attack on the system of slavery, then, threatened far more than slaveowners' wealth. Assaults on the morality of slaveowners, on the efficiency of slave labor, or on the continued expansion of slavery, all threatened the assumptions, beliefs, and the very identities of those who lived in the slave society. Even small farmers who owned no slaves understood their place in society in reference to slavery, and their hopes for the future often revolved around acquiring slaves. Only the slaves themselves might respond favorably to these attacks on their world. As the *Planters' Weekly* explained in December 1860, Lincoln's election imperiled "our liberties, our lives and honor . . . our all." The wonder is not that Greene County ultimately supported secession, but that the leaders were so moderate in seeking to preserve their world.[25]

The citizens of Greene County accepted political conflict as a necessary part of republicanism, but the growing factional conflict between the secessionist and cooperationist parties demanded a demonstration of unity. Greene County's leaders began to work to avoid a rancorous election of delegates to the state convention. Attorney James L. Brown, either on his own or at the behest of others, acted as a middleman between the factions. Brown attended both groups' nomination meetings in mid-December and successfully lobbied for a compromise slate of three delegates. The three nominees were Mercer president Nathaniel M. Crawford, Colonel Richard J. Willis, and Dr. Thomas N. Poullain. In June 1860 Crawford owned $24,400 worth of property, Willis owned 93 slaves, and Poullain, Greene County's wealthiest man, owned 134 slaves, a large plantation, and the Scull Shoals cotton factory. Both secessionists and cooperationists found these three men acceptable, for although they were "leading men," all three usually stood apart from politics. In the best republican tradition these three wealthy slaveholders were to represent the interests of the county in the state convention at the capitol.[26]

Professor Sanford's diary clearly reflected his depression and fear as he observed these events and recognized the growing possibility of war following Lincoln's election. He began to suffer "sick headaches," something he never complained of before, that only music played by his wife or daughter could ease. The village of Penfield formed an infantry company, the Dawson Grays, and asked Sanford to lead their drills. This Sanford did, but on several evenings after drill he suffered "severe sick headaches." With each passing day Sanford understood that reconciliation with the North became less likely, and he prayed earnestly for God to intervene and save the country. Unlike many in Greene County, he apparently had some concept of what war might bring, and he dreaded it.[27]

On Christmas day 1860 Professor Sanford celebrated with his family and then drilled the Dawson Grays that evening. He reported "a considerable turnout of recruits together with quite a crowd of darkeys who were much delighted." The slaves, enjoying their Christmas holiday, must have known something of the crisis that brought out so many new recruits. Isaiah Greene, a slave of Richard Willis, recalled that slaves talked about the political situation before the war began, and Minnie Davis, who belonged to the Crawford family, remembered her mother praying for the Yankees to come and set her and the other slaves free.

Such were the structures of slavery and the blindness caused by the ideological assumptions of slaveowners, however, that even as perceptive a man as Sanford never recorded a question or speculation as to what the slaves felt or thought.[28]

Wednesday, January 2, 1861, dawned rainy and cold, but Professor Sanford braved the weather to cast his vote for the single slate of candidates to the state secession convention. "Feel very anxious," he wrote, "in regard to the State Convention, but trust that God will give our Rulers wisdom." A week later the *Planters' Weekly* reported that most of the convention delegates favored immediate secession. The editor then wrote that he hoped Georgia would not be scourged with war and pestilence as a result.[29]

On January 16, 1861, the convention gathered at Milledgeville. Of the 301 elected delegates, 86 percent owned slaves, and almost half owned 20 or more slaves. Virtually all agreed that Georgia had to respond to Lincoln's election, but they could not agree on the exact course to be followed, and the convention divided into two factions. The secessionists, led by Robert Toombs, Thomas R. R. Cobb, and Eugenius Nesbit, called for immediate withdrawal from the Union to join the already seceded states of South Carolina, Alabama, Florida, and Mississippi. The cooperationists, led by Herschel V. Johnson, Alexander Stephens, and Benjamin Hill, proposed instead that all the slave states work together to present demands to the federal government. These demands, they argued, should include popular sovereignty for new states, protection of slavery in the territories, protection of the interstate slave trade, and strict enforcement of fugitive slave laws. If the federal government refused to accept these demands, then the slave states, acting together, should secede.[30]

The test came following a motion by Benjamin Hill calling for adoption of the cooperationist plan. Crawford voted in favor of the motion, while Willis and Poullain joined more than two-thirds of the delegates in voting against it. Crawford joined the cooperationist camp, while planters Willis and Poullain favored immediate secession. When it later became clear that the majority of delegates favored immediate succession, Crawford and most of the other cooperationists dramatized Georgia's unity by signing the Ordinance of Secession.[31]

When word of secession reached Greensboro, its supporters' celebration swept the town into a frenzy. The Greene Rifles drilled and then fired their cannon late into the night. Seven miles to the north, at Penfield, Professor Sanford listened to the echoing rumble of cannon fire and began to ponder the future. He found the enthusiasm of the young men worrisome and the prospect of war frightening. Later that evening, unable to sleep, he confessed to his diary that "while as a Georgian I shall submit to the action of the state, still I cannot rejoice in the dissolution of the Union."[32]

Throughout the winter and spring of 1861, military organization accelerated in Greene County. The Dawson Grays and the Greene Rifles obtained arms and uniforms, and Sanford requisitioned eighty smoothbore muskets from the state for a new unit, the Mercer Cadets. Greensboro attorney George O. Dawson organized and led a new company, the Stephens Light Guards. Then, in what many considered an unprecedented action, on April 26 the Greene County Inferior Court authorized $5,000 worth of bonds to support the soldiers of Greene County. The inferior court also created committees of leading men to help the indigent families of soldiers called away to war.[33]

Daily life continued in a relatively normal way even as Greene County prepared for war. On March 23 the Sanfords attended their slave George's wedding to Rosette, a slave of local planter Augustus Sharpe. Two weeks later, upset by poor student performance in class, Sanford lamented, "I began to wish I was in almost any other business . . . verily, teaching is pretty trying." Despite the appearance of normality, however, these were exceptional times. The drive to organize the county did more than prepare the people for war. It also began to build a spirit of unity and common purpose among a people in the midst of a dangerous crisis. For many, this push for organization laid the basis of a new Confederate nationalism. Certainly there were other reasons for its development; for example, most southerners shared a common economic and ideological identity on which to build a national identity. But southerners also already had a national identity with the United States, and many struggled, as Professor Sanford did, to cling to their American identity. Events in the winter and spring of 1861, however, began to transform that identity.[34]

Throughout January, February, and March of 1861, Professor Sanford continued to worry in his journal about "our Nation," and "our Country," meaning the United States. Though he occasionally mentioned the Confederacy, he apparently felt little or no identity with it. He watched the Mercer student body melt away as more and more young men left to join military units. The students elected him captain of the Mercer University Cadets, and he led them in drill. Despite these events, Sanford still maintained his American identity and prayed for God to restore the nation without war.[35]

Just as class consciousness is a dynamic process that grows out of particular historical circumstances, so too do events form and shape the national consciousness of a people. The preparations for war, the opinions of neighbors and colleagues, and the press reports of Northern intentions all began to chip away at Sanford's commitment to the Union. Lincoln's call for 75,000 troops in mid-April shocked Sanford and caused him to reconsider his loyalty to the United States. Soon after, word of fighting in Virginia hastened this process, and by mid-May, the once reluctant Sanford had developed a strong identification with his "countrymen," meaning southerners in the Confederacy. "Verily," he wrote, "the Black Republicans seem to be the most abominable miscreants that ever disgraced humanity. . . . Georgia did not secede a minute too soon."[36]

Ritual ceremonies, especially surrounding the departure of troops for the war, also played an important role in the development of Confederate national identity. Generally, elite women invented and organized these ceremonies and through them helped create a Confederate nationalism. At first these women took on only modest tasks, avoiding activities that would draw them inappropriately into the public sphere. Professor Sanford's wife, Maria, for example, joined with other leading women from Penfield to provide every soldier in the Dawson Grays with a uniform and socks. This group also began to sew a beautiful embroidered battle flag for presentation to the Dawson Grays. The distribution of clothing took place privately, and the women arranged for a man to represent them at the public flag presentation ceremony. Only as the war continued and the needs grew more dramatic did these women begin aggressively to enter the public sphere.[37]

On the morning of April 29, 1861, the Dawson Grays formed up on the front lawn of Mercer University to receive the ladies' battle flag. Professor Joseph Willett acted for the women in making a short speech and then handed the flag to Captain Robert L. McWhorter, who had been elected to lead the Dawson Grays. McWhorter, ever the politician, responded with some brief but gallant remarks praising the women and their support of the Confederate cause. The ceremony continued as the company formed up and marched behind their new flag to the railroad depot in Woodville, where they boarded trains for Virginia.[38]

The women of Greenesboro organized a larger and more elaborate ceremony for the departure of the Stephens Light Guards on June 3. This time the soldiers received a flag decorated with the emblems of dozens of young ladies "to urge them on to deeds of noble daring." Professor Henry H. Tucker presented the flag and gave a speech "on behalf of the Ladies." After Captain George Dawson thanked the women, the crowd followed the soldiers to the depot for a drawn-out, tearful, and dramatic departure. Obviously moved, one editor of the *Planters' Weekly* tried to paint the scene with words. "The whistle blows," he wrote, "one long mingled shout burst upon the air, and they are gone; speeding on their way to meet their country's foes. Farewell! Farewell! until our country is free."[39]

Professor Sanford, like hundreds of others, traveled to Greenesboro to watch the departure. He approved of the young soldiers' eagerness for battle, many of whom were concerned that the war would end before they got a chance to fight. That night, after he returned home, Sanford prayed for God to help the soldiers drive back "the fanatical hordes who are seeking to subjugate us." Later he continued, "the more I reflect upon it, the more I am satisfied that the cause of the South is founded on *justice*, *truth*, and *right*."[40]

Sanford's views had changed dramatically over the course of just a few months. During the winter he clearly questioned the need for secession, and his national identity lay with the federal union. By June 1861 he fully identified with the new Confederate nation, and he was not alone. Most citizens of Greene County probably experienced a similar transformation. Attorneys Rolin Stephens and Frederick Fuller, who owned and edited the *Planters' Weekly*, clearly went through the same process. The previous winter they had urged caution and a cooperationist approach to the crisis, and they expressed real fears of secession bringing war and pestilence. But by June of 1861 they had become ardent Confederates.

June 5 was the last issue of the *Planters' Weekly* because Frederick Fuller left for war with the Greene Rifles at the end of the month. Fuller explained his new understanding of the situation in the newspaper's last issue. "This war is emphatically a peoples' war," he wrote, "and the people must sustain it or perish. Our base and merciless enemy boasts that they will divide our lands among them, and claim our wives and daughters as their own." He concluded, "I, for one, would rather shoot my wife and daughter and die in the breech than be conquered." Fuller proved sadly prophetic. After rising to command the Greene Rifles, he died literally in the breech at the bloody angle of Spotsylvania. The other editor of the *Planters' Weekly*, Rolin Stephens, delayed going to war until March 1862. The delay proved of little benefit; on July 1, 1862, he died in the charge at Malvern Hill.[41]

Ceremonies of departure were not the only patriotic rituals organized by women to support the war effort. Allegorical plays, heavily laced with symbolism of the new nation, were produced in communities across the South. One one occasion, however, the message was not what the organizers hoped to convey. The women of White Plains in southern Greene County organized a patriotic spectacle for the evening of September 20, 1861. The appearance of a beautiful young girl dressed to symbolize the new Confederate nation highlighted plans for the evening. Laura Alfriend, the fourteen-year-old daughter of a local planter, was chosen to represent the "Southern Confederacy." Night fell, and only candle footlights lit the stage as the curtain slowly went up to reveal a patriotic tableaux. Laura Alfriend, costumed and holding a Confederate flag, stood perfectly still in the center of the stage. Somehow, as she stood there, her dress caught fire, and horrified onlookers watched as flames enveloped her and the Confederate flag burned in her outstretched hands. After lingering five days, Laura Alfriend died, "spreading a general gloom over the community." [42]

September's gloom may have come from more than Laura Alfriend's death. The first major engagement of the war at Bull Run had resulted in a southern victory, but it had not ended the war. Bull Run also forced many to realize what war really meant. John C. Reid, a Greensboro attorney, served through the war as an officer with the Stephens Light Guards from Greene County. While moving forward at Bull Run his company came under a withering crossfire, and in less than five minutes twenty of the sixty-four men who entered action that day were killed or wounded. "I shall never forget," Reid wrote later, "how pale, stiff, and thoroughly dead Gus Daniel looked as I glanced down when I stumbled over him. This was the first dead man I saw." After the battle, as he tried to help the wounded, he found his friend Thad Howell. "A bullet had struck his forehead, and the brains were oozing out," wrote Reid. "His heels drummed on the ground constantly, but he was utterly unconscious." George Butler, a less-educated man, struggled to explain his shock and horror after the battle in a letter to his sister: "i can't tell how many was killed our loss was considerable i never want to See Such A sight a gain the ground was covered with the ded and the grones of the dying." [43]

In a series of letters to his fiancée, John Reid pondered his experience at Bull Run, apparently understanding for the first time how terrible war could be. He drew a detailed map of his regiment's role in the fight, "resolved upon showing the terrific results to the 8th Georgia of inexperienced conduct." Over the following months Reid reviewed "over and over every military book I could buy or borrow," determined that his men would never again suffer due to his lack of knowledge and inexperience. Meanwhile, in Greene County, Governor Brown ordered the Mercer

Cadets to return their muskets for use by active troops. In August a public rally in Greenesboro called for the people of Greene County to donate their rifles to the Confederacy. The county, which had already sent three companies of men to war, began organizing two more companies. The dream of a swift victory had passed. Some began to understand how unprepared the South was for war and that it would take more than patriotic allegories to fight it.[44]

The Winter of the Heart Is upon Us

In March of 1863 it took more than four Confederate dollars to buy one gold dollar. A private serving in the Confederate army, if paid, earned $11 per month, or a gold wage of $2.68. That March twelve women entered a butcher store in Atlanta and asked the price of bacon. "One dollar a pound," replied the storekeeper. Several women took out guns, and one held her pistol to the storekeeper's head, asking how he expected the poor wives of soldiers to pay such prices. Meanwhile, the other women packed up $200 worth of food. When everyone had loaded up, the gang fled, leaving the terrified butcher unharmed.[1]

The editor of the Augusta *Daily Chronicle and Sentinel* argued that, while this "Amazonian band" might not be important in and of itself, it frighteningly represented "an intimation of the direction toward which we are drifting." Like many others in the Confederate South, the editor feared that war had begun to destroy the values and structures of southern society. In particular, he argued, the equanimity with which many people accepted this crime committed by desperate women boded ill for the future. "If we suffer the foundations of law and equity to be undermined," he wrote, "we shall be in danger of evils at home fully as much to be dreaded as the assaults of the enemy."[2]

War on a titanic scale did threaten the "foundations of law and equity" in Greene County and across the South. As southern leaders struggled with military affairs, they also confronted the challenge of remaking the South's dependent cotton economy into an independent, diversified economy able to support modern war. This effort to remake the southern economy forced many southerners to reconsider their assumptions about private property, the free market, and the law. Though the Confederate government had considerable success in reshaping the economy, so that the South was largely self-sufficient by 1863, the process itself caused social change. Inevitably, a growing conflict developed between those who supported a continued free market and absolute private property, the central elements of a commercial market economy, and those who were willing to abandon these things in the name of southern independence.[3]

During the summer of 1861 Greene County began experiencing one of the first and most persistent economic effects of the war: inflation. Though some merchants raised prices hoping to profit from the war, the dramatic decline in the value of the Confederate dollar resulted mostly from the new government's fiscal policies and doubts about the new nation's survival. The Confederacy printed enormous amounts of currency but lacked the resources needed to support the money. Most southerners, however, preferred to blame rising prices on "speculators" and "profiteers."[4]

In August 1861 Isaac Harman, a Jewish merchant in Penfield, raised prices in his store. Several days later ten Mercer University students confronted Harman outside his store, condemned him as a Jew exploiting his neighbors, and beat him. Harman responded with assault charges against the students. Before the community could digest these events, Harman and his Jewish partners also filed theft charges against another Mercer student, sending Penfield and Greene County into an uproar. Professor Shelton P. Sanford felt "very troubled by the difficulty between some of our students and Mr. Harman, a Jew." The day after the assault Sanford sat on a university justice court that disciplined the students, and Harman later dropped the charges. This "difficulty," however, revealed that the exigencies of war had already strained the bonds of community in Greene County. Isaac Harman and his associates had operated their store in Penfield peacefully for years, until the stress of war awakened a latent anti-Semitism. Suddenly, Harman the merchant could be seen as an outsider with business connections in New York, as someone who acted like a speculator. If he were a speculator, he represented the very forces arrayed against the South. Severed from the community it had once been part of, Harman's business declined so much over the next year that Harman eventually left Greene County.[5]

Several days after the incident, Sanford mused on the problem of rising prices. The greatest threat posed by speculators, he decided, was that their actions could disrupt the good order of a community, creating division and chaos. Sanford, like many, did not see that the problem of inflation had sources in more than mere speculation. Inflation stressed the usually stable structures of the community, and rising prices exacerbated class divisions among whites at the very time the new southern nation needed unity. As inflation widened the gap between planters and small farmers, it confirmed a growing perception of the southern revolution as a rich man's war and a poor man's fight. At the very least, growing economic inequality among whites encouraged some to question the validity of the free market and property rights in the midst of war.[6]

In March 1862 the Greene County grand jury, concerned about the same problems as Sanford, struck a blow against "profiteering" within the county. The jurors handed down two indictments for extortion: one against Henry Atwood and Thomas Rokenbaugh, who managed the Curtwright Manufacturing Company at Long Shoals, and the other against Dr. Thomas N. Poullain, who owned and managed Fontenoy Mills at Scull Shoals. Both factories had raised their prices substantially for cotton yarn and cloth. Greenesboro merchants had paid the higher prices, for outside supplies from the North and Europe had been cut off by the war. These merchants and others, however, convinced the grand jury to investigate. The grand jury found that the prices charged were "unjust, exorbitant, and unreasonable . . . contrary to the good order, peace and dignity" of the community and handed down the indictments. Though the market supported the prices charged by the mills, the grand jury refused to let the workings of the free market take precedence over their perception of community interest.[7]

William A. Lofton, the state's solicitor, approached these extortion indictments with caution. Perhaps grand jury foreman John G. Holtzclaw, a prosperous farmer and gristmill owner who rose from yeoman origins, could afford to offend a man as powerful as Dr. Poullain. Lofton, a politician and lawyer, could not. Knowing that not everyone agreed with the grand jury's attack on the free market, and perhaps not agreeing with it himself, Lofton simply did not proceed with the cases and continued both to the next term of court. A new grand jury assembled in September 1862, and Lofton awaited their action in the matter.[8]

The September 1862 grand jury chose Rowan H. Ward as their foreman. A wealthy planter, Greene County's state senator, a former Whig, and a leading proponent of scientific agriculture, Ward firmly believed in the free market. In their presentments, the September grand jury repudiated the actions of the previous grand jury. Controlling prices or profits infringed on basic individual property rights that should never be violated, argued the grand jury. Producers had to be free to charge whatever the market would bear. Reasoning within the assumptions of commercial market capitalism, the jurors could offer no solution to the problem of rising prices. "We confess that we know not where an effectual and safe remedy is to be found," they explained, "save only in the unselfish patriotism of our fellow-citizens." At the next term of court the extortion cases were entered into the record as nolle prosequi, meaning that Lofton simply refused to prosecute the case.[9]

The state also tried to control prices. During 1861 the price of salt soared throughout the South. Southerners needed salt to cure meat, and price increases threatened to limit the production of needed provisions. In late 1861 Georgia governor Joseph Brown took action, authorizing state authorities to seize supplies of salt and pay a fixed price to the owners. This program briefly stabilized prices, but many found such interference in the market unconscionable. An outraged *Daily Chronicle and Sentinel* charged that Brown's disregard of market forces and the rights of private property put Georgia on the road to tyranny. Then, in early 1862 Governor Brown tried to control the upward-spiraling price of corn. The *Daily Chronicle and Sentinel* again condemned his action, arguing that price controls would actually harm the poor, for there would be no corn available at all if prices could not draw it to market. Governor Brown's attempts to control prices failed, as did local attempts in Greene County, not only because of some opposition to limits on the free market, but also because the factors causing inflation were beyond state and local control. Only sweeping financial reforms by the Confederate Congress combined with military victory could have controlled inflation in the Confederacy.[10]

These early local actions to curb prices or limit profits, though perhaps futile, demonstrated many Georgians' ambivalence about the workings and effects of the commercial market economy. As the war progressed, however, direct government intervention in the economy became a necessity, and the assumptions of the market economy seemed to impede the war effort. Some southern ideologues argued that market-based values had corrupted northern society and that only independence could save the South from similar corruption. There were also many people across the South who did not share the values of the commercial market economy. Tens of thousands of Georgians, for example, lived in the northern highlands or the southeastern pine barrens in communities largely outside the commercial market economy. These people held values drawn from their subsistence economy that many people in Greene County and across the plantation belt of Georgia looked to with nostalgic longing. Even in Greene County itself, some people maintained a subsistence way of life, rejecting the benefits of the commercial market. Attacks on the values of the market economy would find great support among these people.

During the summer of 1861 several correspondents to the Athens *Southern Cultivator* called for farmers to withdraw from the market economy and seek self-sufficiency. "Reconcile yourselves to get along with as little money as possible," suggested one writer; "put your female slaves to work spinning, and [work] to make bread and meat." In this way, he argued, the South could win independence. The Reverend Charles W. Howard of the *Southern Cultivator* went further, arguing that the war was the best thing that could have happened to the South. Some would die, he admitted, and the war would cost millions, "but it will have been money well spent . . . so developing our resources as to render us commercially an independent people." War would force the South to escape dependency, resulting in both political and economic independence.[11]

On Saturday, March 15, 1862, a number of Greene County planters, farmers, and professional men gathered in Greenesboro to discuss ways to respond to the challenges of war. After hearing addresses by Mercer professors Henry H. Tucker and Nathaniel M. Crawford, the meeting took up several proposed resolutions calling for decisive action to confront the South's problems. "Whereas the crop of provisions raised by us does not supply the demand even in ordinary times," explained the resolutions, "and [with] the great granaries of the northwest closed to us, to continue the culture of cotton to the exclusion of grain is virtual surrender to the enemy." Confronting their community's dependence on the world market and on food grown elsewhere, Greene County's leaders sought a road to immediate self-sufficiency. They also saw the potential costs of failure, for "the skill of our officers and the valor of our troops are of no avail without bread."[12]

Only one thing could begin to solve the problems created by their own and the South's dependency, the planters declared in their resolution. Southerners must abandon the market economy built around cotton and begin to produce all the provisions and goods needed for war. In support of this resolution, Greene County's planters pledged that "as a matter of duty to ourselves, to our country, to our world, and to our God, we will devote all our energies to the raising of provisions." Cotton could be grown only for the grower's use and not for the market. Anyone who continued to produce cotton for the market "gave aid and comfort to the enemy" and made "war upon his neighbors." The planters also resolved to end the practice of distilling grain into alcohol to suppress the production and distribution of alcohol in Greene County and to encourage the South's troops to give greater respect to the Sabbath. Finally, they asked the state legislature for appropriate laws to put these resolutions into effect statewide.[13]

During the first year or more of war, voluntary efforts to control cotton production seemed to suffice. Planters and farmers across Georgia agreed to limit production of cotton and emphasize food crops. In neighboring Clarke and Hancock Counties planters promised to grow at most one-half acre of cotton per hand. In other counties farmers promised to limit cotton production or stop growing cotton altogether. Such patriotic voluntary restrictions produced dramatic results. Even those who doubted the meaningfulness of the actions, such as Dolly Lunt Burge in Morgan County, planted corn instead of cotton. Statewide, Georgia produced about 700,000 bales of cotton and 30 million bushels of corn in 1861. In 1862 cotton production fell to only 60,000 bales, but corn production doubled to 60 million bushels.[14]

Such dramatic voluntary efforts did not assure a change in the focus of the southern economy, however. Farmers and planters could at any time resume growing cotton. Just as conscription came to seem necessary for a successful southern war effort, so too did laws controlling the production and distribution of agricultural products. These impositions began in the summer of 1861, when the Confederate Congress prohibited shipments of cotton to the North and restricted shipments of cotton overseas. They hoped to create a "cotton famine" that would force European intervention in the war, but these laws also legitimated using legal restrictions on the market economy and property rights as part of the war effort.[15]

In 1862, following the suggestions of planters across the state, first Governor Brown and then the legislature prohibited the distillation of grain into alcohol. In late 1862 the legislature passed a law limiting cotton production to a maximum of three acres per hand, with a $500 fine for violations. The Confederate Congress also acted, passing impressment legislation in March 1863 that legalized the army's already common practices of confiscating local food supplies to feed troops and of taking slaves for labor. Fixed prices, usually far below market value, were to be paid in return. In April 1863 the Confederate government began a direct tax in kind, requiring all farmers to give one-tenth of their produce to the government. They also enacted an 8 percent property tax and a graduated income tax. Though many criticized these modifications to absolute property rights and a free market, others saw them as necessary to the war effort. The Augusta *Constitutionalist* went so far as to argue that if the government would simply confiscate all property and manage the entire economy, putting every person on rations like soldiers, the war could be won in six months.[16]

Radical intervention in the economy by the government produced results, especially in the field of industrial production. By 1863 the Confederate government had built the world's largest gunpowder works at Augusta and enough arms factories so that the South was self-supporting in the production of small arms. This system of government-owned war production spread to Greene County, where the government bought the old buildings of the Greensboro Manufacturing Company for the arms firm of Leech and Rigdon. Manufacturing copies of the 1851 Navy Colt revolver, Leech and Rigdon began operations in early 1863, producing pistols in Greensboro until they moved to Augusta in early 1864. Leech and Rigdon provided a concrete example within the community of Greene County of the potential efficiency of government-regulated economic development, the sort of success that had induced the *Constitutionalist* to call for complete government management of the economy.[17]

Many planters in Greene County strongly supported the war effort even if they did not enter combat. In the summer of 1863 one Greene County correspondent decried those focused on making money from the war and held up the example of Thomas P. Janes as a model of self-sacrifice. Janes grew no cotton, sold grain to the government at far below market price, and distributed corn and wheat free to the destitute families of soldiers. David C. Barrow also distributed food to the poor neighbors of his Greene County plantation, and his 1864 tax statement shows he produced virtually no cotton on his Greene County land. Others, however, were not so happy to support the war. Joseph Printup left his Gordon County plantation in northwest Georgia because of the continued depredations of soldiers and moved to a farm in Greene County. He was sick and tired of supporting the war and decided to "plant cotton on William's place, all the law will allow." As the demands of the government continued, as inflation grew, as tens of thousands died, many in Greene County probably came to agree with Joseph Printup, who wrote in 1864, "I have done enough for the war."[18]

In the name of winning independence the people of Greene County accepted direct challenges to the prevailing economic and social assumptions of their culture. Conscription forced white men into involuntary servitude, laws controlled prices and markets, the army confiscated private property virtually at will, and a state-supported program of rapid industrialization began to transform the agrarian economy of the South. The reorientation of agricultural production to food crops undoubtedly changed the lives of Greene County's slaves, as did the departure of white owners and overseers for war. More than 800 men left to fight in the war, many never to return, and their absence began to reshape the community. The responsibility of managing farms and businesses and of maintaining the day-to-day life of the community fell increasingly on the women of Greene County.

Women from poor families sometimes struggled merely to survive, with no husbands, fathers, or brothers to help. Many farmers' wives had to manage affairs for the first time, and some women who had never before worked in the fields took up the plow or the hoe. Even wealthy women, with fathers or husbands still in Greene County, took on new tasks to aid the Confederate cause. Through the spring and summer of 1861, individually or in groups, women made uniforms, socks, bandages, and other necessities for the troops. As the demands of the war grew, however, these individual and informal efforts proved insufficient. On July 16, 1861, a group of women in southern Greene County formed the Soldiers' Relief Association of White Plains, the first independent, public women's organization in Greene County history.[19]

Soon women in Greensboro, Penfield, Union Point, and several rural militia districts formed their own organizations. The women who worked in these organizations came from a variety of backgrounds. A list of 162 free women and 17 slaves (three of the latter men) who knitted socks for soldiers in January 1863 named not only the wives of planters and wealthy farmers but also several wives of landless farmers. Relief association members came from different backgrounds and followed the same patterns of deference in their organizations as men did in theirs. The women of White Plains elected Mary Jarrell, the wife of a wealthy local planter, as their president. In Union Point, Jennie Hart, wife of merchant-turned-planter James B. Hart, led local efforts. The Greensboro Benevolent Society elected Eliza King "directress," for apparently local women accorded her the same respect as men did her husband, lawyer and Masonic Grand Master Yelverton P. King. Women from planter and professional families dominated these organizations, and as the war continued, the influence of these wealthy women grew, for they had access to resources far beyond that of poorer women.[20]

In October 1861 Mary Jarrell argued with pride that "the women of this county are doing more for our absent soldiers than the men." Yet, she explained, the women of Greene County "have done their duty unostentatiously . . . with busy hands and womanly devotion to their noble work." Mary Jarrell, and probably many others, struggled with women's new roles in the public sphere and tried to put her own and other women's actions into the context of domesticity. Not only did women move into the public sphere through their relief work, but those who were wives of farmers and planters had to engage in business and manage their property as well. Even if they had an overseer or black driver to help them in their tasks, ultimate responsibility rested on the women's shoulders. In October 1861 the wife of a small planter probably revealed the concerns of many women in Georgia. She wrote to her husband in Virginia, "I am overseeing a little more. . . . [The slaves] don't respect [the overseer] half as much as they do me." Then she complained that the slaves would do better work without the overseer but that she could not "stay without some man on the place." Her husband told her to use her own judgment and get rid of the overseer if necessary. A few months later he told her he could not keep up with the farm from a distance. "You'll have to get along almost by yourself," he explained, "so you must be man and woman both while the war lasts." [21]

The local relief organizations needed coordination, and the women looked to their county seat for guidance. In 1862 women centralized authority by creating the Soldiers' Relief Society of Greene County. Eliza King served as president, and under her leadership the various organizations in Greene County worked together to produce needed clothing for soldiers and to help the families of poor men away in the army. This organization focused on the needs of the county's own men and families, but other women realized that efforts could be expanded to reach any soldier in need. [22]

In Union Point twenty or so women led by Jennie Hart decided to help more than just local soldiers. Union Point lay halfway between Atlanta and Augusta and served as the junction for the railroad line to Athens. Countless soldiers passed through Union Point on their way to war or on their way home. On September 29, 1862, the Wayside Home, a combination hostel, hospital, and canteen, began operations, staffed by Jennie Hart's volunteers. Over the next two years these women provided food and lodging free of charge to almost 35,000 Confederate soldiers, serving about fifty men a day. When trains halted only briefly, volunteers boarded them to take the soldiers food and water. Many sick and wounded soldiers left the trains at the Wayside Home, and some died there. Thousands of men signed the register and in their comments spoke of the services as "most welcome," "unexpected," and "revivifying." One soldier called the volunteers "visions of angels." [23]

Many women from the county's elite families had experience managing large households, and they put these skills to work for the Confederate war effort. Other women contributed things as simple as chickens, turnip greens, or their skill in sewing. Weekly lists of donations to the Wayside Home appeared in the *Chronicle and Sentinel* and told the story of an effort spanning all classes of women. Dozens of items were donated during the week ending December 21, 1862. George S. Tunnell's mother, representing a relatively prosperous family, gave two chickens, two pounds of butter, and two dozen eggs. Mollie Derham, from a less prosperous family, gave a basket of potatoes. Lucy Bently of Weldon, Virginia, sent six pairs of wool socks. Many individuals gave gifts of money, which the volunteers used to purchase supplies. Coordinating and distributing these and scores of other items donated each week required great skill, and apparently the women carried it off without a hitch.[24]

As the war continued, the support of women became increasingly important. In November 1862 the government sought formal control over the production of uniforms by creating the Confederate Clothing Bureau in Augusta, Georgia. By February 1863 more than 1,000 women worked there for wages, producing clothing for the army, and thousands of volunteers contributed their time and their skills to the bureau. Local organizations continued to support their own communities' troops as well. In March 1863 the Dawson Grays, serving in Virginia, passed resolutions thanking the women of Greene County for their support. Because of the women's devotion, explained the soldiers' resolutions, "we are encouraged to go forward more cheerfully in the performance of [our] duties." Union soldiers understood the vital emotional and physical support women gave the Confederate cause and justified depredations across the South as a way to discourage women's support for the Confederate war effort. During their sweep across Georgia and the Carolinas, one of Sherman's officers told a woman protesting the destruction of homes and farms, "You women keep up this war, we are fighting you."[25]

In some cases women assumed roles beyond the bounds of extended domesticity. In 1861 twenty-year-old Emma Berrian Heard married Dr. John Howell of White Plains. In her husband's hometown Emma joined the local relief association and served as secretary. She refused to be known as Mrs. John Howell and signed all official correspondence as a man would, "E. B. Howell." Emma also taught at the White Plains Academy, and in 1863 when the last male teacher left to fight in the war, she became principal of the school. Emma Howell was the first female principal in Greene County, and to some it seemed strange that a woman would have such authority. The *Constitutionalist* explained that because of the war's need for manpower, "we are left no resource but to have female teachers." These opportunities for women such as Emma Howell to exercise authority outside the domestic sphere must have caused some to question the prevailing structure of women's roles in southern society.[26]

Despite the growing desperation of the Confederate cause, some women found their experiences during the war liberating. Major Daniel Printup of Greene County was captured by Union forces and imprisoned at Johnson's Island. While there, he wrote his cousin Anna Pickett about his worries that his wife could not deal with the responsibilities of the plantation. Anna replied, "I hope your wife in all her trials finds herself equal to them, and like many others, finds out for the first time what she is capable of doing."[27]

Many women were forced to find out their own capabilities. Dosia Harris remembered that her master left for a time during the war while his sons were away in the army. His wife, Mary Davis, took over the plantation. "She had a fine pacing mule," recalled Dosia, "[and] every morning she got on dat mule and rid out to her plantation. She evermore did oversee . . . de plantation." Dosia Harris thought Mary Davis a sharper and stricter manager than her husband or her sons. As women rose to the challenges posed by the war, some became successful in their own right and probably gained new confidence in themselves.[28]

Through organizations such as the Soldiers' Relief Society and the Wayside Home, as well as by managing farms and businesses, women participated in the world of business and war. They also implicitly entered the public sphere of politics, for their efforts not only supported the Confederate war effort but also demonstrated political support for the war and the new nation. Though clearly class conscious, these local women's organizations united many white women across class lines and unquestionably encouraged a sense of sexual solidarity among southern white women. Ella Gertrude Clanton Thomas of Augusta thought of returning to her Catholic faith in July of 1864 but found her "longing checked by the idea that priests are *men*." Men, including her husband, could not understand women's sufferings due to the war. Even if the female solidarity induced by war proved ephemeral, the initiative and independence displayed by many women suggests that they were not part of an oppressed class of plantation mistresses. Rather, these were confident women, sure of themselves and already accustomed to exercising power within their households. It was the exertion of power outside of the household that most found exceptional and that many women struggled to characterize as "womanly."[29]

As women's importance to the war effort grew, so too did a powerful ideology of cheerful feminine sacrifice and devotion. These concepts dominated public discourse in the South throughout the war and led many women to greater efforts in support of the war. Greene County's Dawson Grays were encouraged by aid from women, and their resolution of thanks also encouraged more women to make sacrifices for the cause. The weekly notices of Wayside Home activities in Augusta newspapers presented the sacrifices of the women working there as models for other women. The ideology of cheerful sacrifice even required women to hide their suffering from soldiers at the front. One correspondent to the Turnwold *Countryman*, of neighboring Putnam County, chided women for writing discouraging letters to soldiers. "I am not surprised at their feeling badly," he wrote, "but they should not write gloomy letters." [30]

As the war continued, as inflation, scarcity, government demands, and casualties grew, the ideology of cheerful sacrifice wore thin. In the midst of personal desperation, especially during the last year of war, many women in Greene County gave up their aid activities. On June 30, 1864, the Wayside Home at Union Point closed, largely due to a lack of resources. That same year Emma Howell abandoned the effort to run the White Plains school, feeling success was impossible. In Greensboro some women continued to work aiding the wounded soldiers who flooded the town during the battles around Atlanta. Every store and church, and even the Female College, served as hospitals for the wounded from the summer of 1864 until the end of the war. This was grim work, as Ella Thomas discovered in late July 1864, when the threat of a raid on Greensboro forced the removal of many casualties to Augusta. Thomas went to the Catholic church to help and "found a state of destitution I had never imagined before." Wounded men filled the church, straw spread on the floor serving as their beds. Shocked, Thomas saw every type of wound: "some with arms and legs cut off, others with flesh wounds, two men dying." The next morning she returned to the church and found one man she had tried to comfort the day before dead and "swarming with flies." Ella Thomas never again tried to aid the wounded and asked later, "Oh God, will this war never cease?" [31]

As the ideology of cheerful sacrifice collapsed, the echoes reached soldiers at the front. Daniel Printup, a prisoner of war, received a moving letter from his two young sons in Union Point. "Ma is very sad about you being in prison," they wrote; "she is afraid that she will never see you again." When her husband was ordered to the battles around Atlanta, Ella

Thomas angrily wrote: "Am I willing to give my husband to gain Atlanta for the Confederacy? No, No, No, a thousand times No!" As the collapse of the Confederacy drew near, the impact of many women withdrawing their support for the cause must have hastened its end.[32]

In August 1862 Miles Tidwell wrote a long and powerful letter to his former Mercer University classmate, George S. Tunnell of Greene County. He spoke of those taken by the war—their mutual friend George Heard, who died at Bull Run, Tidwell's brother Frank, who died in Virginia, and others. Distraught and rambling, Tidwell asked why God would let a war kill such good men. "Oh, this cruel, cruel war," lamented Tidwell, explaining that his hopes for the future, his trust in Providence, even his belief in God had been crushed by the war. "Now the raven of despair is ever croaking at my heart," he wrote. "Alas, the winter of the heart is upon us, and surely death must be insatiable."[33]

No one expected war to be so terrible, its demands to be so great. The Dawson Grays, Stephens Light Guards, and Greene Rifles all left Greene County for Virginia during the spring and summer of 1861. In 1860 there were about 1,075 white males aged thirteen to forty-five in the county, so these three companies represented almost one-third of Greene's military-age white males. They were not enough. In October, following a call from Governor Joseph Brown, volunteers formed two new companies for state service to defend Savannah. Workers from Dr. Poullain's cotton mill joined one company led by Peter Northen, an elderly veteran of the War of 1812. William A. Florence, a young attorney with no military experience, led the second company. These men signed up for six months of military service so that they could be home in time for spring planting and then marched off to defend the coast. Most were later drafted into other units.[34]

Again, the war demanded more. On March 1, 1862, Professor Sanford attended a public rally in Greensboro to raise another company of troops for the war. Only fifty-five men volunteered. Three days later a second rally managed, in light of the looming threat of conscription, to raise enough additional men to fill Greene's quota. This company, the Greene County Volunteers, marched off to Virginia armed with twelve rifles and eighty-six shotguns. In less than a year after the beginning of hostilities, Greene County had sent more than 600 men to war. The absence of 60 percent of Greene County's military-age white males must have greatly disrupted the community.[35]

These community-based military units offered some advantages to the soldiers by providing a cohesiveness and an infrastructure of support lacking in other units. Further, these companies served as a focus of pride for a community, a visible symbol of its support for and participation in the war. However, units tied to specific localities also had disadvantages. During most of the war volunteer units had the right to elect their own officers. Quite naturally the men tended to elect political and social leaders from their own communities, often the very men who helped recruit the unit. Unfortunately, many of the men elected lacked the ability to exercise military command. The Greene Rifles elected Phillip B. Robinson as their captain, and he led them off to training camp in the spring of 1861. Robinson did not prove a competent leader and soon resigned his command and returned home. Robert L. McWhorter, elected captain of the Dawson Grays, proved a poor company commander, but he had great skill at raising supplies. In early 1862 McWhorter received a promotion to major and assignment to the Quartermaster Department, where he could more fully exercise his abilities.[36]

Being part of a community-based unit also made it difficult for men to rise above their civilian station in life. Everyone knew everyone else's social status, so men from poorer families found advancement difficult despite their performance or abilities. More important for the families at home, military disasters disproportionately affected the people of the involved units' communities. In September 1863 Greene County's Stocks Volunteers, Company B of the Fifty-fifth Georgia Regiment Volunteer Infantry, surrendered at Cumberland Gap. The sixty-two men captured were sent to Camp Douglas, Illinois, as prisoners. There, one-fourth died and the remainder suffered terribly from sickness and malnutrition during the winter of 1863–64. This capture of one small company caused great distress for dozens of families in Greene County. Ironically, the remaining members of the Stocks Volunteers, who because of wounds or leave had not been with the company at Cumberland Gap, were assigned to guard duty at Andersonville.[37]

Because of the changing organizations of local militia units and because some men from Greene County served with units organized elsewhere, a complete count of men from the community who served in the Confederate armed forces proved impossible. Greene County sent six full companies and part of a seventh company of regular infantry to war, as well as a company of cavalry. More than 800 men served with these eight regular companies. Several hundred more men served in militia units from Greene County. Men from all strata of society fought in the war, and the wealthy men who avoided combat did so generally because of old age, for few wealthy men avoided war by hiring substitutes. In a sample of 575 soldiers from Greene County, only 17 men were substitutes. Virtually all of the county's military-age males of all class backgrounds, plus many older men and some boys, served in the Confederate armed forces or the militia during the war.[38]

The sample of 575 soldiers who served in four companies from Greene County gives some idea of the experience of these men at war. The Dawson Grays and the Stephens Light Guards left for war in the spring of 1861, while the Greene County Volunteers and the Stocks Volunteers left in March and May of 1862. Of the 575 men who served with these four units, 173, or 30 percent, died in the war. Another 81 men, or 14 percent, were discharged during the conflict as permanently disabled by wounds or injuries. Fourteen men officially deserted, though many more were not present with their units at the end of the war. Only 141 soldiers, or less than 25 percent of those who had served, surrendered with these four companies at Appomattox. Of those who survived to surrender, more than one-quarter had been wounded at least once during the war.[39]

Combat had a variety of effects on the soldiers. Charley Sanford, Professor Shelton P. Sanford's son, joined the Irwin Artillery in the summer of 1862. He fought at Fredericksburg in December but then contracted typhoid and spent a month in a Richmond hospital. In late January 1863 he returned home on a forty-day furlough. Gone was the excited, talkative teenager of the summer before. Charley spoke little and avoided his family by spending most of his time at home alone hunting. Unable to talk with his troubled son at home, Professor Sanford accompanied him back to Virginia and spent several days with his battery, but he never broke through the wall that separated them.[40]

John C. Reid served with Greene County's Stephens Light Guards throughout the war. His account of the company he ultimately rose to command is the tale of men increasingly brutalized by war. These men from Greene County examined dead bodies with interest to see if bullets passed through, obediently hanged a comrade accused of desertion, and ate rations directly out of haversacks still looped over Union dead. One particular incident, which took place in the trenches at Petersburg, is perhaps the best example of the war's effect on these men. The men of Reid's company had adopted a starving pointer dog and shared their precious food with him. Then the dog disappeared, only to return several days later obviously well fed. The men of the company caught the dog, tied him up, and tried him for desertion. Mocking army legal procedure, the men presented evidence that the dog must have gone to the Union trenches for food, as southern soldiers lacked the food to fatten him up. The mock court found the dog guilty and sentenced him to be shot. With great seriousness, the men then executed the dog.[41]

Between 250 and 300 men from Greene County died in the war, and about 100 men were permanently disabled. War accustomed many men to violence and brutality and left some psychologically unhinged. Unlike the experience of many American soldiers in the twentieth century, military service during the Civil War did not liberate the soldiers from the restraining bonds of their communities. Instead, serving in locally organized units led by already existing elites only reinforced the men's place in the hierarchy of their society and strengthened that hierarchy by giving it the legitimacy of military organization. Hundreds of Greene County's men returned from war accustomed both to violence and to a reinforced social hierarchy.[42]

Greene County's slaves first felt the effects of war when scores of masters and overseers left for military service in the spring of 1861. A few slaves went to war as well, for most well-heeled officers took servants with them. Auss Davis, Dosia Harris's father, went to war as William Davis's servant. Dosia recalled her and the other children's excitement when the men returned on furlough. They thought her father's missing finger especially fascinating, for it had been shot off in battle. When John C. Reid left for Virginia in 1861, he took Lit, one of his father's slaves, with him. The war slowly transformed Lit's role as Reid's manservant into one of company servant, and eventually he cooked for all the men. Lit died of disease in 1864 while he was with the company in Virginia, though no roster of the Stephens Light Guards records his service.[43]

The vast majority of slaves, however, remained in Greene County working in the fields. Over time, the war began to change their lives just as it changed the lives of the community's white inhabitants. Slaves suffered the war's shortages and declining standard of living as much if not more than their masters. Work routines changed as farmers grew less cotton and more corn. Perhaps most important, despite the efforts of white women and men who remained behind, slaves simply could not be supervised as closely as they had been before the war. Because of the absence of so many men, on larger farms and plantations more slaves than ever before took up the duties of overseers, while on smaller farms slaves undoubtedly began to direct their own work.[44]

The war also began to reshape slavery in subtle ways, and some slaves gained greater control over their own lives as a result. In 1859 the Georgia Railroad owned sixteen slaves, several of whom lived in Greenesboro. As white workers left for war, the railroad replaced many workers with slaves, so that by the war's end the railroad controlled more than 300 slave workers. Many of these slaves lived in Greene County, and others traveled through the county regularly. In September 1863 the Greene County grand jury complained about the railroad's treatment of these slaves. Owned by a corporation, not an individual, these slaves lived in relative freedom outside of their working hours. Worse, complained the grand jury, the railroad gave these slaves money to purchase their own food. These practices, argued the grand jury, tended to undermine the institution of slavery and to demoralize other slaves in the community.[45]

That same September, in neighboring Hancock County, the chief justice of the Georgia Supreme Court, Linton Stephens, worried about the changing nature of slavery. Stephens tried to punish several slaves on his plantation for stealing but met arguments and resistance; one slave went so far as to pull a knife on the overseer trying to enforce Stephens's will. He complained about the incident in a letter to his brother Alexander Stephens, vice president of the Confederacy, and later wrote that "our negro population is becoming extensively corrupted. . . . I believe the institution of slavery is already so undermined and demoralized [that it] is tending to disintegration and ruin." As if to confirm his fears, in October 1863 Hancock County authorities arrested thirty-four slaves charged with plotting insurrection. Newspapers reported that more than 100 slaves participated in secret meetings to plot insurrection and escape. The ringleaders were slave artisans who hired their own time from their masters and lived virtually free lives. After the scare died down, the superior court had most of the slaves whipped and then released. Four slaves, however, were tried for insurrection and sentenced to death.[46]

Even as some Georgians struggled to maintain the traditional structures of slavery, others began to work for reform. President Nathaniel M. Crawford and Professor Henry H. Tucker of Mercer University led a campaign to reshape Georgia's laws of slavery to conform to Christian principles. In 1862 Crawford called for a repeal of Georgia's law prohibiting slave literacy, arguing that every human being had the right to read God's word. The legislature debated this issue but never acted on it. Then, Crawford and Tucker fought successfully to repeal a new law prohibiting slaves from preaching. Finally, they began to campaign for laws to recognize and protect slave marriages. Essentially, Crawford and other religious leaders struggled with the contradictory legal nature of the slaves. At law, slaves were at times merely property and at other times persons, and this conflicted with Crawford's image of slaves as brothers and sisters in Christ. The contradictions within the slave system, Crawford felt, had to be resolved, and war provided an opportunity for such reforms.[47]

A remarkable development in early 1864 highlighted the growing acceptance of religious freedom for slaves among Greene County's white people. For decades, slave members had outnumbered white members of the Greenesboro Baptist Church, but the slaves had little influence on the nature or content of church services. Dissatisfied with this situation, a group of slaves and free blacks decided to organize and build a church of their own. Unlike the African church at Penfield, this independent church was created by black believers acting alone. Led by slaves Frank Massey, Henry Porter, Umply Stocks, and Jack Terrell, these black people collected money to buy land and build a church. On January 27, 1864, Nancy Bickers, a wealthy white widow who owned sixteen slaves, sold the church one and one-quarter acres of land on the southern edge of Greenesboro. The new church asked Levi Thornton, a slave, to serve as pastor. Members called their new church Springfield Baptist, probably referring to the established seventy-year-old African American church of the same name in Augusta.[48]

Despite some changes, slavery continued to function in Greene County during the war. Along Georgia's coast Union troops freed thousands of slaves, and in northwest Georgia the proximity of Federal forces from 1863 on began to destroy slavery in that region. Several families relocated with their slaves to Greene County, usually moving to farms near or on relatives' land. James J. Printup tired of the problems of running a farm in northwest Georgia, so during the winter of 1863–64, he moved his slaves to a farm near his brother's place in Greene County. He wrote his brother Daniel explaining his reasons for the move and the problems he faced with his slaves. "I don't know whether I wrote you about John And Jesse," Printup continued. "They both run off and I have not heard from them since." Printup explained that he had no doubt they were with the Union troops at Chattanooga or Nashville and then confessed, "I was astonished at Jesse [running away], he having but one arm."[49]

Like many slaveowners, Printup knew that some of his slaves might run away, but he could not comprehend the depth of their longing for freedom. That Jesse, handicapped as he was by having only one arm, would dare to run away surprised Printup. But slaves all across Georgia—including Greene County, where Printup thought his slaves were safe—passionately desired freedom. The extent of that passion, however, and the willingness of former slaves to suffer hardship in the name of freedom would become clear only after emancipation.

We Have No Chance of Justice
before the Courts

On November 15, 1864, William Tecumseh Sherman's army of 60,000 men began its march from Atlanta to the sea. The next morning, Sherman and his staff paused on a hill to admire the scene. "Behind us lay Atlanta," Sherman wrote, "smoldering and in ruins, the black smoke rising high in the air and hanging like a pall over the city." The general then turned to watch his soldiers march past. Sherman's men were healthy, well rested, and in high spirits. A band began to play "The Battle Hymn of the Republic," and soldiers joined in singing. "Never before or since," wrote Sherman, "have I heard the chorus of 'Glory, glory, hallelujah!' done with more spirit or in better harmony of time and place."[1]

William T. Sherman had no intention, however, of leading a march of liberation through Georgia. He angrily rejected suggestions that the blacks were his allies, and during the campaign for Atlanta, he had shown little sympathy for slaves. Now, setting out on a potentially difficult march, Sherman thought of the slaves along the route as a possible hindrance to a military campaign. His first priority, argued Sherman, was the defeat of the Confederacy. Escorting slaves to freedom did not fit into his plans for the march. Many of his officers and soldiers agreed. As one Michigan private explained, "ain't right . . . to have them thinking we're here just to free the slaves. We're fighting secession. This slavery business has just been hung onto us."[2]

When Sherman's men entered Covington, in Newton County, at the northern edge of the plantation belt, they found that the "negroes were simply frantic with joy." The ecstatic slaves even mobbed the general, eventually forcing him to use back streets to pass through the town. "Whenever they heard my name," Sherman recalled, "they clustered around my horse, shouted and prayed in their peculiar style." Sherman only partly understood what he and his men meant as a symbol to the slaves of Georgia. Despite the general's feelings or those of a private from

Michigan, the slaves knew that the war for union had become a war for freedom. General Sherman and his men provided tangible evidence of that freedom.[3]

Even as slaves celebrated the arrival of Sherman's forces, Confederate leaders struggled to discern his plans. The right wing of his army seemed headed south toward Macon; the left wing appeared to be headed east toward Augusta. Frantic messages flew back and forth between the Confederate commanders, some convinced Macon was Sherman's objective, others that he intended to take Augusta. The Confederates mustered troops and appointed generals in the hopes that they could somehow anticipate Sherman's goal. Only Robert E. Lee guessed correctly from the start, cabling Jefferson Davis that "Savannah will probably be Sherman's object."[4]

The left wing of Sherman's army, under General Henry W. Slocum, marched east along the Georgia Railroad to Madison. There, General John Geary's Division received orders for detached duty. At five o'clock on the morning of November 19, Geary's men left their wagon train and marched east toward the Oconee River and Greensboro. Confederate scouts harassed Geary's troops but could not prevent them from destroying more than 5 miles of railroad, 530 bales of cotton, and 50,000 bushels of corn that day alone. One detachment of Union troops marched north and burned the Appalachee River ferry between Morgan and Greene Counties, while another detachment destroyed the Georgia Railroad's bridge across the Oconee. The next morning, November 20, Geary's main body descended on Park's Mill. They burned the ferryboats, the mill, and all other buildings except for James B. Park's home, spared because Park was a Mason. Wheeler's cavalry fired on Geary's men from across the river, but they were soon driven away. Geary then put a detachment across the river that marched to Greensboro, driving the Confederate cavalry before it and capturing the town. The Union troops held Greensboro for several hours that Sunday and convinced many people that Sherman intended to march on Augusta. Its mission done, the Union detachment marched back to the river, crossing in canoes to rejoin the division.[5]

Sherman's troops then turned south, away from Greene County, and headed toward Milledgeville. Small units of Confederate cavalry followed, raiding the army's flanks and rear. Among these raiders were Captain Alexander Shannon's Scouts, thirty handpicked men from the Eighth Texas Cavalry. Private Enoch John kept a diary of the Scouts' actions as they followed Sherman's army, picking off and ruthlessly killing isolated groups of Union soldiers. On November 22 the Scouts marched south along the Oconee River between Greene and Putnam Counties, trailing the rear guard of Sherman's left wing. Disgusted because they found no Yankee foragers to kill that day, Private John simply noted that the Scouts "followed on and only whipped about 1,000 negroes who were on their way to the enemy."[6]

Joseph Addison Turner, whose plantation lay in Putnam County, just across the Oconee River from Greene County, tried to hide his mules and slaves from the northern soldiers. He drove the mules into the swamp, but because it was Sunday, he failed to round up his slaves in time to make them hide in the swamp as well. Three young male slaves ran away with Sherman's men, although Turner believed two of them were forced to leave by the soldiers. Most slaves who followed Sherman's troops soon discovered that, while his soldiers may have symbolized freedom, they did little to help slaves escape. Sherman's forces accepted a number of strong young black men for pioneer work, and some units made room for a few black women as camp followers, but the rest of the slaves were simply left behind. Most who tried to follow could not keep up with the swiftly marching soldiers and soon began to drift back to their owners. A few days after Sherman passed, Dr. John Curtwright at Long Shoals in Greene County wrote Turner that four of Rowan Ward's slaves had returned home. Turner himself noted that many other peoples' slaves had returned, but his three men never came back.[7]

Across Georgia's plantation belt thousands of slaves abandoned home and family to follow Sherman's troops. For Greene County's slaves, however, Sherman's march must have seemed both tantalizing and disappointing. The Union army only brushed the county's borders before turning south and marching away. For a slave to follow the Federal forces required a quick decision, leading to escape, evasion of Confederate pickets, and crossing the Oconee River. Despite the challenge, some made it. Two of James B. Park's slaves ran away with the Union troops. Dosia Harris recalled that Si, a slave on Samuel Davis's plantation, also "run 'way wid dem yankees when dey come through." Si made it to Savannah, where "dey made a black yankee soldier out of him." Other slaves were not so lucky and, like Rowan Ward's, returned home after failing to keep up with an army that did not want them.[8]

Most slaves in Greene County had no chance to escape and remembered only the depredations of Sherman's men. Though the county suffered just one brief raid by Sherman's main force, stragglers and deserters roamed the county for days after the army passed. At Richard Willis's plantation, Isaiah Greene led soldiers to his master's hidden whiskey and other provisions in exchange for a stick of candy. Joseph McWhorter's slaves successfully hid the plantation silver from raiders, but Federal soldiers took all the livestock and meat. Some slaves may have used the soldier's ravages as a chance to strike at their masters. One woman wrote that "all of Uncle J.'s negroes left, . . . [and] Aunt L. gave all her money, jewelry, and watch to old Joe to take care of, and he marched off with them." In Putnam County, Mrs. Johnson's gin house caught fire several days after the Federal troops had passed. She blamed Yankees, but Joseph Turner felt certain her own slaves burned the gin. Despite several stories of loyal devotion among the slaves, many whites expressed great bitterness about the disloyalty of slaves in the months after Sherman's march.[9]

Colonel Rowan Ward's militia company from Greene County followed Sherman's men almost to Sandersville and then returned home, rounding up Union stragglers along the way. They brought six men back to Greene County as prisoners of war, but in other cases captured stragglers met summary execution. Shannon's Scouts often simply shot down stragglers, especially those engaged in pillage or helping slaves to escape. Joseph Turner reported that four Union soldiers captured near Eatonton "misbehaved in the presence of some ladies," and for their indecency, they were "summarily disposed of" by local citizens.[10]

In Greene County some thought Confederate soldiers a worse plague than the Northern raiders. Trying to slow Sherman's expected advance toward Augusta, General Wheeler's men destroyed the railroad in Greene County and burned several small bridges. They took food, horses, mules, and livestock from whomever they chose. Having experienced the depredations of both the Union and Confederate forces, one man from Greene wrote to the *Countryman* that "the whole land mourns on account of Wheeler's Cavalry. . . . Here in middle Georgia they are dreaded fully as much, if not more, than the yankees." Eventually, however, all the stragglers passed. The Confederate cavalry moved on, the local militia returned home, and master and slave in Greene County began once again to work out their changing relationship.[11]

An uneasy peace ruled Greene County for the next six months. Unlike the "burnt country" to the west and south that marked Sherman's passage, the people of Greene County had sufficient food for the winter. The challenge they faced was not so much physical as it was cultural and ideological. Slaves desired freedom and had an idea of what emancipation could mean for their lives, even if they did not foresee the challenges freedom would bring. Masters increasingly realized that some sort of emancipation loomed in the future and most shared a conviction that it would be disastrous. "Slave labor is necessary for the production of cotton," argued one worried correspondent to the *Countryman*. Editor Joseph Turner explained that with emancipation "the rich will become richer and the poor poorer, and white skin will no longer secure a man against servitude." Most slaveowners seemed to have maintained substantial authority during the last six months of war, but both master and slave knew that the relations of labor were changing. In some cases slaves asserted their rights to greater religious freedom by attending the new independent Springfield church or even demanding partial wages for their labor. Slaves saw these acts as steps toward freedom, but many masters worried where the slaves' impudence and "demoralization" would lead.[12]

Uncertainty about the future caused many white Georgians to fear the deterioration of their authority over the slaves, seeing in it a harbinger of the disintegration of society. In January 1865 "a negro dressed in the height of fashion" refused to help fight a warehouse fire in Augusta. His direct disobedience of orders and the symbolism of his dress led to his being mobbed by the crowd. In March, Governor Brown responded to slaveowner complaints about the growing difficulty of managing slaves by authorizing a picket around Savannah to prevent the escape of slaves into that city. These soldiers were not sent to besiege the Union troops in Savannah, they were instead sent to keep slaves out. In April authorities captured a band of outlaws in their cave outside of Augusta. Five of the bandits were white and seven were black, yet they had cooperated and worked together. And as if black and white consortium were not enough to confirm for many Georgians the collapse of southern civilization, Confederate soldiers returning home after Lee's surrender rioted and broke into government storehouses in Augusta. The rioters also attacked blacks on the street, perhaps transferring their anger to the target that seemed to benefit most from their defeat.[13]

Word of Lee's surrender set off celebrations among some of eastern Georgia's slaves, but most slaves remained under the direct authority of their masters for several more weeks or months. In Athens slaves celebrated word of Appomattox by dancing around a liberty pole, but the next morning they found the pole cut down, and many worried about their masters' response to the celebration. In Greene County the Reverend Hardy Peek called his slaves together and told them they were free. The slaves celebrated by singing and marching up and down the road that passed the plantation. Slaves from other farms joined them, and Joe

Peek, who the slaveowners had never allowed to preach, gave his first sermon to the freedpeople gathered by the road.[14]

Despite some celebrations of emancipation, slaves in Greene County soon returned to work as they had before. Other masters in Greene County were not so forthcoming as the Reverend Peek. William McWhorter recalled that "Marse Joe never did tell his Niggers dey was free," and Isaiah Greene told of masters who kept their slaves in bondage six months after Lee's surrender. Though slaves knew about the collapse of the Confederacy, in most cases emancipation did not become a reality until Union soldiers arrived.[15]

Union troops entered Greene County on May 5, 1865, almost a month after Lee's surrender and more than two weeks after Johnston's surrender in North Carolina. The troops did not come to free the slaves but to pursue Confederate President Jefferson Davis. Davis and his party passed through Greene County on the fourth and would continue to flee southward until captured near Irwinville, Georgia. More Federal troops followed, passing through to other locations. Some of these units celebrated the war's end in their own way. On May 7 Federal soldiers forced a train off the tracks of the Athens branch near Union Point and robbed the passengers. A traveler who passed through Greene County in the middle of May reported that "the yankees have committed such depredations that the whole country is destitute and the people desperate." In Washington, Georgia, twenty miles from Union Point, Eliza Andrews fearfully noted in mid-May that the same soldiers who had looted Greene County were on their way to her town. The next day she heard that near Greenesboro local citizens had ambushed Union plunderers, wounding several. Greene County tradition maintains that the officer who led these troops fraternized with black women, so he was shot from a window of the Statham Hotel in the center of Greenesboro. True or not, disorder and violence filled the month of May despite or, in some cases, because of the presence of Federal soldiers.[16]

On June 7, 1865, the 175th New York Volunteers, who were encamped near Savannah, received orders to march to Augusta, Georgia, and then to take up occupation duty in the subdistrict of Greenesboro, which consisted of Greene, Glasscock, Hancock, Lincoln, Taliaferro, Wilkes, and Walton Counties. In September, Wilkes and Lincoln Counties were taken out of the subdistrict, but Jasper, Morgan, Newton, Putnam, and Walton Counties were added to occupation troops' subdistrict. Because the railroad between Augusta and Greenesboro was still useless, the 175th New York marched to Greenesboro and took up its duties there on June 26.[17]

The 175th New York Volunteers came from Staten Island, and about 80 percent of its original complement were foreign born, mostly in Ireland or Germany. Sent to New Orleans in 1862, the regiment entered combat on April 12, 1863, and suffered terribly from disease during the Port Hudson campaign. In the assault on Port Hudson's fortifications on June 14, 1863, the 175th New York suffered 25 percent casualties and was withdrawn from combat soon after. A broken regiment of less than 350 men remained, so in October the regiment was consolidated into a three-company battalion. For the next year the troops served in occupation duties in Louisiana, perhaps gaining familiarity with the process of "reconstruction" there. In the fall of 1864 they traveled up the Mississippi and Ohio to the railroad in Charleston, West Virginia, and from there to Baltimore, where they boarded ship for Savannah. By the time these men reached Greenesboro in the summer of 1865, they were experienced occupation troops, but the unit also suffered from low morale and a simple desire to go home. Numbering less than 200 men, the 175th New York found the task of managing the transformation from slavery to freedom in ten counties overwhelming.[18]

Captain Charles McCarthy, Irish born, commanded the 175th New York at Greenesboro. He also served as assistant provost marshal for the entire subdistrict, his work mainly consisting of traveling from county to county and administering the amnesty oath to those who qualified. McCarthy sent small detachments of soldiers to occupy each county seat in his subdistrict, while about 100 men remained at his headquarters just east of Greenesboro in the home of John Cuningham, a once-wealthy planter whose family was evicted. McCarthy created four-man mounted patrols that rode throughout his subdistrict visiting plantations and encouraging the freedpeople to contract for work. Willingly or not, these soldiers were the true instrument of emancipation in Greene County.[19]

As Northern soldiers roamed Greene County they brought final word of emancipation. Dosia Harris told how her mistress, Mary Davis, hurried to hide her best mule and her money before the Union troops reached her plantation. "When dem yankees finally did git dar," Dosia recalled, "dey was singin' a song 'bout freedom, . . . and dey called all de slaves together and told 'em dey was free as jack rabbits." When Federal troops arrived at Joseph McWhorter's plantation, the slaves were working. "One of dem yankee sojers rid through the fields whar dey was wukin' and he axed 'em if dey didn't know dey was free," explained William McWhorter. On Richard Willis's plantation the soldiers explained that the slaves were now as free as their mistress. "She can't whip you anymore," said a Union soldier.[20]

Most slaves already knew about emancipation, but visits by Federal troops gave emancipation substance and reality in the presence of the master. The Federal presence not only had a powerful psychological effect on both master and slave, it also began the process of moving freedom into the realm of the living law. In a formal sense the collapse of the Confederate army and government in April freed the slaves in Greene County, but it took time for freedom to become a reality. Not until the middle of May in Washington, Georgia, did Eliza Andrews report that "people are making no effort to detain their negroes now." In rural areas slavery often continued until the arrival of occupation troops. Most slaves in Greene County worked through May and into late June before beginning to make contracts with their masters. For all the pretensions of legislators and leaders in Washington, D.C., emancipation as just a presidential proclamation had little real effect. The realm of the living law is social, and only when laws exist in both the conceptual and behavioral sphere do they take on significant reality. The working out of this enormous legal change in the status of black people and its transformation into a behavioral reality dominated events in Greene County throughout the summer of 1865, while the reorganization of labor relations took almost a decade.[21]

Before the Civil War, masters and slaves lived in a noncommercial paternalistic relationship. The slaveholders participated capitalistically in the world market economy, but slaves had only indirect ties to the commercial world. Emancipation legally severed this paternalistic, noncommercial relationship between masters and slaves. The Northern emancipators expected former masters and slaves to quickly structure a new market-based relationship centered on the principles of free labor. On May 26, 1865, planters and "leading citizens" met in Augusta's Masonic Hall with Federal representatives to discuss this new commercial relationship. Union army chaplain Mansfield French and Captain John Emory Bryant represented the Freedmen's Bureau at the meeting. Created in March 1865, the bureau had among its many duties the responsibility of directing the transformation of slavery into free labor. Chaplain French and Captain Bryant explained how free labor worked, referring at length to the success of free labor among the freedmen in the sea islands off the Georgia and South Carolina coast. French specifically suggested a contractual sharecropping arrangement that had worked well in the sea islands. The landowners provided the land, seed, and draft animals and then split the crop equally with the laborers.[22]

The next morning 5,000 freedpeople gathered on Augusta's parade grounds to hear French and Bryant. French gave a free-labor sermon, explaining in a patronizing tone the freedpeople's obligations under the new system. He rebuked the former slaves for their idleness, for their devotion to display in dress, and for seeking material things. The free-labor system, he explained, rewarded only the virtuous: those who worked hard, practiced thrift, and avoided public display. French argued that free laborers should work harder, longer, and more effectively than slaves. He also emphasized the necessity for written contracts and the principle that a contract bound the parties until completion. Those who broke a contract would be compelled by the law to complete it or to pay damages to the injured party. After the speeches, the freedpeople celebrated with singing and clapping. "It was a wild, thrilling sight," Bryant wrote his wife. "These people are smart. They know what freedom is as well as I do."[23]

Perhaps the former slaves had a coherent idea of freedom, but many had only the most basic understanding of what a contract meant. In the countryside, far from Augusta, the ideas of contractual relationships filtered down to the freedpeople in only the simplest terms. Former slaves apparently wondered why they should sign contracts binding them to work when they were supposed to be free. In many cases the occupying military forces provided little guidance. On Richard Willis's plantation in Greene County a Union soldier told the slaves to "sign a paper so that you will receive pay for your work" and nothing more. Most northerners viewed slavery as an unnatural system, and with slavery destroyed, many expected free labor to spring up effortlessly in its place. The conquerors quickly realized, however, that the people of the South needed guidance before they would realize the inevitability and the advantages of free labor.[24]

In early June, John Emory Bryant issued labor regulations for the Augusta region, including Greene County. In them he sought to define the new commercial relationship that should exist between the freedpeople and their former masters. The regulations laid out a suggested schedule of wages for six days of labor each week. Freedmen should make their own contracts, continued the regulations, and then submit the documents to Bryant's office for approval. The regulations also prohibited personal punishment of laborers by their employers, requiring all parties to submit to the rule of law to solve conflicts. Violators of these regulations, asserted Bryant, "will sooner or later be investigated and punished." Bryant's regulations reflected the belief of Freedmen's Bureau commissioner O. O. Howard that the principles of contract and of equal justice under law would accomplish the transition to free labor.[25]

Others were not so sanguine about the possibility of a change to workable free labor. Joseph Addison Turner spoke for many planters in and around Greene County when he argued that slaves would "live to curse the day they were set free." "The nigger's only idea of freedom is freedom from work," explained Turner. Contracts for labor, he argued, could never be enforced, for growing cotton "requires constant and unremitting labor. Negroes will not work unless they are forced to do so, and they can not be forced to do so unless they are slaves." Turner expected only failure and ruin from the contract system and saw only one solution to the labor question—re-enslave the freedmen.[26]

Turner simply could not believe that free workers would provide landowners with the labor needed to raise cotton. His assumptions about the improvident and indolent nature of black people came directly from the ideological structures of slavery, assumptions ironically reflected in chaplain Mansfield French's speech to the freedpeople. The mere legal fact of emancipation could not reshape Turner's beliefs or those of men like him. James Roark characterized the persistence of the ideological assumptions of slavery into the postbellum era as "a blackened chimney standing amid charred ruins." A more appropriate characterization, however, is foundation stones remaining after a fire. By their very arrangement the stones influence the shape of any new structure built upon the ruins. Antebellum ideological assumptions about the nature of slaves, the labor relations needed to grow cotton, and the proper social relationship of laborers and masters, all necessarily influenced the new order built upon the ruins of the old.[27]

Captain Bryant's labor regulations also asserted the right of freedpeople to move at will, particularly in order to reunite families. This process had already begun in Greene County, as husbands, wives, and children assembled together in family groups. Other freedpeople simply left masters they did not like or experimented with the freedom to move. In Greensboro a black squatter community, which whites derisively called Canaan, sprang up around the Springfield Baptist Church. It attracted a growing population of not just former house servants and town slaves but also freedpeople from the country as well. Living in town offered the former slaves more personal liberty than the countryside and let blacks experience for the first time life in an independent, supportive community. The contract labor system allowed many freedpeople to live in this community and walk back and forth to their work each day. Canaan continued to grow as more and more former slaves moved away from their former masters in an effort to make freedom a personal reality. These freedpeople soon built the Ebenezer African Methodist Episcopal Church within yards of the Springfield Baptist Church, making these two institutions the physical core of the growing black community.[28]

When Sidney Andrews, a New Englander touring the defeated South, visited Greenesboro's Canaan in November 1865, he found it hard to understand why so many freedpeople chose to live together in squalor when they could have remained with their former masters and enjoyed a better standard of living. "What did you leave the old place for, Auntie?" he asked an elderly freedwoman. "What fur? [En]*Joy my freedom!*" replied the old woman. For all his empathy, Andrews still could not understand the meaning of personal autonomy and community independence to people who had been slaves, nor could he understand valuing this autonomy above one's comfort and standard of living. Pondering the slaves' choices, which did not seem rational to a white New Englander, Andrews asked a crucial question, "What is the 'freedom' that war has brought this dusky race?"[29]

As Greene County's landowners and freedpeople made contracts during the spring and summer of 1865, they began to define and give substance to some aspects of "freedom," at least as the landowners saw it. Most landowners had little or no money, so they contracted with their laborers for share-wages. Alfred Parrott's master informed the slaves of their freedom and then offered them one-third of the crop already in the ground to stay on as his laborers. Thomas R. Thornton also offered his workers share-wages, and the provisions of the contract he made reveal much about Thornton's understanding of the meaning of freedom for his former slaves.[30]

On June 3, 1865, Thornton contracted with twenty-eight of his former slaves. Under the agreement, all who were able to labor, including children, were to do "whatever they are told to do." In return Thornton promised food, clothing, and lodging until the end of the year, and he pledged treatment "as kind as he has done heretofore." At the completion of the contract the freedpeople would receive one-sixth of all the food crops. The contract further provided that workers who were "idle or disobedient or disrespectful or dishonest or unfaithful or get drunk or in any way fail to perform their part of the contract shall be instantly dismissed from service." Following such dismissal, the former worker would have "to leave the premises, and shall receive no wages or other compensation for past labor." Not surprisingly, the contract failed to specify any remedies for the freedpeople in case Thornton breached his part of the contract.[31]

This agreement provided for little more than contractual slavery, yet it seems representative of the usual contract made during the first season following emancipation. Only the methods of payment varied to any great degree among these contracts. Confederate currency and bonds had no value following the surrender, but a few planters had enough money to promise their workers cash payment at the end of the year. The day after Union troops told his slaves of their freedom, Richard Willis made the freedpeople an offer. If they would stay on the plantation and work as they had before emancipation, Willis would give each family $75 at Christmas. Most of his former slaves took the offer, but Willis offered Isaiah Greene's stepfather only $50, for the man was "afflicted." Isaiah's stepfather refused the offer, believing his family should be treated the same as the other families. Willis finally agreed to pay him the same amount as he would an able-bodied man. Paternalism had not vanished along with the legal status of slavery and even managed to creep into the commercial relationship between Willis and his workers.[32]

Some landowners, however, felt little paternalistic concern for their newly freed slaves. On June 1, 1865, Micajah Pollard contracted for money wages with Elizabeth and Rebecca Lindsey. He agreed to work until Christmas and would receive $6 a month for his labor. After he worked five months, though, the Lindseys forced him to leave the farm and refused to pay him his wages. In a different sort of contract, Richmond Peek agreed to work for his former master, James C. Peek. In return for the labor of Richmond, his son, and three daughters, James Peek pledged to give them 12 bushels of corn and 158 pounds of pork, worth about $70. The family fulfilled their part of the contract, laboring the full period for Peek, but their employer then refused to give them the provisions they had earned. In both of these cases paternalistic concerns obviously faded in the face of economic reality, or perhaps simple greed.[33]

Facing problems of disease and starvation among the thousands of refugees crowding into Augusta, John Emory Bryant could hardly regulate or control every contract in eastern Georgia. He begged his superior, Assistant Commissioner Rufus Saxton, for help, proposing that the Freedmen's Bureau provide full-time legal counsel for freedpeople in every city in Georgia. Saxton did not have the resources for that, and because of his continued pressure for more resources to help the freedpeople, advocacy of their cause soon resulted in the army removing him from command of the bureau in Georgia. In Greene County there was no Freedmen's Bureau agent until early 1866, so the county's black people turned to the local occupying forces for help structuring their first contractual relationships with white landowners. The Irish and German immigrants in the 175th New York, however, showed little interest in the contract problems between whites and blacks. Most cases were ignored, and those few of seeming importance were referred to the provost marshal in Augusta.[34]

The problems Greene County's freedpeople encountered with the contract system belied hopes for a quick transition to free labor. Through contracts many employers sought to force black laborers to work and live in conditions similar to slavery. These contracts rarely provided for regular wages and usually bound the employee to work for an entire year before receiving any money or a share of the crop. Many black workers surely began to question just what sort of "free" labor this was. Worse, those freedpeople who had grievances against employers in 1865 discovered that they could not bring actions or testify in Georgia's civil courts. Only through a white patron acting as "next friend" could a black person file a claim against a white person in Georgia's courts, and only the white patron could testify. The Freedmen's Bureau and the provost marshal had courts in Georgia that would hear freedpeople's cases, but both were far away, in Augusta. The anger and frustration many freedpeople felt as a result of abusive contracts and powerlessness in the legal system became the basis for growing political consciousness among Greene County's former slaves.

Greene County's freedpeople were not alone. Across Georgia black people faced the same problems. During 1865 and into 1866, black Georgians could not exercise any of the rights of citizens. No black person could vote, testify in court, serve on a jury, or practice law. Freedpeople also suffered many of the restrictions they had lived with as slaves. The military commander of Milledgeville required former slaves to have passes from their employers to travel and permission from their employer to sell anything, and he arrested and returned blacks who were under contract but left their employers. This commander went so far as to order that freedmen who used "any disrespectful language to their former masters will be severely punished."[35]

In December 1865, the Augusta *Colored American* published a call by freedmen for a convention to meet and "consult together" on "how to secure the rights of citizenship." The *Colored American* argued that black Georgians should not merely ask for equal rights, they should aggressively demand equal rights. "We council no fawning nor bowing because of former associations," explained the paper. On January 10, 1866, delegates from all of Georgia's major cities and several rural counties assembled in Augusta's Springfield Baptist Church. In his opening address the Reverend Ulysses L. Houston explained that the Freedmen's Convention "met to ask for free laws. . . . The laws which now govern us [are] oppressive and cruel, we want them changed." Valentine Thomas, Charles Martin, Edward Powers, and Abram Colby represented the freedpeople of Greene County at the convention. The freedmen spent most of the first day organizing committees and arguing about the rules of order. On the second day General Davis Tillson of the Freedmen's Bureau spoke to the convention.[36]

Davis Tillson took de facto control of the Freedmen's Bureau in Georgia during September 1865. Convinced that the bureau under Saxton had gone too far in favoring the freed slaves, Tillson began his own investigation into how the bureau might promote his vision of the freedpeople's role in society. Tillson toured the state, talking with freedmen, planters, and former state officials. In late October he visited Georgia's ongoing Constitutional Convention and asked the all-white assembly for their suggestions as to how the Freedmen's Bureau might be made more successful. Returning to Augusta, Tillson drew two conclusions from his tour. First, the bureau needed many more local agents if it intended to carry out its tasks statewide. Under Saxton there were just a few agents in upcountry Georgia, most of whom were overburdened with work. Second, the bureau and white landowners needed to cooperate more closely to make the free-labor system work. Working together, the bureau and the landowners could use contracts to bring the freedpeople into the market system. To accomplish these goals Tillson asked the white delegates at the Constitutional Convention to recommend men who could serve as bureau agents. He also promised planters that he would compel the freedpeople to work, thus solving their major concern about free labor in Georgia.[37]

In December 1865 Tillson issued orders that set wages for freedpeople, and he required all freedmen to make contracts for the next year by January 10, 1866, or the bureau would make contracts for them. Apparently Tillson did not believe that the new minimum wage of twelve dollars a month for men and eight dollars a month for women would induce all the freedmen to make contracts. Tillson also began appointing agents across Georgia, eventually more than 200, almost all of whom were white southern men. In this way Tillson expected to expand the bureau's reach to every community of the state while he gained the support of Georgia's white landowners.[38]

In his speech to the Freedmen's Convention Tillson waxed rhapsodic about the great future black people had in a free-labor Georgia. Most whites had only feelings of good will toward the freedpeople, explained Tillson, but they were discouraged by so many freedpeople's unwillingness to work. The year 1865 proved a disappointing one for want of labor, argued Tillson, so during the coming year the freedpeople must prove themselves worthy of freedom by working very hard. Hard work would greatly benefit the former slaves, for "work is the talismanic power which can remove your poverty and ignorance" asserted Tillson. Meanwhile, until black people *proved* they could work hard, become educated, and accumulate wealth, they should not concern themselves with unimportant matters such as equal legal rights.[39]

Tillson returned to the convention the next day and spent several hours answering questions from the freedmen. Tillson responded along the lines of his speech, but the unsatisfied delegates continued to quiz him. At one point bedlam reigned as several questioners showered Tillson with queries and challenges at the same time. Finally, the chairman intervened and ruled that only the head of each county's delegation could ask questions. After answering a few more increasingly pointed questions, Tillson left the convention.[40]

After the general's departure, the Freedmen's Convention took up the report of its Committee on the Condition of the Colored People. In many parts of Georgia, reported the committee, black people still labored under conditions of servitude similar to slavery and were afraid to acknowledge themselves free. White landowners broke up freedmen's meetings and prevented the creation of schools by the freedpeople. In some parts of the state freedmen still needed travel passes from their former owners, and landlords often drove workers away after the harvest without paying them their wages. Freedpeople were killed and beaten so often, concluded the committee, that "murder and other horrid outrages are the ordinary sufferings of our people." General Tillson clearly knew about the sorts of outrages reported by the committee and even referred to them in his address. Despite these injustices, he did not think that Georgia's black people needed to seek equal rights.[41]

Rejecting General Tillson's advice to work hard and forget about seeking equal rights, the Freedmen's Convention organized the Georgia Equal Rights Association and elected John Emory Bryant, who had resigned from the Freedmen's Bureau, as president. The association's purpose was simply "to secure for every citizen, without regard for race, descent, or color, equal political rights." "We claim for ourselves that we are endowed by our creator with all, and the same, inalienable rights that are other men's," explained the freedmen. The freedmen also planned to establish branches of the Equal Rights Association in every county to promote equal rights, assist the destitute, and work for the "education and elevation of the people." The convention demanded justice against those who abused black workers, contract protection for laborers, the right to sit on juries, and the right of suffrage. They also called for black representation in the state government, arguing that "it is unreasonable to suppose that those who once deprived us of our natural rights will now help us."[42]

As its first act the Equal Rights Association sent an address to Georgia's new postwar legislature meeting in Milledgeville. "As we are willing to bury the past and forget the ills of slavery," the freedmen explained, "we expect your encouragement by the creation of such laws as are equitable and progressive." Knowing that the legislature's decisions concerning the legal rights of freedpeople could shape their future, the freedmen argued that they were already citizens, born in Georgia and bound by history to the white people of the state. As such, argued the freedmen, they should be entitled to vote, sit on juries, practice law, and exercise all the rights of full citizens.[43]

If the Georgia legislature noticed the freedmen's plea for equal rights, their actions did not show it. Meeting from December 1865 through March 1866, the legislators ratified the Thirteenth Amendment to the U.S. Constitution as they were required to do by President Andrew Johnson's administration. Then the legislature turned to questions about the social and political role of free black people in Georgia. Unlike most other southern states, the Georgia legislature avoided creating a "black code" of direct legal prohibitions and restrictions based on race. Instead, attempting to be more subtle, they created a system of positive rights organized by categories of "persons." "Persons of color," which included everyone with "one-eighth or more of negro or African blood," had the right to marry, to divorce, to make and enforce contracts, to sue or be sued, to own property, and even to be witnesses in legal cases involving a person of color as a party. Other categories of "persons" given positive rights included corporations, aliens, residents not aliens, and citizens. Citizens included "all white persons born in this state." Male citizens had the right to vote, to serve on juries, and to hold public office. And just in case someone missed the point, the law emphasized that "Persons having one-eighth or more negro or African blood are not white persons."[44]

In light of northern reaction to "black codes" in other southern states, the Georgia General Assembly carefully worded the laws passed that first session so as to make few distinctions on the basis of race. Only legislation prohibiting interracial marriage and defining the rights of persons of color made such distinctions. All other laws, including a greatly revised criminal code, made no mention of race. Clearly, however, the legislature intended many of the new laws to structure and control the social and economic roles of Georgia's black people. While formally racially neutral, these laws reflected a belief that the control and punishment of black laborers had simply been moved from the private sphere to the public sphere.[45]

A new apprentice law allowed local courts to bind abandoned or orphaned minors to labor for masters until the age of twenty-one. Of course, many freedpeople under the age of twenty-one were "abandoned minors" because former masters had sold their parents. The legislature made "insurrection," arson, burglary, and rape capital crimes. They also criminalized the enticement of workers under contract and legislated against vagrancy. The law defined vagrants as "persons wandering or strolling about in idleness . . . without visible means of support." That such a person might merely be looking for work did not concern the legislators, who provided that vagrancy could be punished by fines, whipping, up to a year of hard labor for the county, or by binding the vagrant out to labor for anyone willing to pay the county a fee. Finally, anticipating a flood of cases involving the freed slaves, the legislature created county courts to deal with petty cases. These courts immediately took up the task of labor discipline within the public sphere.[46]

Meanwhile, open conflict broke out between Greene County's white and black communities. Sending delegates to the Freedmen's Convention in Augusta symbolized the determination of the county's freed slaves to seek justice, an aggressiveness that spilled over into relations with employers. Across most of east Georgia's cotton belt, landowners offered freedmen contracts for the year 1866 at between $3 and $8 per month, payable at the completion of the contract. They specifically ignored General Tillson's standard of $12 per month. Though hundreds of laborers left the region seeking higher wages in southwest Georgia or points farther west, most freedmen remained and had little choice but to accept the offered contract terms.[47]

When the delegates to the Freedmen's Convention returned, they began to build a tightly organized Equal Rights Association in Greene County. Through the association these leaders attacked abusive contracts.

One delegate, preaching at Springfield Baptist, in Canaan, told his listeners to demand justice from their employers. A start, he suggested, would be to demand wages dating back to the Emancipation Proclamation of January 1, 1863. Some freedpeople did exactly that and used planters' refusals to pay back wages as the basis for a strike. Then the Freedmen's Bureau state superintendent of education, G. L. Eberhart, visited Canaan and encouraged the laborers of Greene to go further, telling them they had the right "to break their contracts as they saw fit." More workers joined the strike and in some cases abandoned entire plantations in their efforts to secure just contracts. By February 1866 the freedmen's strike had halted agricultural labor in much of the county.[48]

In Greenesboro, frightened by growing militancy among the black people in Canaan, Mayor Wiley G. Johnson ordered a roundup of guns belonging to the freedpeople. The town marshal confiscated dozens of firearms, but the situation only grew more heated, and violence loomed. In the midst of these problems the first Freedmen's Bureau agent for Greene, Taliaferro, and Morgan Counties, Jonathan T. Dawson, arrived in Greenesboro. He reported to General Tillson that "everything was in greatest confusion" and pled for help in resolving the strike and the conflict over the freedmen's guns. In March General Tillson's direct intervention forced town officials to return the freedpeople's firearms, and that crisis ended. But when Dawson attempted to convince the freedpeople to return to work under their contracts, he found that "it would be at the risk of his life for him to attempt to compel them to abide by their contracts." James Davison, a local white leader, blamed the strike and the problems with freed workers on "pernicious intermeddling" by the Equal Rights Association and sought help from the bureau in suppressing it. Greene County's freedpeople, however, believed that they should return to work when they chose, not when the bureau or their employers told them to. Finally, employers renegotiated their contracts with workers, in some cases offering as much as $.50 or $1 per day, minus deductions for food, clothing, and other items. In April the strike ended, and the freedpeople returned to work, many under new contracts.[49]

Greene County's Equal Rights Association soon emerged as one of the most successful county organizations in the state, and Abram Colby became its leader. Abram Colby, the son of a white planter, had lived independently as a barber in Greenesboro for more than fifteen years. Though virtually illiterate, Colby apparently had great personal charisma and speaking ability, and he emerged as a leader of Greene County's black community and served as a delegate to the Freedmen's Convention in January 1866. As the freedpeople struggled against unfair contracts during the first half of 1866, Colby used this issue to build "one of the largest and most enthusiastic branches" of the Equal Rights Association.[50]

G. L. Eberhart, the Freedmen's Bureau's state superintendent of education, wrote Abram Colby on February 24, 1866, to inquire about the strike and stories of violence in Greensboro. Colby wrote back, denying that there were any "freemans going wild and struggling about and all this." Then, he tried to explain the problems facing the freedpeople:

> I do not see the most distant shadow of right or equal justice here in Greensboro. . . . Mr. Dawson put some freedmen in jail last Monday because they refused to work under contracts for 7 and 8 $ per month—Their masters come and took them out of jail yesterday in the very same form [and] dragged them back to their plantations with as much power and assurance as could have been exhibited three or five years ago.[51]

Clearly, Abram Colby did not see Dawson, the local Freedmen's Bureau agent, as a supporter of the freedpeople, so the Equal Rights Association went its own way. Meanwhile, the freedpeople grew ever more politically active.

During the summer of 1866 Henry McNeal Turner, a black leader and minister from Macon, spoke to Colby's Equal Rights Association. A large crowd of people gathered in Canaan to hear Turner's call for black activism and self-reliance. He encouraged the freedmen to actively protect themselves and, in particular, to drive out of their midst white men who exploited black women. His remarks angered a group of armed whites listening to the meeting, but when they attempted to attack Turner, they were faced down by armed freedmen. "I never saw more firearms among one set of people in my life," Turner marveled. "I have not seen so determined a set of colored people as they are at Greensboro."[52]

Jonathan Dawson barely had time to organize a Freedmen's Bureau court in Greene before April 1866, when Federal authorities returned most judicial functions to the State of Georgia. The newly created county court became the venue for the vast majority of cases involving Greene County's freedpeople. Columbus Heard sat as judge, and Thomas W. Robinson served as solicitor of the court. Heard fought with the Stephens Light Guards during the Civil War, was wounded at Gettysburg, and spent the remainder of the war in a Union prison. Thomas W. Robinson was a young man in his early twenties and had commanded a militia company during the war. He later emerged as a leader of Greene County's

Ku Klux Klan. Both men came from prominent planter families, and they administered justice to the freedpeople in a manner reminiscent of plantation slave discipline, merely moving those principles from the private sphere to the public courtroom.[53]

Unlike the superior court, the county court made limited use of juries, and so the outcome of cases closely reflected the beliefs and personality of the judge. From the beginning, Judge Heard revealed his determination to deal strictly with the freedpeople. Henry Brook, "a person of color," was found guilty of stealing one-half bushel of corn. Judge Heard sentenced him to thirty-nine lashes. Henry Allen took two watermelons from his employer's garden. Judge Heard gave him three months at hard labor on the county chain gang. Lousia Park used obscene language in the presence of Mary Simmons, a white woman. For her crime Lousia received thirty lashes, though they were administered inside the jail to preserve her modesty. Major Jackson pled guilty to stealing nine pieces of bacon from John Wright's smokehouse. Judge Heard ordered thirty-nine lashes and a fine of $100. In lieu of the fine, Major Jackson could serve on the chain gang for twelve months. These cases typified the harsh punishments given for petty crimes before the county court. Twenty-one cases of vagrancy also came before the court during June through December 1866. In all vagrancy cases the defendants were black, and in seventeen cases the court found them guilty. Some of those convicted received thirty-nine lashes and an admonition to go and sin no more; others spent three months on the county chain gang. In this way the county court imposed strict order, attempted to shape labor relations, and allowed men who had been members of the planter class to define the outlines of black people's freedom.[54]

The county court handled not only minor criminal cases but also civil suits involving less than $200. During June through December 1866 nine freedpeople sued their employers for unpaid wages or breach of contract. In all but one case the black plaintiffs lost and had to pay costs, an expensive lesson for people who were desperately poor. Like most Americans, Abram Colby and other black leaders in Greene County believed in the law's abstract promise of equal justice. The law claimed to stand apart from the social structure, above it and autonomous, and so could arbitrate between the various interest groups in society. This pluralist conception of law led the freedpeople to hope they could secure legal rights and justice through the legal system. By the summer of 1866, however, the county court had demonstrated the sort of justice black people could expect at the hands of their former masters. Realizing that the freedpeople would never have legal justice as long as white southerners controlled the legal system, the local Equal Rights Association tried to secure outside help.[55]

In August 1866 Abram Colby and three other freedmen appealed to General Davis Tillson for help in their problems with the legal system. "We humbly ask you to give us the right of tribunal to settle business between colored and others without going to court," the freedmen's petition read. "We know from what we have seen that we have no chance of justice before the courts. We ask of you, sir, some right to defend ourselves and make those who contract with us stick to the contract. Our former masters are determined to oppress us." Finally, the freedmen closed with a plaintive postscript: "If there is nothing else can be done, can't we have an attorney, if we have to support him, so that we may have fairplay." Colby signed the letter and apparently believed that if freedpeople had equal access to the legal system, if only just an attorney to represent them, the legal system would fulfill its promise and afford them justice. General Tillson never responded to Colby's letter.[56]

During his tenure as agent, Jonathan Dawson showed little sympathy for the freedpeople. General Tillson issued orders prohibiting whipping as a punishment in Georgia, yet throughout 1866 Dawson never complained about or reported Greene County for flogging so many black defendants. Nor did he seem concerned by the unfair treatment black defendants suffered at the hands of the county court. During his tenure in office, well over 100 black people were beaten at the whipping post outside the jail behind the courthouse. Agents in other counties did protest. In Oglethorpe County agent J. G. Robinson wrote General Tillson about the unfairness of the local county court and its common use of whipping as punishment. This injustice, he argued, resulted from all-white juries made up of "nigger haters."[57]

Dawson not only failed to protect the freedpeople from abuse by the criminal justice system, he also failed to protect them from fraud by their employers. The crop of 1865 had been poor, but the crop of 1866 proved disastrous. The freedpeople's strike ended in time for spring planting, but the county lost half its crop of winter wheat and virtually all of its oats. Then, cotton planting revealed that much of the seed was rotten and would not germinate, resulting in only one-fourth of the usual stand of cotton. Landowners also reported problems with their laborers, arguing that the freedpeople worked only half as much as they did in slavery. Finally, drought during the summer of 1866 hurt both the cotton and the corn crops. One correspondent from Greene worried that the cotton crop would be so small that it would not bring enough money to feed the county. Some freedmen, he said, faced starvation. In these circumstances, during the fall and winter of 1866, many employers drove workers off the land, refusing to pay them wages or to divide up the crops.[58]

The black people of Greene County, however, were not compliant victims. Instead, the process of commodifying their labor, the oppressive contract system, the unequal laws passed by the state legislature, and the "justice" meted out by the county court, all accelerated the development of active political consciousness among Greene's freedpeople. By virtue of their society's racial ideology and the experience of slavery, they already had a well-developed class identity. Greene County's freedpeople also quickly learned that they could not depend on the federal government to bring lasting change to their lives, nor could they rely on their former masters. If there was to be meaningful change in Greene County, the freedpeople realized that they would have to make it happen.

The Time for Action Is at Hand

After the surrender at Appomattox, Captain John C. Reid set out for home on foot. Three weeks later he reached his father's plantation outside Philomath, just east of the Greene County line. There, despite his parents' joy at his safe return, Reid found an oppressive air of dread. Reid's parents lived in a limbo of uncertainty, believing that they had lost everything and fearful about the future. Soon, John Reid himself began to sink into depression. Before the war his closest friends—his brother, James Reid of Sparta, John Lofton of Lexington, William Florence, Rolin Stephens, and Reid's partner, Frederick Fuller, all of Greenesboro—had been fellow younger members of the bar. Every one of these friends died in the war. Only the help and advice from his wartime bride saved Reid from falling into complete despair. She convinced him to leave the discouraging atmosphere of his parents' home and move to her hometown of Lexington, in Oglethorpe County. There she awakened in him a resolve to practice law again.[1]

Other members of the community began to rebuild their lives as well and struggled to make sense of their changed world. In October 1865 Greene County's voters elected Yelverton P. King, Miles W. Lewis, and Nathaniel M. Crawford, all prominent prewar leaders, as delegates to the Constitutional Convention in Milledgeville. In November voters elected Robert L. McWhorter and John W. Swann, both successful antebellum planters, to the new state legislature. In December the Greenesboro post office reopened with James W. Godkin, the prewar and wartime postmaster, in charge. Clearly, the white people of Greene County sought the continuity of the world before emancipation. Try as they might to structure a new world that resembled the old, however, Greene County's white population could not escape the fact that emancipation wiped out 60 percent of the county's wealth and changed the basis of labor relations. Despite attempts to create a recognizable world, defeat and emancipation meant that fear and despair haunted the white population of Greene County.[2]

In September 1866 the Greene County grand jury, led by foreman Robert L. McWhorter, expressed these concerns and fears: "We cannot congratulate ourselves as in other days on a bright and hopeful future. We have just emerged from a mighty revolution, . . . the consequences of which cannot even be imagined. We began the War in good faith, we were honest, and upon its result we stayed our future and our sacred honor. But we have been beaten, by our defeat we have lost millions in Confederate issue, millions in the emancipation of our slaves, we have virtually lost [everything]." Columbus Heard, the newly appointed judge of the county court, expressed his feelings more bluntly to a friend in South Carolina: "We of the South are for this, and perhaps succeeding generations, a ruined people."[3]

One of the unimagined consequences was taking place even as the grand jury met. Abram Colby and the Equal Rights Association organized the freedmen of Greene County for political action. Though the ultimate goal of the Equal Rights Association was political equality, local organizations had more immediate issues to deal with. The most pressing local issue for Greene County's freedpeople, and for freedpeople in many parts of Georgia, was the unresponsive legal system and unfair treatment by employers. Black laborers who contracted to work during 1865 or 1866 often suffered blatant economic exploitation and abuse. This resulted, in part, from the freedmen's own ignorance of the contract system or perhaps merely their ignorance of the cost of a year's subsistence for a family. Some individuals contracted for absurdly low wages or tiny fractions of the final crop. Other freedmen were victims of outright fraud by employers. Especially common was the practice of driving black people working on share-wages off the land before the completion of the contract and then insisting that the freedmen had breached the agreement. In either case, blacks found that the courts usually supported the employers.[4]

The Union League and the Equal Rights Association attracted increasing numbers of black members during 1866 as the need for political action grew clearer. In May the Augusta *Weekly Chronicle and Sentinel* reported that scores of black people had begun to pour into the city, "all wending their way to the Mecca of freedom—the headquarters of the Georgia Equal Rights Association." White Georgians not only disparaged the ongoing politicization of the freedmen, they misunderstood it as well. A year later, "M," a correspondent from Greene County, reassured readers of the *Weekly Chronicle and Sentinel* that the vast majority of black people had no real interest in politics. As an example he recounted a conversation with a "respectable negro" at Greenesboro's depot. Asked if he intended to go to a political meeting in Augusta, the freedman replied that he had no interest in such meetings. When "M" asked the freedman what he wanted, he replied, "to farm and make bread and meat," an answer "M" thought comfortingly apolitical.[5]

If "M" saw no political significance in the freedman's answer, the freedpeople themselves increasingly realized that the desire "to farm and make bread and meat" embodied a direct challenge to the existing state of society. Freedpeople across the South expressed a desire for land and personal independence through subsistence farming. By implication, they had little interest in producing for the market system or working for wages. Most Freedmen's Bureau officers and most landowners, however, expected the former slaves to labor for wages producing cotton for the market, so both the bureau and landowners worked toward that end. The bureau also sought fair treatment for all black workers, a goal landowners would not accept. In Greene County white landowners managed to frustrate most of the bureau's efforts to win fair treatment for the freedpeople.[6]

In January 1867 Colonel Caleb C. Sibley took control of the Freedmen's Bureau in Georgia, replacing Davis Tillson, who retired to a plantation in Bryan County. Sibley discovered that many agents appointed by Tillson had never really worked to help the freedpeople; instead, they milked their positions by charging fees for their services. Sibley began to clean house and reorganize the bureau in Georgia, replacing agents he found unsatisfactory. In April he replaced Greene County's agent Jonathan T. Dawson with William A. Moore, who set up his office in Crawfordville, the judicial seat of Taliaferro County. Moore's appointment brought him $1,200 per year, and he complied well with the administrative demands of his office. Moore kept detailed accounts and each month sent a full report to General O. O. Howard. Each report included the required phrase, "my duties are to assist Freedmen in obtaining justice and to encourage Industry, Education, and Temperance." Soon, however, some of Greene County's black people began to question Moore's performance as agent.[7]

Despite his administrative abilities, Moore proved incompetent in his duties. In June of 1867 a half-dozen Greene County freedmen complained about delays and inaction by Moore. Colonel Sibley ordered an investigation, which resulted in the appointment of subagents for Greene and Morgan Counties to assist Moore in his work. David A. Newsom, the son of a Greene County slaveowner, took the position as subagent in Greene County and opened his office in Woodville. He proved a distinct change from Moore and engaged in a fascinating struggle to remake the legal system by providing quick and simple remedies to the freedpeople's complaints. Newsom actually went into the field to investigate claims, a change from prior agents' practices. He also involved white men from the community as referees on technical questions, such as whether the crops on a farm showed evidence of sufficient labor by the freedpeople. Newsom's most focused campaign, however, was against the apprenticeship law. The forced separation of children from their kin disgusted him, and Newsom fought to have apprenticed black children returned to their families.[8]

Newsom's frustration grew as he struggled with white resistance to his actions. In September 1867, soon after his appointment, Newsom wrote Colonel Sibley asking for help. "The Sheriff and other officers of Greene Co. refuse to cooperate with me," Newsom complained, and whites treated his orders "with contempt." Newsom also learned to avoid the "inefficient" agent Moore and wrote directly to his superiors in Augusta, to Colonel Sibley, or even to General Howard. Despite his energy and the support of the military government, the bureau's powers and resources proved too limited for Newsom's goals. Again and again white employers refused to heed his orders, and Newsom's efforts were wasted. In May 1868 Newsom moved on to local politics, while Colonel Sibley finally removed the incompetent agent Moore and appointed John H. Sullivan in his place.[9]

Sullivan immediately encountered frustrating problems. Sullivan took office on June 1, and on June 3 he wrote his superior about his inability to compel the appearance of white witnesses and parties. The next day he complained that he could not even get a warrant served. On the night of June 9, several men tried to break into Sullivan's house while he slept and left a written death threat. On June 10 he sent summons to white defendants charged with whipping a freedman forty or fifty lashes. "The defendants," Sullivan wrote, "upon ascertaining from the bearers that the envelopes contained summons from the Bureau, commenced abusing said bearers, and told them to take the letters back and tell the Agent to stick them up his ——." As a venue for the freedpeople to seek justice in Greene County, the Freedmen's Bureau failed abysmally.[10]

Problems of logistics, authority, and jurisdiction severely limited the potential impact of the bureau in Greene County. The bureau could not even depend on its own agents in the county. A more basic problem, however, grew out of ideological contradictions in the organization's own goals. On one hand the bureau sought to achieve an instant conversion to contractual free labor across the cotton South, and most bureau officials hoped to move the freed slaves into the larger market economy as quickly as possible. On the other hand they sought to secure equal rights and justice for the freedpeople in court systems controlled by their former masters. General Howard, commissioner of the Freedmen's Bureau, saw no conflict between these two goals. Yet the very contract system promoted by the bureau gave employers a "legal" means of maintaining authority over the former slaves, authority that could be enforced through the "color blind" actions of the courts.[11]

The black workers who refused to make contracts stood outside the market and so seemed to threaten the success of the free-labor system in the South. Workers without contracts moved freely from place to place, took day labor as it suited them, and sometimes decided not to work. Such workers could not provide the disciplined day-to-day labor needed to produce a substantial surplus of cotton or other products for the market. Both southern landowners and northern emancipators labeled such workers vagrants and felt they should be forced to work. In 1866, Georgia passed its first vagrancy law. Ironically, the free-labor system willingly used compulsion to force individual workers into the market system. This irony, sadly, proved tragic for many freedpeople across the South, including Greene County. In their eagerness to commodify black labor and quickly bring workers into the market economy, the Freedmen's Bureau's leaders exposed the freedpeople to incredible abuse and exploitation. The freedpeople soon realized that their goals of personal autonomy could never be won through programs of the Freedmen's Bureau. Instead, they needed a complete reorientation of existing social processes, and only politics seemed to offer the chance to peacefully effect such sweeping change.[12]

By October 1866 the Equal Rights Association had spread to more than fifty counties in Georgia, and some county meetings had attracted over 2,000 freedpeople. As John Emory Bryant explained, the meetings were "schools where colored citizens learn their rights." Newspapers, including the association's own Augusta *Loyal Georgian*, were often read aloud at the meetings and political issues discussed. In particular, the meetings focused on obtaining suffrage for Georgia's black people. Because of the bureau's freewheeling discussions of politics at their meetings, their focus on freedpeople's rights, and their continual pressure for black manhood suffrage, the Georgia Equal Rights Association met increasing white opposition in Greene County and across the state. The pressure and occasional violence directed against the association convinced the delegates at its second statewide convention in October 1866 to limit political activities temporarily and focus instead on the issue of education for the freedpeople.[13]

Other events, however, derailed the association's attempt to limit political conflict with whites. On November 9, 1866, the Georgia legislature decisively rejected the proposed Fourteenth Amendment to the United States Constitution. Both John Swann and Robert McWhorter, Greene County's representatives, voted against the amendment. In response to Georgia's and other southern states' recalcitrance on this and other issues, in early March the United States Congress passed the Reconstruction Act of 1867 over a presidential veto. This act established military governments in the defeated South, including Georgia, with specific preconditions for the resumption of civilian rule. The conditions included the elimination of the Georgia legislature's carefully constructed categories of persons and required that black men be accorded the full rights of citizenship and suffrage. In future elections, Greene County's black men who were of age would vote.[14]

The conditions that would result in the end of military rule astonished most white people in Greene County. Not only had they lived within a culture that justified slavery as a benefit to an inferior race, but they also lived within the larger world market system, where a complex system of "scientific" racial hierarchy was used to explain the economic relationship between different groups of people in the world economy. In the summer of 1867 a front page article in the Greenesboro *Herald* quoted Harvard University's Louis Agassiz on scientific differences between the races. "The whole physical organization of the negro differs quite as much from the white man as it does from that of the chimpanzee," wrote Agassiz. "The chimpanzee has not much further to progress to become a negro than the negro has to become a white man." In light of such "scientific truth" the newspaper commented on the insanity of considering blacks equal to whites and then lamented, "we poor Southerners have fallen into the hands of a strange people."[15]

Voter registration in the spring and summer of 1867 only emphasized the strangeness of this new situation. The *Loyal Georgian* called for Georgia's black men to organize and register to vote, explaining that the Union League and similar organizations made a fine basis upon which to build a Republican Party. "Friends, the time has come for work," explained the paper. "The enemy are organizing to defeat us, let us work as hard as they." In Greene County 1,002 white men registered to vote, but 1,528 freedmen registered. By sheer numbers, black voters could control Greene County elections.[16]

This threat spurred white Democrats to action, and they called a mass meeting of all white voters at the courthouse "to take counsel together to direct black suffrage in the right channel." The organizers emphasized the importance of the meeting by pointing out that "*Inaction is political death.*" The meeting itself, however, revealed that white leaders did not fear an indigenous, self-directed black political movement, for they believed that black people were incapable of such action. Instead, the Democrats feared that Republicans would manipulate and use black voters. The mass meeting resolved that since someone had to control the black voters, the Democrats should attempt to gain that control. As the editor of the *Herald* argued, "the colored vote is a powerful element, and will be controlled by some influence. Why should it not be controlled by those who are affected by it?" [17]

Black voters, however, were not so easily controlled as the whites imagined. Abram Colby's Equal Rights Association combined with the local Union League to build a solid base for black political activity. The freedmen in Greenesboro organized a militia company that held drills at night. Though they apparently never received any arms from the state, the mere existence of the company suggested increasing solidarity among the freedmen. Democrats soon found that they simply could not control the mass of black voters as they had planned. Rebuffed in their attempts to approach black voters, Democratic leaders devised another response to the requirements of military Reconstruction. They adopted a strategy of noncooperation, a sort of nonviolent resistance that attempted to deny the Reconstruction government legitimacy by refusing to participate in it. [18]

The largest noncooperative movement was a statewide boycott by white voters of the election for delegates to the new state Constitutional Convention required under the Reconstruction Act. During the election, held October 29 through November 2, 1867, 102,283 Georgians voted in favor of the convention and elected delegates, while only 4,127 bothered to vote against a convention. In Greene County the "radical" candidate ran unopposed and received 1,249 votes, all but one from black voters. As the *Herald* proudly announced, only "One White Man Voted!!" One thousand white men boycotted the polls, reported the paper, and the only white man who voted in Greene County was the candidate, J. W. Tom Catching, who voted for himself. [19]

The freedpeople's celebration of their newfound power at the polls, ended in tragedy, however. While they paraded through the streets of Greenesboro, hurrahing and firing guns into the air, "a pistol in the hand of Tom Catching went off." The shot severed the middle finger of

Catching's hand and killed a black child standing in the crowd. The following week brought more tragedy. A black man named Allen Jackson argued with William Curry, a poor white artisan, on the street in Greensboro. Enraged, Curry drew his gun and killed Jackson. A mob of freedmen grabbed Curry and began to beat him but were stopped by the town marshal, who arrested Curry and took him to jail. More than 200 angry black men gathered outside the jail demanding Curry be hanged immediately, threatening to break in and do it themselves. The marshal and his men took up positions to defend the fortresslike building, and the jail bristled with rifles. Seeing that assault would be futile, the frustrated crowd soon dispersed. When some white citizens of Greene County tried to post bail for Curry's release, the military authorities intervened and denied bail. A month later, however, Curry mysteriously escaped the jail's three-foot-thick walls and disappeared.[20]

The last few months of 1867 had frightened Greene County's white leaders, waking in many a resolve to do whatever necessary to "save" their society. Military control of civil government, organized black militia drilling in Greensboro, an election controlled by black voters, unrestrained freedmen reveling in the streets, and a potential lynch mob of black men, all convinced Greene County's white leaders to change their tactics. Clearly, Greene County's black population intended to participate fully in the body politic and to make the community responsive to their needs. White leaders called for action to forestall this threat. "From the demonstrations made by the colored population we think it high time that some precautionary measures be adopted by the citizens," commented the *Herald*. The county Democratic Party put it more bluntly: "The time for inactivity is gone, the time for action is at hand."[21]

The new strategy of action by white conservatives began early in 1868. Democrats began to organize their voters to contest the upcoming April election of state officers. Thomas Stocks, Miles W. Lewis, James R. Sanders, James B. Park, and Professor Henry H. Tucker, now president of Mercer University, emerged as leaders of this new political movement, uniting the antebellum political factions. "The ball is now in motion," argued Greene County Democrats. "Let every man bestir himself and see what can be done to defeat the wicked designs of the negro Radical party."[22]

Some Democrats did more than merely bestir themselves. On February 27, 1868, a simple one-line comment in the *Herald* announced that "Gen. N. B. Forrest was in Atlanta on the 24th." General Nathan Bedford Forrest, among his many accomplishments, led the Ku Klux Klan.

Apparently, he visited Atlanta in February 1868 to finalize the organization of the Klan in Georgia.[23]

Dudley M. DuBose, Robert Toombs's son-in-law and law partner, of nearby Wilkes County, became Grand Titan of the Klan for Georgia's Fifth Congressional District, which included Greene County. He asked John C. Reid, who had moved to Lexington, to head the Klan in Oglethorpe County. Reid later explained how the Klan organized in Georgia. Each county contained several militia districts, and the Klan found this arrangement convenient for its purposes. DuBose and Reid established dens consisting of five to twenty Confederate veterans in each militia district. Since most Georgia counties had eight to twelve militia districts, any county Klan organization could on a few hours notice raise between 50 and 200 armed and mounted men. Accustomed to discipline and violence by their military service, these men raised no objections to the Klan's methods.[24]

The Klan carried out its attacks only at night, usually against "a troublesome negro, a pestilential Scalawag, or a bogus Ku Klux." Typically, the Klansmen threatened and whipped their victim, though on occasion they tortured or even castrated their target. Those who resisted were often killed. The Klan also broke up Union League meetings and political gatherings of freedpeople, intimidated black voters by terror, and on occasion murdered Republican leaders. In order to prevent the identification of members, "operations" usually involved men from outside the immediate neighborhood of the action, and for politically sensitive operations, dens were brought in from other counties. To make identification even more difficult, Reid's Klansmen wore black or brown masks and robes for concealment, though Abram Colby reported white robes and masks among Klansmen in Greene County. Because he was well known as the solicitor of Oglethorpe's county court, John C. Reid took extra care to disguise his own appearance and voice. On the whole, Reid argued, the Klan served as a needed police force that sometimes engaged in "guerilla warfare."[25]

As Reid proudly explained, the leadership of county Klan organizations usually reflected the leadership of the local Democratic Party. Abram Colby testified that the leadership of Greene County's Ku Klux Klan included James R. Sanders, a wealthy and influential planter; John E. Walker, the county's leading physician; and Thomas W. Robinson, the solicitor of the county court. The editor of the *Herald*, Henry M. Burns, also had close ties to the Klan, as his associate editor unwittingly revealed in an article explaining the editor's absence. All of these men were well-known leaders of the Democratic Party in Greene County, and they probably saw no conflict between the goals of their political party and the goals of the Klan.[26]

Thomas Robinson most likely served as the head, or "Grand Giant," of the Klan in Greene County. Not only did Abram Colby report that Robinson led the group of mounted Klansmen he observed, but Tom Robinson fit the profile of county Klan leaders given by John C. Reid as well. Grand Titan Dudley DuBose, an attorney, tended to choose successful young lawyers who had connections within the judicial system and the experience of military command to lead county organizations. Besides being solicitor of the county court, Thomas Robinson had commanded a militia unit during the Civil War. He also had married into the wealthy and powerful Park family, and his older brother, Philip B. Robinson, was superior court judge for the Ocmulgee Circuit, which included Greene County. Of the members of the county's bar in 1868, only Thomas Robinson fit the profile given by Reid.[27]

As for the other members of the local Klan, during the 1930s Greene County historian Thaddeus Brockett Rice proudly produced a list of eighty men "who freed Greene County from Carpetbag rule," hinting that these men had at one time or another at least cooperated with the Klan. The names included Judge Columbus Heard of the county court, Miles W. Lewis, Rowan H. Ward, John Swann, James B. Park, Thomas P. Janes, Joel F. Thornton, and Sheriff Charles C. Norton. Interestingly, the delegation sent to the Fifth Congressional District's Democratic Convention in October 1868 included Miles W. Lewis, James R. Sanders, and John Swann, and it was headed by Thomas W. Robinson.[28]

While the Democrats and the Ku Klux Klan organized, some ambitious white men concluded that greater opportunity lay with Greene County's new Republican Party. Only eleven local white men openly cooperated with the Republicans, but all were from prominent local families or were well known themselves, except for John Sullivan, who was a carriage maker and wheelwright before the war. Most had also been slaveowners or came from slaveowning families. J. W. Tom Catching, the delegate to the Constitutional Convention of 1867–68, owned twenty-nine slaves in 1860, and his brother Rufus owned more. David A. Newsom and Greene Thompson came from prosperous slaveowning families, and John Mitchell owned seventeen slaves in 1860. These men had different reasons for joining the Republican Party. J. W. Tom Catching and John Sullivan seem to have truly wanted to help Greene County's black people, and they stood up for freedpeople's rights even against their own interests. David A. Newsom had mixed motives, showing real concern for the suffering of black people but looking out for himself as well. The most successful of the white Republicans, Robert L. McWhorter, simply saw the Republican Party as an opportunity for advancement. Events would show he cared little about the freedpeople.[29]

Born into modest circumstances, Robert L. McWhorter began work at age nineteen clerking in a Penfield mercantile firm. In three years he became a partner in the firm and married Cordelia Janes, the daughter of one of Greene County's wealthiest planters. After Cordelia's death he married again, this time to the daughter of a wealthy southwest Georgia planter. By 1860 McWhorter owned a large plantation, mercantile interests, fifty-five slaves and, as a member of the "opposition party," had served two terms in the Georgia House. In 1861 he led a company of soldiers from Penfield to war, where he rose to the rank of major. After surrendering at Appomattox, he returned to Greene County determined to rebuild his fortunes as a planter and politician.[30]

Perhaps the most hated and the most loved politician in Greene County, Robert L. McWhorter seemed always to land on his feet. McWhorter represented Greene County in the Georgia General Assembly from 1865 through 1867, supporting the discriminatory laws passed during the first postwar legislative sessions and voting against the Fourteenth Amendment to the Constitution. In early 1868, however, he shocked the county and his colleagues by joining the Republican Party. Robert L. McWhorter may have had some compassion for the black people of Greene County, but he also saw black voters as a group that could be easily exploited. Besides, McWhorter always thought of himself as an outsider, and at heart was an aggressive and combative man who enjoyed the role of "opposition" leader. As a leader of the Republican Party in Greene County, he could once again confound his enemies while riding the Republican tide to power.[31]

McWhorter and the other white Republicans joined with Abram Colby's Equal Rights Association and the Union League in early 1868 to build a Republican Party in Greene County. Save for a few white leaders, this organization consisted almost entirely of black men. In March 1868, at their first county convention, the Republicans nominated Abram Colby and Robert L. McWhorter for Greene County's two seats in the Georgia House of Representatives. David A. Newsom stood for the office of ordinary, John Mitchell for tax receiver, and Greene Thompson sought the office of tax collector. The new Georgia Constitution of 1868 had eliminated the county inferior courts, giving most of the inferior court's powers to the ordinary. Under the new Constitution the ordinary and the tax officials controlled county governments, so these men, if elected, would control Greene County.[32]

A week after Colby and McWhorter's nominations a brief notice appeared in the *Herald*. Headlines in bold capitals read "K-K-K" and told readers that "Bob McWhorter will take pleasure in explaining the meaning of the above letters. Give him a call." As the targets of Klan harassment, both men also received Klan threats that promised "to kill or drive every damn Radical out of the county." Warnings to the freedmen appeared in the newspaper as well, telling blacks that "when voting time comes you had best go to your old master and . . . he will tell you what to do." But these threats and suggestions had little effect on Greene County's black voters, who turned out in mass. Colby, McWhorter, and the rest of the Republican ticket trounced their opponents by a two to one margin in the April 1868 election. Across Georgia Republican representatives won a majority of seats in the General Assembly, and the Republican candidate for governor, Rufus Bullock, received 7,000 more votes than his Democratic opponent.[33]

The Republican victors often faced harassment and ridicule in their own communities. David A. Newsom, elected judge of the ordinary court and thus the most powerful county official under the new Constitution, was assaulted on the street by John Dunn, a white farmer who cursed Newsom soundly for his association with black voters. David Newsom brought charges in superior court against Dunn, but a jury found Dunn not guilty. Abram Colby later named Dunn as a member of the Ku Klux Klan. In Penfield someone stole Robert L. McWhorter's fine Kentucky-bred walking horse, and McWhorter later found the poor animal in a nearby swamp completely shaven of hair. Students from nearby Mercer University began to provide all night "serenades" outside McWhorter's Penfield home, doing their best to keep him from getting any rest. One song that appeared in the *Herald* parodied McWhorter by having him collapse from drink in a freedmen's tavern. The chorus went as follows: "Clasped to old Abe in a loving embrace, The hairs of his kinky head doth tickle Bob's face, And Abe wishing Bob more sober to keep, Hugs him to sleep, Bummers, hugs him to sleep." Unfortunately for Abram Colby and other black legislators, Robert L. McWhorter proved less friendly to them than the song implied.[34]

On July 4, 1868, when the legislature assembled in the new capital of Atlanta, 29 of the 172 members of the house were black, and three of the Senate's 44 members were black. On the first day of business Robert L. McWhorter won election as Speaker of the House by a margin of two votes. As time passed, he came to be known as a moderate Republicans, one of a group of white Republican legislators who held a swing vote position between the conservative Democrats and the radical Republicans and their black allies. These men could select which party's agenda to support, though they usually proved as conservative as most Democrats.[35]

Abram Colby became a member of the Committee on Agriculture and Internal Improvements, but he spent most of his time learning his job and refining his political skills. Colby could still barely read, so his teenage son William, who could read and write, acted as his secretary. On July 21, 1868, Colby and McWhorter joined a majority in the House ratifying the Fourteenth Amendment, an act that ended Military Reconstruction in Georgia. In August Colby proposed a bill allowing county officers to choose which newspapers would carry local legal advertisements. Though seemingly a small matter, the fees for county legal ads could mean financial survival for Georgia's struggling black and Republican press. The House tabled the bill and never took it up again.[36]

Abram Colby and the other black legislators had high hopes when they began the legislative session of 1868, but their hope did not last long. The Georgia Constitution of 1868 failed to specifically grant blacks the right to hold public office in Georgia, and conservatives argued that blacks were thus ineligible to sit in the legislature. By August the Democrats managed to convince many "moderate" Republicans of their position. The Greensboro *Herald* observed, "there are Republicans [who] are acting with the Democratic wing . . . we can safely say to the people of Greene that their representative has resolved to shape his course with the Democratic party." Robert L. McWhorter, Colby's fellow Republican from Greene County, would cooperate with the Democrats on the issue of eligibility. In September, Speaker McWhorter managed to be absent when the matter came to a vote, and the Speaker pro tem who took his place ruled that the twenty-nine black legislators could not vote on the issue of eligibility. Thirty white Republicans voted with the Democrats or abstained. By a vote of eighty-three to twenty-three the legislature expelled its black members, and replaced them with their Democratic opponents from the April elections. James B. Park took Abram Colby's seat in the House.[37]

This reversal of fortune stunned the black legislators. Like Abram Colby, most had trusted their white Republican allies. Henry McNeal Turner, speaking for Colby and several other black assemblymen, addressed the House on the expulsion issue. "The Anglo-Saxon race, sir, is a most surprising one," Turner said, directing his remarks to Speaker McWhorter. "No man has ever been more deceived than I have been for the last three weeks. The treachery exhibited by gentlemen belonging to that race has shaken my confidence more than anything that has come under my observation from the day of my birth." Turner threatened, pleaded, and reasoned, but under it all lay his enormous outrage. "How dare you make laws by which to try me and my wife and children, and deny me a voice in the making of those laws." Finished, Turner asked for permission to leave the chamber, approached the Speaker's chair, brushed the dust from his feet, and walked out the door.[38]

The Greenesboro *Herald* crowed that "The people of Georgia have reason to rejoice . . . they now have a legislature composed of white men." Even more important, argued the paper, the Republicans would split, for the freedmen now knew they could not trust the white radicals. McWhorter and other white Republicans had simply used the black voters, who would soon discover that the Democrats were their only true friends. Abram Colby and the other expelled legislators, however, did not turn to the Democratic Party, nor did they give up. In October 1868 they assembled at Henry M. Turner's request in Macon to form the "Civil and Political Rights Association," a new organization comprised only of black members. Together, they began to campaign for Federal help in regaining their seats in the Georgia General Assembly and in suppressing violence against black people in Georgia. Their campaign would ultimately bear fruit in December 1869, but until then the freedpeople could look only to the courts for help. There they found little succor.[39]

When Republicans won control of the state government in the April 1868 election, conservatives across Georgia feared a complete change in the workings of the legal system. The Constitution of 1868 allowed the governor to appoint superior court judges, and conservatives assumed that Republican controlled courts would not give white people "justice." Ironically, their fears reflected a clear understanding of what happened to black people in conservative controlled courts. Responding to these fears, attorney R. J. Moses of Columbus toured the state arguing that white people should simply refuse to participate in the "radical" justice system. Instead, lawyers and judges should set up a private system of binding arbitration that would be made part of the freedpeople's employment contracts, avoiding the courts completely.[40]

But conservative fears about the "radical" courts proved unfounded in Greene County. Governor Rufus Bullock appointed Philip B. Robinson superior court judge for the Ocmulgee Circuit in 1868. Robinson, the minister of Greenesboro's First Baptist Church, may indeed have had more sympathy for the plight of black people than his brother, Klan leader Thomas W. Robinson. In any trial before the superior court, the ideas and assumptions of jurors would have an important role. Even if Philip Robinson intended to offer equal justice to the people of Greene County, his influence would have at best been limited.[41]

In fact, as superior court judge, and later as county court judge, Robinson dealt harshly with the freedpeople who came before his court. The outcome of civil cases involving black people before his court offered the freedpeople little hope. Other than as plaintiffs or defendants, freedpeople had no role in the functioning of courts in the county. In fact, no black man ever served on a jury in Greene County during Reconstruction, though jurors were supposed to come randomly from the list of county taxpayers. A few black people who could afford a lawyer brought civil suits against employers who refused to pay their wages, but black plaintiffs seldom won. As General Alfred H. Terry, who oversaw Georgia's Reconstruction during 1869 and 1870, explained, "in civil cases between parties of the opposite color Sambo generally goes to the wall."[42]

Criminal cases gave similar results. Greene County's grand juries refused to even admit the existence of the Ku Klux Klan, and juries seldom convicted whites accused of crimes against black people. Two criminal cases from the September term of superior court in 1869 characterized the problem. Nancy and Ruben Jackson, convinced that their employer had cheated them, led a small group of freedpeople to Thomas Winn's house where they waved clubs and threatened him. Arrested and charged with inciting to riot, Nancy and Ruben each received a $50 fine or ninety days at hard labor. At almost the same time a group of white men, led by William Nunn, Lucius Nunn, and Don Irby, gathered outside the meeting of a black church in Union Point firing guns into the air and yelling threats. The members of the church pressed charges, but the three men were found not guilty of disrupting worship services.[43]

Even as the freedmen struggled to gain justice in the courts, a wave of Ku Klux Klan–inspired violence swept across Georgia. Democrats were determined to win the November General elections, and from August through October 1868 the Freedmen's Bureau reported 142 attacks on Georgia's black people, including 31 murders. Klan activity in Greene County became so open that on October 24, 1868, the Mercer University baseball team played at Penfield against the Ku Klux club of Covington. Mercer won, sixty-five to thirty-two. In the weeks before the election the Klan rode nightly, beating and terrorizing freedmen. As Robert

McWhorter's brother Joe explained, "the K K Democracy are determined to prevent the negro from voting. A great many negroes are hid out
in the woods every night for fear of losing their lives." Though the Klan
focused on intimidating black voters, they also acted to punish black
workers who challenged their employers. Outside Penfield a disguised
group of twenty mounted men beat a black man to death for complaining
to the Freedmen's Bureau about his employer, and then beat a black
woman until she miscarried for the same crime. One week before
the election, the editor of the *Herald* reminded the "colored voters of
Greene" of the violence, telling them "to remember the fate of poor Tray,
may the Lord have mercy on his soul," when deciding whether to vote.[44]

From January 1 through November 15, 1868, the Freedmen's Bureau
reported fourteen acts of violence by white people against freedpeople
in Greene County. Of these, only four, a murder, a shooting, a pistol-
whipping, and a beating, came to trial. In all four cases white juries
acquitted the white defendants. In one case, Fanny Peek was severely
whipped by William Farrell, and Peek successfully brought charges
against Farrell. The jury acquitted Farrell, who returned home and
whipped Fanny Peek again. The second time she did not bother pressing
charges. Ten of the cases reported by the Freedmen's Bureau, including a
murder, never made it to court. As John Sullivan explained, "there is no
chance of punishing these violators of law unless the military take it in
hand." Abram Colby expressed the freedpeople's despair resulting from
such unpunished crimes when he told a Congressional Committee that
"there is no use in talking about whipping, they whip them whenever
they want to in my county."[45]

Despite the threats and violence, Abram Colby and the black voters of
Greene County stood together for the November 1868 election. Perhaps
on the advice of John Sullivan, who was the county's last Freedmen's
Bureau agent, black voters organized themselves into companies, and on
election day company after company marched to the polls, their numbers
and unity forestalling white attempts at intimidation. About 1,200 of
Greene County's 1,500 eligible black voters dared to cast ballots. Republican candidates, including Ulysses Grant, won majorities in Greene
County, while in most neighboring counties white intimidation of black
voters facilitated Democratic victories.[46]

Ku Klux Klan violence continued in Greene County, and John Sullivan
asked the grand jury to investigate. On November 30, 1868, after months
of open Klan activity, the grand jury announced "we have made a diligent
inquiry and can learn nothing to satisfy us as to the existence of any such

bands." Even if the leading citizens who sat on the grand jury were not themselves Klan members, they obviously did not want to limit its activities. A disgusted Agent Sullivan had already explained to his superiors that "there is no chance of having these violators of law and order punished" in Greene County.[47]

In several neighboring counties the Klan helped restore white political dominance in the November 1868 election, but Republicans, many of them black men, continued to hold most local offices in Greene and the surrounding counties. Despite the terror, despite the lack of protection from the legal system, the black people of eastern Georgia did not simply cave in to the pressures of organized violence. In Greene County this proved especially true, as the freedpeople demonstrated remarkable durability in the face of growing violence. Their perseverance showed not just tremendous courage and unity of purpose, it also highlighted the power of the revolution that had swept through the black community in Greene County. Destroying that revolution would take more than a simple campaign of violence.

All Right, Set 'Em Up Again

In late 1868 the Freedmen's Bureau asked for reports on violence from its agents across Georgia. R. C. Anthony, the bureau agent in Warren County, twenty miles to the east of Greene County, reported the murder of a freedman and the violent dispersal of a Republican meeting. Returning to Warrenton after the meeting, Anthony described the scene that greeted him there:

> On my return to town I saw 25 or 30 mounted men with double bar-relled guns and revolvers. These were from Glascock Co., and I learn that they had been sent for to help keep the peace. They were welcomed by speeches at the Court House, one speaker swinging a revolver over his head saying, "This is the law and this shall rule this country."[1]

During 1869 the Ku Klux Klan tried to establish the law of the revolver in Greene County. Local groups and Klansmen from neighboring counties fought to destroy black political leaders and to reassert white elites' control over the freedpeople. The attackers burned houses, beat dozens of individuals, and murdered several freedpeople. David A. Newsom, a white Republican elected county ordinary in April 1868, grew increasingly concerned about the violence. In July 1869 Klan attacks near his homeplace outside Union Point injured black people he knew, and both Newsom and James B. Hart tried to protect their workers and halt the violence. Soon, both men received death threats from the Klan. Newsom wrote Republican governor Rufus Bullock asking for help. Explaining the situation and the death threats, Newsom told the governor, "I feel much intimidated." The governor promised help, but the Klan attacks continued. In August Klansmen from Taliaferro County attacked and beat George Battle, a black leader in Union Point. Newsom wrote the governor a report of the attack, even risking giving the names of some of the Klansmen involved in the assault. Again, nothing came of Newsom's report. After this cry for help, Newsom never again reported Klan activity to the governor, apparently silenced both by Klan threats and by the ineffectual response by the governor to the violence.[2]

The Ku Klux Klan violence in Greene County may have begun as a political campaign of terrorism, but it quickly took on the personal causes of the Klansmen as well. In particular this meant punishing black people who refused to accept an economically and socially subservient role. William Lumpkin, the son of a planter, recalled his indignation at black people's refusal to conduct themselves submissively. "On the streets of Union Point," he remembered, "a darkey pushed me off the sidewalk and spit on me. . . . We were helpless." Though reading law at the time, Lumpkin began riding with the Klan at night, frightening and intimidating troublesome freedpeople. Disguised and on horseback, Lumpkin enjoyed the power that came with terror and felt helpless no more.[3]

Greene County's ex-slaves understood the political intentions of the Klan and in many cases were able to stand up to political terrorism. The attacks stemming from violations of social codes or as a response to economic success, however, were far more galling. Many Klansmen feared that education would teach black people to live above their station, so teachers who worked with the freedpeople were harassed and in several cases driven from the county. Klansmen also burned the freedpeople's school at Penfield, leaving them no "place to hold their meetings as school except in the woods." In other cases freedpeople were attacked simply for trying to live as free people. William McWhorter recalled that "jus' as de Niggers was branchin' out and startin' to live lak free folks, dem nightriders come 'long beatin', cuttin' and slashin' 'em up." Such attacks not only punished freedpeople for economic success or for conducting themselves inappropriately, but in some cases the attacks also helped force black workers into patronage relationships with local whites for protection. John C. Reid and his fellow Klansmen may have viewed themselves as proud minutemen or political policemen, but the freedpeople thought them worse than thieves.[4]

Minnie Davis, who was born a slave in Greene County, remembered the Ku Klux Klan's campaign of terror. "We were afraid of the Ku Klux Klan riders," she explained. "There were lots of killings going on for a long time after the war was supposed to be over." Isaiah Greene told of how his uncle and some other freedmen found an abandoned wagon full of money in the creek. The Ku Klux Klan began to pursue those who found the money. They eventually found an informer, who named

Isaiah's uncle as the leader. "One night," Isaiah told an interviewer, "they kidnaped and carried him to the woods where they pinned him to the ground, set the dry leaves on fire, and left him." The fire severely burned Isaiah's uncle's feet, and then he broke free and escaped. Later, all his toes had to be amputated because of the burns.[5]

As the acknowledged leader of Greene County's freedpeople, Abram Colby grew increasingly frustrated by the lack of response to the violence. In August 1869 Colby wrote Republican governor Rufus Bullock begging for help. "I don't know what course to pursue," he confessed. "On saturday last they taken out 20 men, and they shot an innocent person on last thursday night. . . . Governor, the Clu Clux [*sic*] is found riding in our county every night." Colby then pleaded, "Governor, pray send protection to our county."[6]

On the nights of September 17, 18, and 19, 1869, the Klan led a large-scale attempt to eliminate radical leadership in the county. In surprise raids, they tried to capture Greenesboro's American Missionary Association teacher as well as local black leaders, including Abram Colby. Wagonloads of students from Mercer University were brought from Penfield to assist in this effort. The Klansmen found the white A.M.A. teacher, a northern man named R. H. Gladding, and abused and threatened him. Gladding had violated social norms not just by teaching in the freedpeople's school, but also "one rainy day, to the town's horrified amazement, he was seen to walk down Main Street, his umbrella over a Negro woman." Because Gladding was a northern man with connections to the military authorities, the Klansmen handled him carefully. Not so the elderly man who simply boarded Gladding in his house; the Klansmen dragged him out and beat him severely. But despite a massive house-to-house search by Klansmen and students through Greenesboro, the black community successfully hid their leaders from the mob. After the attack, Gladding wrote Governor Bullock for help, explaining, "I do not deem my life safe unless I can be protected, and therefore ask that proper protection be given to myself and my school."[7]

The military authorities had not responded to David Newsom's call for assistance, nor had they responded to Abram Colby's cry for help. Gladding, however, was a teacher working for the powerful American Missionary Association, so in response to his demand Federal authorities sent a company of sixty-five soldiers to keep order in Greene County and to protect Gladding's school. These infantrymen spent the next several months chasing mounted men back and forth across the county, never catching any Klansmen nor finding many witnesses that would testify against the Klan. It was a frustrating experience that left both the soldiers and the freedpeople of Greene County very discouraged.[8]

Henry M. Turner heard report after report of the violence, and he responded. "We advise our people," he wrote in October 1869, "to the extent of their power, to defend themselves against any and all these outrages." Greene County's black people often tried to defend themselves and even fought back against the violence. When the Klan murdered a freedman in the southern part of Greene County, armed black men launched an attack on the home of a local Klansman, wounding him in the gunfight that followed. The wounded man then hid under the floorboards of his house while armed freedmen searched for him to finish him off. Hancock County authorities arrested most of the blacks involved in this "insurrection," and thirteen freedmen later received sentences of four years in prison. Jordan Williams, a black resident of the area, wrote to Governor Bullock, explaining that there was no "insurrection." The attackers acted, "believing it to be indispensable for their own safety and liberty in the county of Greene," argued Williams. He asserted the freedpeople's right to respond to "crimes committed upon their people when the civil authorities permitted those who committed outrages upon the colored people to go at large."[9]

Unable to defeat Colby politically and unable to frighten blacks into political submission, Democratic leaders in Greene County decided to try another approach. On October 27, 1869, a group of Greenesboro merchants, knowing that Abram Colby might soon be reseated in the legislature, offered him $5,000 to join the Democratic Party or $2,500 to resign his seat. Colby refused the bribes, saying "I will not go back on my people for all [the wealth] in Greene County." Two nights later, on October 29, Klansmen broke open the door of Abram Colby's house and found him in bed, asleep. A robed and masked Klansman put a pistol to Colby's head and demanded that he surrender. "Of course I surrender," Colby replied. After terrorizing Colby's family with their guns, the Klansmen took him deep into some nearby woods, stripped him, and began beating him systematically. Twenty-three men took turns whipping him until Dr. John E. Walker, one of the Klansmen, pronounced Abram Colby dead. Two men reportedly complained to Tom Robinson, their leader, "Captain, we have not struck him a lick." "Go on and lick him; he is a dead man," replied Robinson. After the two men beat Colby some more, the Klansmen mounted and rode away.[10]

At eleven o'clock that same night two freedmen demanding help woke the detachment of eleven federal soldiers encamped in Greenesboro, sent there to protect Gladding's A.M.A. school. The Ku Klux Klan, said the freedmen, had broken into Abram Colby's house, and they feared for his life. Lieutenant George Hoyt, who was the commander, dressed and let the freedmen into his tent. At first he did not believe their story, but after questioning them further, Hoyt decided that they told the truth. Leaving three men to guard the camp, the lieutenant and seven men set out with the informants to rescue Abram Colby. Hoyt's patrol had marched about half the distance to Abram Colby's house when they met Colby's brother. He told them that "it was all over." He had followed the Klansmen to the edge of the woods, heard the beating, his brother's screams, and then a gunshot. Abram Colby was dead, said the brother. Lieutenant Hoyt convinced the brother to show him the place. The soldiers searched the woods for over an hour, finding no sign of Colby or the Klansmen. Exhausted and cold, the soldiers finally returned to Greenesboro.[11]

But Abram Colby did not die that night. He later recalled lying on the ground, semiconscious, the beating having continued so long that he could no longer feel the blows. "Doctor Walker came up to feel my pulse," remembered Colby. "Finding my wrist all wet and bloody, he did not feel my pulse, but said 'he is dead.'" After the Klansmen left, Colby managed to drag himself to a nearby cabin, whose inhabitants helped him. The next day Colby's brother took word to Lieutenant Hoyt that Abram survived the attack, and Hoyt visited Colby's hideout that afternoon. He found Colby in bed, unable to move, his back cut to shreds. "He was in very bad condition," reported Hoyt. The beating left Abram Colby with internal injuries and constant pain. The damage to his spine was so extensive that he lost the use of his left hand and had difficulty rising from a bed. In spite of these injuries, constant threats, and more attacks, Abram Colby continued his work as a leader of freedpeople in Greene County and eastern Georgia.[12]

The Greensboro *Herald* never reported the attack on Colby, just as it never reported other attacks in the county; but the military investigation that followed and a $5,000 reward offered by Governor Bullock for the arrest of the attackers certainly meant the event was well known. Colby named Dr. Walker, Jerry Sanders, Thomas Robinson, and several other prominent local men as among those who attacked him that night. Other than Abram Colby, however, no one else dared identify his attackers.

In June of 1870, a black woman named Anna Wynn tried to poison Thomas W. Robinson by putting strychnine in his drinking water. Both Robinson and his wife Mary drank a little of the water and became very ill. Again, the *Herald* did not report the gist of the incident, nor did superior court records indicate Anna's motives. She may have meant to assassinate the leader of Greene County's Klan, or perhaps she had other reasons for trying to kill Robinson. Whatever her motive, Anna received five years in prison for her crime.[13]

In December 1869, Congress reimposed military rule in Georgia, and General Alfred H. Terry took command of the state. Terry ordered the reseating of Abram Colby and the other expelled black legislators in January 1870. The black legislators tried to pass a bill creating a black militia to protect the freedmen, but they failed. Other bills intended to protect black citizens' civil rights, to ensure black men the right to jury duty, and to provide equal access to transportation all failed to pass the legislature. In fact, though Republicans dominated the legislature throughout 1870, they accomplished little that helped the freedmen in their ongoing struggle for justice. General Terry had little sympathy for the problems facing the black legislators. "If with a majority in each branch of the Legislature favorable to them, they cannot pass measures for their protection they had better suffer for a while," argued Terry. Abram Colby had a different view, explaining that "the white Republicans were too weak for us." General Terry never understood that white Republicans like Robert L. McWhorter had no intention of helping black Georgians secure their civil rights.[14]

Despite his crippled hand and constant pain, Abram Colby continued an active role in state and local politics. In the spring of 1870 Colby spent six weeks in Washington, D.C., as part of Governor Bullock's effort to continue military rule in Georgia. Colby met with Republican leaders, including President Grant, and tried to explain the problems of poverty, violence, and powerlessness facing Georgia's freedpeople. The military, he argued, was the only protection black people could trust. Most of the politicians refused to believe Colby's stories, especially his accounts of violence. As he later explained, "We tried Senator Sherman, and he thought it quite impossible that things were so bad as we told him." Colby's mission failed, but it moved him into the inner circle of Republican leaders in Georgia.[15]

As the December 1870 election loomed, Greene County's Democrats hoped that the split between Robert L. McWhorter and Abram Colby would destroy the local Republican Party. Colby's growing influence in the

Republican Party only exacerbated the conflict between his supporters and those of Speaker McWhorter. Meanwhile, the Republican Party began to come apart statewide. John Emory Bryant broke with Governor Bullock over Bullock's plans to have military rule continue in Georgia so as to avoid a general election that Bullock would likely lose. Bryant may not have understood that elections would result in Republican defeat statewide as well, or perhaps he could not resist the opportunity to take control of the Republican Party in Georgia. For whatever reason, in October 1870 Bryant held his own Fifth Congressional District nominating convention in Augusta. Delegates from Burke, Hancock, and Greene Counties, including Abram Colby, openly opposed the nominations made at Bryant's convention, and so supporters of Governor Bullock held their own Fifth District nominating convention in Greenesboro on November 3, 1870. Robert L. McWhorter chaired the convention while two freedmen, Abram Colby and Luke Crittle, represented Greene County. Colby's influence with the Bullock faction showed in his appointment to the Credentials Committee and in his election to represent the Fifth District in the Republican Party Central Committee. Jack Heard and Richmond Thompson, both freedmen, were elected to represent Greene County in the Fifth District Party Committee. After nominating their candidates for Congress, the convention pled for peace at the polls during the upcoming election and fully endorsed the actions of Governor Bullock over the past year. The problems between Colby and McWhorter, however, remained unresolved.[16]

Because of the conflict between Colby's and McWhorter's factions of the local Republican Party, the county nominating convention was postponed until December in the hope that unity could be restored. The *Herald* exulted that "the Radical party of Greene County is on a burst; emphatically—it has burst into fragments" and believed that Democrats would triumph in the December election before the Republicans could reorganize. On November 14 Henry McNeal Turner spoke to a mass meeting of freedpeople in Canaan, calling for continued Republican unity. If black voters rejected McWhorter, argued Turner, then a Democrat would surely take his place in the legislature. The black community had to stand with the Republican Party, or all would be lost. He also warned black voters against Democratic plays for their votes, telling them to "avoid the men who used to whip you and run you down in the swamp." The *Herald* gleefully latched on to Turner's warning, reminding black voters that the McWhorter family had the reputation of having been the "most tyrannical" of masters during slavery.[17]

Most black voters still doubted the "two-faced McWhorter" and looked to Abram Colby for guidance. Colby remained silent, but on the eve of the county nominating convention, Turner returned to speak in Greenesboro. Again he pled for black voters to unite in the Republican Party and to resist Democratic designs to intimidate them or entice them away. He told voters to support McWhorter despite questions about his actions in the House. Turner went even further, appealing to poor white men to support the Republican Party because, he said, the wealthy oppressed them as well. The editor of the *Herald* considered this argument truly dangerous; he expressed astonishment that Turner had the "sagacity" to appeal to "the poor white trash to join the Radical Party." Turner was attempting to limit the impact of black disunity by striking at white unity in the county, but his appeal had little effect. If Republicans were to win the election in Greene County they would win due to the support of black voters.[18]

The next day, December 3, 1870, the Greene County Republican Nominating Convention assembled at the courthouse. Robert McWhorter's brother, district court judge William H. McWhorter, took the chair. As soon as the proceedings began, J. W. Tom Catching launched a powerful attack on the McWhorter clan, claiming that they had sold out and abandoned the freedpeople of Greene County. The convention almost dissolved in disorder, but the chair finally managed to restore quiet and proceeded to the nominations. By a voice vote the delegates approved a slate of candidates virtually identical to that of 1868, including Robert McWhorter and Abram Colby as candidates for the legislature. The only meaningful change was the nomination of David A. Newsom for state senator. Some delegates questioned the accuracy of the voice votes, but the chairman rejected calls for a show of hands.[19]

The Democrats waited to see the results of the Republican meeting, and then they assembled a few days later with Miles W. Lewis in the chair. They nominated James R. Sanders and James D. Moore for the House and Judge Columbus Heard for the Senate. In their appeal to white voters, the Democrats emphasized economic issues. "If Radicalism triumphs," argued the Democrats, "real estate, stocks of all kinds, and public credit go down, and taxes go up." Democrats also reminded black voters of Robert McWhorter's role in the expulsion of black members from the legislature and his other questionable acts since then. Despite these appeals to members of the other parties, division between Republicans and Democrats continued to follow racial lines. The only real question about the December election was whether black voters would turn out to support a Republican ticket with Robert L. McWhorter on the ballot. Realizing that he also needed a good voter turnout to remain in the House, Abram Colby finally spoke to a mass meeting of freedpeople just days before the election. Colby explained the importance of supporting both Republican candidates and had McWhorter come stand next to him before the crowd, calling the upcoming election "the final struggle." [20]

Saturday night before the election Abram Colby returned home from church, and as he approached his house the dogs in his yard began barking. His son opened the door, and a shot rang out. The bullet narrowly missed Colby and his son. When a fusillade of bullets struck the house, Colby grabbed his gun and ran upstairs to return fire. Before he could respond, the attackers slipped away. Shaken but uninjured, the next day Colby voted in the election, but then his supporters convinced him to leave the county for his own safety. [21]

Despite the violence directed at Colby, Republican sheriff Reed C. Hailes and his deputy managed to keep order at the polling places in Greenesboro and Penfield. Several men were arrested, including Abram Colby's brother Chapman, who was carrying a concealed pistol at the poll. The violence and intimidation that usually faced the freedmen during an election seemed to be held at bay by Sheriff Hailes's protection, and they turned out in large numbers to vote. Republicans received about 1,300 votes, giving them majorities of 400 to 500 votes in all county races. David A. Newsom also received about 1,300 votes for the Georgia Senate in Greene County, but voters in the other two counties of the Nineteenth District heavily supported Judge Columbus Heard, who won the seat. Though he lost his Senate bid, Newsom continued to serve as Greene County's ordinary. Most important, the voters overwhelmingly re-elected Robert McWhorter and Abram Colby to the Georgia House. [22]

Outside Greene County, however, Republican political power began to collapse. After the election of December 1870, Democrats held 81 percent of the seats in the Georgia House and 86 percent of the seats in the Georgia Senate. Governor Bullock delayed the meeting of the new legislature as long as possible, but after almost a year he could delay no longer. In October 1871, facing impeachment by the new Democratic legislature and several felony indictments, Rufus Bullock fled the state and returned to New York. In November, eleven months after being elected, the Democrat-controlled legislature assembled in Atlanta bent on "redeeming" the state and removing all taint of "radical rule." It quickly arranged for the election of a new governor, and Democrat James M. Smith was elected without opposition. Over the next year the legislature considered and passed hundreds of bills as the newly triumphant Democrats attempted to reshape the state and undo the effects of Reconstruction. Although Abram Colby and several other black Republicans were also members of the legislature, they were an isolated minority and virtually powerless.[23]

In Greene County, however, black voters continued to exercise their power. Because of continuing Klan violence directed at his house, Abram Colby moved with his family to Atlanta in 1871. The following year, Colby could not meet the residency requirements to run again for office in Greene County, so Jack Heard, a younger black leader, ran in his place. Robert McWhorter had by then decisively broken with the Bullock Republicans, abandoned the freedpeople, and begun to seek a new constituency among white voters. Greene County's Republicans nominated Greene Thompson, a white merchant, to take McWhorter's place. Phillip Clayton, one of Greene County's wealthiest men with many financial connections to the Northeast, also joined with the Republicans and was nominated by them for the Eighth District's seat in Congress as a reward for his work in Greene County.[24]

Again black voters dominated the elections in Greene County. In October 1872 Jack Heard and Greene Thompson won seats in the Georgia House, and Republicans won all local offices they contested. Freedmen also turned out in large numbers in November to vote for Phillip Clayton and Ulysses S. Grant, both of whom won large majorities in Greene County but lost in every other county of the new Eighth District. Defeated for a third time, Greene County's Democrats hung Phillip Clayton in effigy at the courthouse, damning him for his financial and organizational contributions to the Republican cause. Against great odds, the freedpeople of Greene County had won another political victory, but some began to suspect that such victories were hollow.[25]

Abram Colby had realized that political victory and resistance to violence gained little for Greene County's freedpeople. Without access to and equal justice from the legal system, Greene County's black people had no chance of gaining control over their lives. Colby had resisted terrorism, but the violence continued. He had won political victory, but he found himself powerless. Only the legal system offered hope for justice, and by late 1871, Colby knew even this hope was futile. In the fall of 1871 a Joint Congressional Committee investigating political terrorism in the South came to Atlanta. Abram Colby, along with dozens of other freedmen, testified about the situation in Georgia. When asked why he never went to court about the Klan attack, Colby explained that he knew of no judge or court who would punish his attackers. Even the federal grand jury called in Atlanta to investigate the violence included Klan sympathizers such as James R. Sanders, a leader of the Ku Klux Klan in Greene County who had run against Colby in the 1870 election. The legal system in Georgia would never give black people justice, Colby argued, and only the resumption of military rule could give the freedpeople any protection. The faith Abram Colby once had shared with other Americans in the importance of the rule of law and in the equity of the legal system and his hope that an attorney representing blacks might allow fair play had all been crushed.[26]

Conservatives also used the legal system to strike at white Republicans. Beginning with the March Term of 1868, creditors began filing suit for antebellum debts against white Republicans. Greene Thompson, David A. Newsom, and Robert L. McWhorter each faced several substantial claims; in every case they lost in jury trials and had to pay large sums to the plaintiffs. J. W. Tom Catching had the honor of being the most pursued debtor among the white Republicans, probably because of his unusually staunch defense of black people's interests even within the Republican Party. In March 1868 Catching faced three lawsuits for debts totaling more than $5,500, and he faced other lawsuits for debts virtually every term of court for the next three years. By the spring of 1872 these actions bankrupted Catching. He sold all of his property under court order and then left Greene County. He later wrote to newly elected Democratic governor James M. Smith for help. He explained that he and his daughter had been forced to leave his farm by fraudulent claims. "Although I know that our State laws," Catching wrote, "if executed, would restore our home and property with heavy damages to be paid by the robbers, I have positively failed to get an officer or lawyer of the County to act in this case." Like the black people he tried to help, Catching found the legal system turned against him, giving him no chance to seek justice. Governor Smith never responded to Catching's plea, and Catching never returned to Greene County.[27]

The true "final struggle" for Greene County's black voters came in the fall of 1874. White manipulation of the economic and legal systems rather than political terrorism crushed the freedmen's political hopes in the election that year. The *Herald* issued a clarion call for Democratic action to win the 1874 election. "Our county has continued under Radical rule," lamented the paper's editor, "while neighboring counties, as much oppressed as ourselves, by united action have thrown off the yoke and are again free and independent." He argued further that "it only requires concert of action among our people to accomplish the same good end. A large majority of the negroes are in the employment of Democrats and if the proper effort is made they can be influenced to vote right." Isaiah Greene recalled that his former master, Richard Willis, used such pressure to influence his workers' votes. Those families who failed to vote correctly "were asked to move off his plantation." Economic pressures like this began to damage black political unity in Greene County so much that at their August 1874 nominating convention, Republicans could not agree on candidates and open conflict broke out over the issue of compromise with the Democrats.[28]

The Republicans finally nominated Jack Heard and former Freedmen's Bureau agent John H. Sullivan for the House, rejecting more radical candidates. But Sullivan seemed quite radical enough to the Democrats. He had organized and still led a militia company of black men. In 1872 his company applied to Governor James M. Smith for recognition and arms under Georgia's new militia law. Governor Smith, as in most such cases, never responded to Sullivan's requests. Through his former association with the Freedmen's Bureau and his leadership of the militia company, Sullivan won great influence and respect in the black community and pursued more radical goals than did Jack Heard, the black candidate. Heard had served one term in the legislature and seemed to have lost hope of changing the lives of freedpeople in Greene County. He advocated black emigration to the West or to Liberia as an alternative.[29]

In the October state election, John Sullivan and Jack Heard lost to planter Democrats Lewis B. Willis and Lorenzo D. Carlton. Of more than 2,500 men registered, less than 1,600 cast votes, two-thirds of them for Democrats. The *Herald* attributed Democratic victory to white solidarity and "black men with white hearts" who voted Democratic. Actually, legal subterfuge made the victory possible. In two of the county's six precincts there were no Republican votes, and in a third precinct only one Republican vote. Local election managers simply allowed whites to vote early, and then because Georgia's election laws allowed local managers to set the hours for voting, they closed the polls. The freedmen, patiently waiting their turn to vote after the white voters, had no opportunity to cast their ballots. Outraged, they looked to Jack Heard for leadership, but he declined to organize any protest. He had instead turned his energy to promoting black emigration to the American West. Greene County's freedmen had to look elsewhere for leadership.[30]

The Monday following the election, Greene County's Democrats and guests from surrounding counties gathered for an official victory celebration in Greenesboro. After band performances and a torchlight parade around the town, the crowd gathered in front of the Dougherty Hotel, where Democratic leaders spoke from the porch. Three of the speakers were black men. Two of the them were visitors from Morgan County, but the third, Ned Statham, lived in Greenesboro and had organized an active Democratic Club among the town's black people. Many Democrats refused to take their allies seriously, however. In fact, the *Herald* reported that the black speakers "were of course, a feature adding fun and hilarity to the occasion." Other Democrats took a more generous view, arguing that their black allies were entitled to more than praise; "they are entitled to material aid in all their laudable undertakings." No one bothered, however, to record what Ned Statham said.[31]

Black Democrats not only had problems gaining respect among white leaders, they also faced exclusion from the black community. Near Union Point, for example, the Lumpkin's ex-slave, Big Dennis, always voted as directed by his former master. As a result, he was a lonely man, an outcast among the freedpeople. Despite the growing numbers of "black men with white hearts," most freedmen continued to support the Republican cause. Rejecting the promise of economic aid for black voters who supported the Democratic Party, many freedmen, especially those around Union Point, led by George Battle, organized for the upcoming November general election.[32]

On the morning of the November 1874 national election, more than 300 black voters awaited the opening of the polls at Union Point. Having missed their chance to vote in the October election, these freedmen were determined to vote before the polls could be closed. Seeing the crowd, local election managers, led by William Reynolds, simply refused to open the polls, which was arguably a legal act under the new state election law passed by the Democratic legislature. By preventing potential Republicans from voting, the election managers helped the Democrats secure a majority in the election.[33]

Angry black voters held a protest meeting the following Saturday night and there turned to a middle-aged artisan named Montgomery Shepherd for leadership. Shepherd spoke to the crowd and then led them in a midnight protest demonstration through the streets of Union Point. Some members of the crowd, armed with pistols and clubs, marched into the white residential section and threatened the homes of several local leaders. At one home a protester pointed his pistol at a member of the local white elite and pulled the trigger. There was the loud pop of a percussion cap, but no discharge, and the laughing protesters left the fainting man on

his porch. At about three o'clock on Sunday morning, the last of the protesters went home.[34]

That same morning, Montgomery Shepherd, George Battle, and several other freedmen were arrested and locked in the local jail. In response
to rumors of an attempt to free the prisoners, a posse of 25 white men
rode up from Greenesboro, and Governor James Smith put 500 militiamen on alert in Augusta. There were two acts of violence: Union Point
election manager William Reynolds was fired on from ambush, and an ar-
sonist set fire to Lorenzo Carlton's barn, but no rescue effort developed.
The prisoners were tried before county court judge Philip B. Robinson.
Each received stiff sentences for riot. Montgomery Shepherd received the
maximum sentence possible, $500 in fines and twelve months on the
chain-gang. Less than a month later a small item in the *Herald* reported
that Montgomery Shepherd, serving his time on the chain-gang, was shot
to death "while trying to escape." The *Herald's* new editor, James B.
Park, dryly commented, "All right, set 'em up again."[35]

Greene County's black people, however, never were able to "set 'em
up again." The "insurrection" of 1874 convinced the county's white
Democrats that black Republican resurgence had to be prevented at any
cost. Intimidation, conspiracy, economic pressure, and legal manipulation had finally given Democrats control of local government in Greene
County, but no one knew how long such control would last. Seven years
of Republican dominance demonstrated just how determined black voters could be, and federal intervention or the rise of a new black leader like
Abram Colby could quickly return the Republicans to power. If black
men were going to be allowed to vote, something more lasting than fraud
and intimidation would have to render their vote meaningless.

Throughout 1875 Greene's Democratic leaders struggled with the
problem of preventing a Republican resurgence. They also faced increasing criticism from within their own party, led by the now-redeemed
McWhorter family. The critics focused on the structure and high cost of
local government, and called for sweeping reform to save the county
money. In a letter to the *Herald* in November, a taxpayer called for the
creation of a county commission to exercise the powers of the former
inferior court. Two weeks later the grand jury issued a similar call. Led
by foreman William H. McWhorter the jurors recommended that the
county's representatives seek a law from the legislature creating a Board
of Commissioners in Greene County. The grand jury also recommended
the abolition of the offices of ordinary, treasurer, and tax receiver in the

county. These measures, argued the jurors' presentments, would save the county thousands of dollars and allow a reduction in local taxes.[36]

A county commission, however, offered far more than just the possibility of saving money. The bill, introduced by Lorenzo Carlton to the legislature, provided that commissioners would be chosen by the grand jury for four-year terms. There would not be a county-wide election of commissioners; the white elites who served on the grand jury would elect them. These commissioners would exercise enormous power, controlling all county property, setting tax rates, managing and controlling elections, and overseeing all county expenditures. The bill followed the example of similar bills creating boards of commissioners in other counties, and on February 19, 1876, it became law. Explaining the workings of the new law, the *Herald* reassured readers that "a negro has never been drawn on a jury in this county." With virtually all the powers of local government resting in the hands of the Board of Commissioners, as it had a decade earlier in the inferior court, local elected officials would have little influence over affairs in the county. There was no threat that voters, white or black, would disrupt the white elite's grasp on the reins of power in Greene County.[37]

The March 1876 grand jury, led by foreman James B. Park, had the honor of choosing Greene County's first Board of Commissioners. After due deliberation they elected from their own ranks James B. Park, Peter W. Printup, and Baldwin Copelan. Park was one of Greene's wealthiest landowners and a successful businessman. In 1860, at the age of thirty-one, Park owned sixty-six slaves. In 1872 he wielded enough influence in the Georgia legislature to have the boundary of Greene County extended across the Oconee River to include his home and mill community that had been in Morgan County. Peter W. Printup moved from New York to a plantation in Greene County before the Civil War. In 1860 he owned $20,000 worth of land. After the war Printup entered business deals with his wealthy relatives in the Northeast and invested in a commission merchant business in Augusta. Baldwin Copelan owned fifty-seven slaves in 1860 but lost most of his wealth during the 1860s. In 1873 his nephew Edward Copelan leased the "Big Store" from Charles A. Davis and entered the mercantile trade in Greensboro as part of McCall, Copelan, and Co. Eventually the Copelan family would join in partnership with the Davis family to become the dominant merchants in Greene County. Baldwin Copelan apparently served on the county commission as a proxy for Edward Copelan and Charles A. Davis. The three commissioners clearly represented the transitional state of Greene's economy in the mid-1870s. All three men still identified themselves as farmers, but all three were heavily involved in commerce, probably making more money from business than from farming.[38]

The county commission insured that white men would control Greene County's government, but black voters could still play a role in state and national elections. Democrats knew that they could still benefit from control of the black vote, so before the 1876 election, they openly courted the freedmen and called for white employers to put pressure on their black workers to "vote correctly." Without a secret ballot, each man's vote was known to the community, and the Democrats put this knowledge to use. Some freedmen began to question the value of struggling at great personal cost to elect Republican candidates who had never really been able to help or protect their constituents. Thus, black voters faced the terrible dilemma of choosing between confrontation or accommodation, and this predicament shattered black political unity in Greene County.[39]

As the 1876 elections approached, white Democrats worked to win as much black support as possible. Frank Peek, "a staunch colored Democrat," played a crucial role in creating organized Democratic Clubs among the county's freedpeople. Torn over the question of cooperation or confrontation, large numbers of freedmen left the Republican Party and aligned themselves with the Democrats. The remaining Republicans gathered in September to nominate candidates for the upcoming election. They could agree on, or perhaps find, only one candidate, moderate black minister and teacher Henry Smith of Penfield. Meanwhile, the Democrats held a lively convention at the courthouse that drew more than 500 participants. The choice of nominees to the Georgia House was hotly contested, and Robert L. McWhorter, former Republican Speaker of the House, was one of the leading candidates for nomination. McWhorter's supporters argued that he had shown himself a true conservative yet would be a vehicle to attract black votes to the Democrats. McWhorter almost won nomination, but after several inconclusive ballots, he withdrew, and attorney William H. Branch and planter Valentine D. Gresham won the Democratic nomination for the Georgia House.[40]

The Democrats won the October 1876 election by a landslide. Branch and Gresham won about 1,500 votes each, while Smith polled only 603 votes. According to the *Herald*, of almost 1,200 black men who voted, about half cast their ballots for Democrats. This figure may have reflected wishful thinking, but there was sufficient division of the black electorate to result in violence. On the Saturday following the election a group of black Republicans gathered in Union Point for a rally. Spotting several black Democrats in the crowd, the Republicans mobbed them. But the intervention of the black Democrats' "white friends" turned the tables, and the Republicans withdrew from the brawl, defeated. Clearly, the unity forged by Abram Colby, the solidarity that made Republican victory possible, had dissolved.[41]

After October 1876, black voters never again threatened to gain control of politics in Greene County. In the November presidential election just one month later, only 100 Republicans bothered to cast ballots. But black voting rights and political power did not simply disappear after 1876; rather, they were weakened during the following decade. The desperate economic situation of most freedpeople meant that they felt compelled to vote for the causes of their white patrons, and on only one occasion during the next decade did black voters stand in opposition to the cause of their patrons. In December 1877 large numbers of black voters turned out to reject the new state constitution they correctly believed threatened their interests; but the Constitution of 1877 won approval statewide. Terror, fraud, and violence had all played significant roles in the destruction of black political power in Greene County, but the increasing economic dependency and economic coercion of black voters combined with white control and manipulation of the legal system proved the most effective means of derailing the freedpeople's struggle for political power.[42]

In the 1870s the modern commercial market economy and its lawyer and merchant servants achieved ascendancy in Greene County. During the decade and a half following the Civil War, the majority of the county's farmers became dependent on the market for their sustenance. Greene County's black people, whether working for wages, as tenants, or on shares, were forced by legal, economic, and social structures to produce cotton for the market. Through the legislature and the courts, white conservatives attempted, with some success, to manipulate the economic transformation for their own political benefit by using its effects to influence black voters. This political struggle only increased the county's reliance on the grain of the Midwest, the industrial products of the North, and the international cotton market. The resulting intensification of cotton cultivation, combined with declining soil fertility and growing population, ended any hope of self-sufficiency and independence for most of Greene County's farmers. Ironically, white conservatives' efforts to control black laborers through the market system facilitated the growth of a structured economic dependency that eventually engulfed not just Greene County's black population, but large numbers of white farmers as well. By 1880 most of Greene County's people, black and white, worked and lived in thrall to a national and international market system they could not control.

The Old Plantation System
Is Played Out

The poverty and suffering of Greene County's freedpeople reflected more than just the racism of their society. Given virtually "nothing but freedom," Greene County's freedpeople found their problems increased by the ongoing transformation of the county's economy. During the late 1860s and the 1870s the people of Greene County became fully dependent on the commercial market economy, not just to sell their cotton but also for the necessities of life. This transformation exposed the majority of Greene County's people to the potentially destructive caprices of the market. For the freedpeople, who were at the bottom of the economic ladder, the costs of this dependency made escape from poverty almost impossible.

Further economic pressure resulted from the collapse of the plantation system of labor. By the late 1860s black people began to refuse to work for share-wages in gangs reminiscent of slavery and increasingly demanded sharecropping and tenancy relationships. These new labor relations offered some black workers more autonomy in directing their own day-to-day work but often increased the workers' personal obligations to their landlords and resulted in little economic advantage to the freedpeople. Ultimately, the dire poverty and new servile relationships of the freedpeople undermined their efforts to gain personal independence and political power.[1]

Following emancipation, most plantation owners tried to continue planting using the factorylike gang labor system that had proven successful before the war. Freedpeople worked in gangs organized for specific tasks and supervised by overseers; little distinguished their daily work experience from that of slavery. During 1866 and 1867 on James R. Sanders's plantation outside Penfield, for example, an overseer directed the work of the gangs and kept track of deductions for disobedience or laziness that would be taken out of the worker's final pay. Many freedpeople might have preferred to work for weekly or monthly cash wages, but they never had an opportunity to do so. Because of a lack of both credit and money as well as the desire of employers to maintain leverage over their laborers, most black workers toiled all year for a share of the final crop. As James Davison of Union Point explained in January 1866, "the contracts on large farms, generally, are made for from one quarter (1/4) to one half (1/2) of the crops." [2]

The share-wage system seemed to offer freedpeople a chance to participate in the profits of farming, but it actually worked to the advantage of the employer. Under the share-wage system employers could limit their labor cost during the year to the amount necessary for worker subsistence. If they furnished their own workers, landowners often recovered much of the furnishing costs with interest. Having no cash income during the year, workers were tied to whatever credit relationship the employer created. Because they had to make it to the end of the year to be paid for their labor, laborers accepted work and living conditions they might otherwise have fled. Employers commonly dismissed unsatisfactory workers without pay, and the courts demonstrated little sympathy toward workers in such situations. The freedpeople, however, began to resist working under such conditions. Many longed for the independence of family farms and spoke often of their desires for small farms, which would provide family subsistence. As Abram Colby explained when asked what the freedpeople of Greene County wanted, "they would all go into the county and farm ... make all they could, and live happily." [3]

Some American leaders understood the freedpeople's desire for land and believed that land redistribution would result in beneficial change for the South. Pennsylvania Congressman Thaddeus Stevens argued in September 1865 that "the whole fabric of southern society must be changed" by Reconstruction. In order to do this, he proposed that the federal government confiscate the property of the South's 70,000 largest landowners. This land would be sufficient to provide every household of freedpeople with a forty-acre farm, and the remainder when sold would pay off the national debt that had resulted from the Civil War. Thus, southern elites who led their states to war would be punished, the taxpayers of the nation would be relieved of an enormous debt burden, and a South of independent small farmers would prosper like a transplanted Indiana. [4]

Stevens, however, failed to win much support for his plan. Citing the experience of emancipation in the British Caribbean, some congressmen argued that giving small farms to the freedmen would allow them to farm for subsistence, and this would mean an end to the large-scale cotton production that was so important to the nation's economy. Others simply could not swallow the usurpation of so many people's property rights or feared the implications of subjecting property ownership to moral tests. The freedpeople's hopes for owning small family farms largely vanished with Stevens's plan, but black workers soon turned to a new vision of independent farming.[5]

Before the Civil War many Georgia farmers rented land and farmed as tenants. Though landless, tenants lived and farmed independently on a parcel of land, sometimes paying rent with a share of the final crop. In 1860, between 10 and 20 percent of Greene County's farmers owned no land and farmed as tenants. These white tenants offered an example of independence without landownership that must have interested the freedpeople. Coastal Georgia and South Carolina provided another example. During the Civil War, Union forces occupied the Sea Islands around Port Royal, South Carolina, and set up an experiment in free labor for the ex-slaves. Some freedpeople actually purchased small farms; others worked as tenants on family-size plots either for wages or paid rent with a share of the produce. Both the example of white tenants in Greene County and the well-known experience of freed slaves in the Sea Islands must have convinced Greene County's freedpeople that a similar system could work for them. Although they still wanted to own land, after the obvious failure of land redistribution plans, most black farmers realized that for the moment tenancy was as much as they could expect.[6]

This conflict between landowners' desire for easily controlled share-wage gang labor and freedpeople's desire for independent tenancy began in late 1867 and 1868, coinciding with the triumph of black political power in Greene County. Many landowners viewed this desire for tenancy as merely a part of the political movement among the freedpeople, a negotiable demand intended to win political advantage. In November 1868 a group of leading white men representing various political views assembled in Greensboro to try to find a political solution to the labor system conflict. Participants meeting "for the purpose of regulating the labor system" included Freedmen's Bureau agent John Sullivan, Republican William H. McWhorter, and Democrats Lorenzo Carlton, James R. Sanders, Rowan Ward, William H. Branch, and Thomas P. Janes. Not a single freedperson joined the group. The meeting revealed that these white men, representing a variety of political perspectives, supported the share-wage system of labor, but they could not agree how best to promote it. Ultimately, this group discovered that the freedpeople's demand for a changed labor system was not just a political ploy. Finding they could not influence the freedpeople, the organization fell apart.[7]

The experience of slavery had convinced most landowners that only a gang labor system could be profitable on a plantation. The idea of black laborers directing their own work seemed absurd, almost funny, were it not so threatening. One Greene County farmer argued, "the ignorant negro, suddenly and involuntarily made his own master" could not possibly farm successfully. As the editor of the Greensboro *Herald* explained, "the difficulty appears to be how to manage free negro labor in order to make it profitable." Editor Henry Burns agreed that the share-wage system offered the best return. "Land owners operate against the best interests of the county by renting lands to the freedmen," argued Burns. "In such a situation labor is badly directed and the land badly cultivated." Worse, Burns contended, such a system had a larger implication, for "this system induces the freedman to feel his importance by occupying the position of a tenant instead of a laborer."[8]

Employer control over black workers diminished as the conflict over the labor system grew. Employers called for vigorous enforcement of vagrancy and antienticement laws, and the new district court, which in 1868 had replaced the county court, responded. Although District Court Judge William H. McWhorter, a Republican, did not enforce the law with such draconian force as had County Court Judge Columbus Heard, black defendants were often convicted of vagrancy in his court and employers won most breach of contract suits. Antienticement warnings appeared in the *Herald*, significantly often headed by the same illustration of a black man with a pole and bundle over his shoulder that had been used in 1860 by the Greensboro *Planters' Weekly* to head advertisements for runaway slaves. Despite legal pressures and warnings, black workers continued to leave their share-wage contracts and demand tenancy arrangements.[9]

Some landowners concluded that free black labor could not work and began to consider replacing the freedpeople with immigrants. In 1869 a letter in the *Herald* from "A Planter" chided the freedpeople of Greene County for their failures as laborers and threatened to replace them with "Chinamen." "Choose now whom ye will serve," concluded the letter ominously. Two months later the *Herald* trumpeted, "The Chinese are Coming." Planters in other counties had brought in Chinese laborers, reported the paper, and were very pleased with the results. In Greene County progressive agriculturist Rowan H. Ward had "ordered" ten

Chinese laborers for a test on his farm, and the paper expected other farmers to soon follow suit. Ward's Chinese, if they ever arrived, must not have proved successful, for the paper never addressed the issue again.[10]

The struggle over the labor system reached a crisis in 1870 and 1871. During the spring of 1870 large numbers of Greene County's black workers broke their share-wage contracts and insisted on sharecropping or tenancy agreements. Employers called on the legal system and community action to help enforce the share-wage system. In January 1871, the newspaper published the entire text of Georgia's antienticement law and discussed the problem at length. "What Shall We Do for Labor?" cried headlines in the *Herald*, and reported that "the planters are very much frustrated with their inability to secure hands." Despite the concerns and efforts of employers, by the spring of 1871 the outcome of the struggle was clear. "The general condition of our labor system is daily becoming more demoralized and unreliable," complained *Herald* editor Henry Burns. "Some of our planters who heretofore have been most successful are absolutely without hands to plant their crops, yet the country is full of negroes loafing around consuming what remains of last year's work, waiting for the [landowners] to offer him half he makes." Black workers might not have control of the land, but they did control their labor and could pressure farmers who needed to plant on schedule by simply withholding that labor.[11]

By holding out for sharecropping and tenancy arrangements during the winters of 1870 and 1871, black workers created a labor shortage that threatened the continued production of cotton for the market in Greene County. With planting time approaching and desperate for workers, most landowners gave into the freedpeople's vision of how labor should be organized. As one planter explained in a letter to the *Herald*, "we hear much about the scarcity of labor. This evil will continue until we settle laborers in permanent and comfortable houses [on individual parcels of land]." The writer went further, arguing that landowners must provide schools for the freedmen's children and allow their families independent control of their plots of land, "or the negro will quit the region."[12]

The members of the Greene County Agricultural and Mechanical Association also recognized the inevitable transformation of the labor system and called on the landowners of the county to accept the change. In an "appeal to the Citizens of Greene County," Rowan Ward and Thomas Janes explained in the *Herald* that "our system of labor has been changed . . . [forcing] the necessity upon us of accommodating

ourselves to the changed circumstances." This meant, as another correspondent pointed out, that "the old plantation system of cotton raising is
played out."[13]

As late as 1877, 80 percent of middle Georgia landowners insisted
that the share-wage gang system was still the "most satisfactory to landowners." Yet, at the same time, almost 80 percent of "laborers" in middle
Georgia worked as sharecroppers or tenants. Black laborers clearly could
influence their work relations with landowners, and some may have seen
this change in the labor system as a victory for the freedpeople. As
Thomas Janes explained, black workers "insist upon working [as ten-
ants] for a 'share of the crop' in preference to hiring for wages . . . because
it gives the employer less control over their time."[14]

By the mid-1870s most plantations in Greene County had been transformed, becoming large landholdings farmed by a number of separate
family units. The organizational coherency and factorylike labor system
that had helped make plantations successful economic ventures were
gone. Though a few landowners maintained a plantationlike environment
by remaining on their farms and closely supervising their sharecroppers
and tenants, most large landowners seem to have left their farms and
moved to Greenesboro or Union Point, exercising only modest supervision over their farms. Landowners may not have liked the new system of
sharecropping and tenancy, but they were forced to accept it by their
laborers. Sharecropping and tenancy, however, did not solve the freedpeople's problems of poverty and exploitation, and the revised labor
arrangements created new problems that were gladly used by landowners
to manipulate their tenants.[15]

Sharecropping exposed the freedpeople directly to the risks and problems of the market system. Sharecropping also forced workers to live on
credit during the year, and interest charges chipped away at their already
meager earnings. Under the Crop Lien Law of 1866, only landlords had
the right to sell farming supplies, food, and other necessities to tenants.
Until 1872, this included sharecroppers. The landlord could assign his
right to furnish to someone else, but many landlords preferred to furnish
their own tenants because it gave them an extra measure of control.
Though most landlords with sharecroppers and tenants seem to have
given up the day-to-day supervision common under slavery, they did
want to control the types of crops grown and the general work schedule.
Furnishing gave landlords a powerful tool, for they had the power to cut
off the supplies of unsatisfactory tenants or to manipulate the prices of
goods furnished to control the tenant's income. Tenants and croppers, so

often seeking independence in the new relationship, found instead that they had to please the landlord to achieve any sort of success. These personal obligations also gave landlords a lever by which they could influence the political and social behavior of their tenants.[16]

The movement of much of the county's black population into scattered individual homesteads had a second, unanticipated effect on black political and social behavior. Following emancipation, freedpeople had poured into Greensboro and Union Point to seek the support of living in a unified community. The physical closeness of people in Canaan, for example, let them resist white encroachment, such as the mayor's attempt to confiscate firearms in 1866. Further, the night riders could easily strike freedpeople living on isolated homesteads, but attacking (or even finding) specific victims in Canaan proved another matter. During the 1870s, as black people moved out of Greensboro and Union Point to take up residence on the land as sharecroppers or tenants, they lost much of the physical and psychological unity their communities had provided. The freedpeople's success in gaining sharecropping labor arrangements inevitably undermined the physical solidarity of the black community.[17]

Despite the decreasing physical solidarity of the black community and the powerful levers of furnishing and the personal obligations of freedpeople, most landowners felt they had too little control over sharecroppers. This did not mean they wanted control of day-to-day farming decisions. Landlords quickly showed that they were willing to allow the sharecropper to direct most normal work tasks. But they were unwilling to give up control over the crop. Landowners wanted to control the kinds of crops raised and in many cases needed ownership of the crop itself to secure liens. But one significant obstacle blocked landlords' control of the crop: the law.

Before the Civil War, Georgia's common law treated sharecropping as a variant of tenancy; the 1866 Crop Lien Law apparently included sharecroppers within the category of tenant. As large numbers of freedpeople successfully demanded sharecropping arrangements, however, landlords began to confront the sharecroppers' rights as tenants. By law, tenants had a possessory estate in the land they rented, which meant they could not legally be thrown off the land if they paid their rent. Tenants also had the right to quiet enjoyment of the land, which meant landowners had no legal right to interfere in the legitimate activities of tenants on the land. Tenants could be removed from the land only through formal eviction proceedings, a sometimes costly and always time-consuming process. Of course, night riders could drive problem tenants off the land, but most landowners desired legitimate and permanent power to do so. Finally, and perhaps most galling to landlords dependent on crop liens, tenants owned the crops raised on their leaseholds. The landowner had only a lien for rent against the crops and no say in how the tenant disposed of the crops. Landowners felt they had not just lost control of their laborers, they had also literally lost control of the crops grown on their land.[18]

Landlords began to challenge the legal rights of tenants in court, and in a series of cases, the Georgia Supreme Court began to limit or even restructure the rights of tenancy. Then, in the case of *Appling v. Odom*, the Georgia Supreme Court made an important conceptual leap that allowed them to avoid confronting hundreds of years of landlord and tenant law. In *Appling*, the court decided that they knew sharecropping when they saw it and that sharecropping was merely a contract, not a form of tenancy.[19]

In 1871 two freedmen, Stephen Odom and John Mozee, contracted to sharecrop with August Mercier, a landowner in Early County, Georgia. Mercier agreed to furnish the land and the mules in exchange for half the crop, and Mozee and Odom agreed to provide the labor for the other half of the crop. Odom and Mozee must have worked hard because they raised a crop of 11 bales of cotton and 100 bushels of corn. Mozee left the farm sometime in the fall of 1871, but Stephen Odom remained. In November 1871, Odom mortgaged the portion of the crop not covered by Mercier's lien for rent to Thomas K. Appling for $270. Appling later foreclosed on the mortgage, and Odom helped Sheriff John Willis levy on his and Mozee's five bales of cotton under a court foreclosure order. Then, Stephen Odom also left the farm.[20]

August Mercier, through his agent, John Milton, had furnished Odom and Mozee with 800 pounds of bacon at the credit price of $.25 per pound, $.10 more than the cash price of $.15. Unhappy that Odom had left without paying his $200 furnishing bill, Mercier sought legal help. In February 1872 Mercier filed a claim on the five bales of cotton Appling took when he foreclosed on the mortgage. Mercier argued that his furnishing lien on the cotton was superior to Appling's mortgage. In April the Early County Superior Court heard the case, and the jury found that Mercier, the landlord, owned the cotton. Appling immediately appealed the result to the Georgia Supreme Court, who heard the case in July 1872. Appling's counsel argued that the jury verdict was clearly contrary to law. As a tenant, Odom owned the crop and could mortgage it to whomever he wished.[21]

The supreme court rejected Appling's argument and affirmed the jury verdict giving the cotton to Mercier. The court did not consider the priority of the liens, nor did they even argue within the framework of landlord and tenant law. Instead, in that occasional clarity of vision that strikes appellate judges, Associate Justice Henry K. McCay announced that "there is an obvious difference between a cropper and a tenant." If this were indeed the case, Georgia's lawyers and judges working prior to 1872 had never seen the difference. The distinction between sharecropping and tenancy only became apparent with the reorganization of labor in the late 1860s and early 1870s. During that time, black laborers increasingly took on the role of sharecroppers, transforming the social and economic context surrounding that legal category. What had been an unimportant distinction in landlord and tenant law became a crucial one once it involved emancipated black laborers.[22]

In his opinion Justice McCay explained that tenants have "possession of the premises exclusive of the landlord." Sharecroppers, however, did not. Sharecroppers did not have the right to possess the land, the right of quiet enjoyment, or the right to own the crops they grew on the land. "The case of a cropper is rather a mode of paying wages, [not] a tenancy. . . . The cropper's share of the crop is not his until he has complied with the bargain." Sharecropping, then, was not a part of landlord and tenant law but a part of contract law. Thus, Stephen Odom never owned the crops he grew and therefore could not dispose of them in any way. This case did not involve a question of priority of liens or problems with the rights of tenants because Odom never was a tenant. He merely had a license to live on the land he worked on under a contract for share-wages.[23]

In some ways *Appling v. Odom* simply legitimized existing practices, but it also clearly undercut freedpeople's hopes of gaining independence through sharecropping. Sharecroppers might live and work on specifically delineated tracts of land, they might make all the decisions concerning cultivation, they might do all the work to raise the crops, but at law, they were just hired hands working for wages. Landlords could interfere in the management of the parcel of land to whatever extent they thought necessary or practical. A sharecropper who failed to comply with the bargain could be expelled—without pay and without messy eviction proceedings. Sharecroppers could not give crop liens in order to obtain independent financing, for they did not own the crop. At law sharecroppers were at the mercy of their landlords for credit and furnishing (although not all landlords took advantage of this power). Finally, if a sharecropper dared to harvest and sell part of the crop, he committed larceny from the landowner. Ironically, Justice McCay, who had the inspiration for this solution to landowners' concerns, was one of the Republican "Reconstruction Justices" appointed in 1868 to protect Reconstruction reforms and the civil rights of freedpeople.[24]

Appling dealt with the problem of crop ownership, but most landowners also worried about laborers breaking their contracts. In fact, the impunity with which workers broke share-wage contracts had contributed greatly to their success in demanding sharecropping and tenancy arrangements. Employers could bring suit for breach of contract when laborers walked out, but since the vast majority of black workers had virtually no assets, such suits had little purpose. Landowners not only wanted to control the crops raised on their land, they also wanted greater power to enforce contracts involving their laborers.

While the struggle over labor continued, Georgia's Democrats finally triumphed in their political struggle with the Republican Party. In October 1871 Republican governor Rufus Bullock fled the state to avoid impeachment and prosecution for corruption. In November 1871 the Democratically controlled legislature met, bent on "redeeming" Georgia from the effects of Reconstruction. As part of their efforts the General Assembly reestablished the county court. County courts had been created during the 1865–66 session after the Civil War as one means to control the newly freed slaves, but in 1868 the Republicans had eliminated these courts, in part to satisfy their black constituents. The Democrats recreated the county court with few differences from the earlier version. The judge and solicitor were to be appointed by the governor, and the courts had jurisdiction in civil cases involving up to $100 and in all nonfelony criminal cases. Two provisions of the new county court law reveal that legislators intended for the court to deal with more than petty crimes and small claims. First, the county court had jurisdiction over "all applications for eviction of intruders, [and] tenants holding over" and the right to foreclose mortgages of personal property and liens without limit as to the amount involved. Second, and most important, the court had the power to register contracts of employment and tenants' leases of land. This was the key, legislators hoped, to controlling laborers.[25]

Under the law, either party involved in a written contract could file that contract with the county court. Once filed, it became a "Court Contract," and the provisions of the contract would be enforced just as a judgment by the court would be. If either party failed to carry out the contract, that party would be in contempt of court and subject to arrest, imprisonment, and could be forced to carry out the contract or to pay damages. As Greenesboro attorney R. R. Thurmond explained in the *Herald*, if employers explain to their workers "that if they fail to carry out their contracts . . . they will be punished either by imprisonment or work on the chain gang, then you will have appealed to them with an argument to which they will listen." In 1874 several dozen contracts were registered with the county court, and fourteen people were arrested and forced by the court to carry out their duties indicated in the contract. Not surprisingly, all fourteen defendants were black.[26]

The new system of enforcing contracts promised immediate effects. As Thurmond argued, "if these court contracts therefore are entered into as a general thing, it will have the tendency to revive our system of labor which for the past seven or eight years has been so uncertain." In addition to the contract registration system, the new county court judge, Philip B. Robinson, ordered the bailiff of the court to "seek out and report all vagrants." Robinson clearly knew his court existed to manage Greene County's black laborers, and he sought to do so. Over the next six months his court handled thirty-five vagrancy cases, and the defendants in every case were sentenced to time on the county chain gang. The system apparently had its intended effect. By January 1876 the *Herald* reported that "laborers are plentiful and at a reduction in price. Able bodied men hiring at an average of less than a hundred dollars [per year]." But even this success did not satisfy landowners hungry for cheap laborers. Only a week later the paper bemoaned the fact that so many freedpeople did not work at all. "If the strolling women and half grown boys and girls could be put to work it would be very much to the welfare of all." Clearly, landowners would never find satisfactory any labor system short of slavery.[27]

Less than ten years after emancipation, most freedpeople found their hopes for autonomy and independence crushed by the redeemers' labor-control system; but not all black workers gave in without a fight. In January 1875 Thomas P. Janes contracted with four freedmen to work as hands on his farm and registered the contracts with the county court. In May, Janes's wife reported the men to Judge Philip B. Robinson as not fulfilling their contracts, so the county court bailiff arrested the men and secured them in the Greenesboro jail. Dr. Janes came back from Atlanta, where he was performing his duties as the state commissioner of agriculture, and made arrangements for the freedmen to be released from jail. He refused, however, to pay them for their five months of work. These men then went to the federal authorities in Atlanta, where they swore out warrants for fraud and false arrest against Janes's sons and the court bailiff. The U.S. marshal arrested Janes's three sons and the bailiff and took them to Atlanta, but after a hearing before the U.S. commissioner, they were released, and the laborers recovered nothing for their work. Once again, the legal system not only proved unable to protect black workers from exploitation, it facilitated it as well.[28]

That emancipation would transform the labor system in Greene County seemed obvious to most observers in the 1860s. That it would also reshape the financial system, however, did not seem so inevitable. Slavery had been the center of the antebellum plantation economy and the basis of the planters' power for years. The slave system provided the labor to cheaply produce cotton on the plantations, and the slaves represented much of the capital accumulated by the planters. Most important, the enormous asset base the slaves represented allowed planters to finance their operations at low rates of interest through factors in Augusta, Charleston, and Savannah. These low-interest loans, advances, and furnishings enabled planters to reap great profits if they managed their affairs properly.[29]

Of just under $9 million worth of taxable property in 1860, almost $6 million represented the value of slaves in Greene County. Emancipation not only destroyed slavery, it also eliminated nearly two-thirds of the county's wealth and demolished the financial structures that made plantation agriculture possible. Some factors attempted to reestablish the old forms of business after emancipation, but most ultimately failed. Slaves, who were easily sold or transported, served as excellent security for loans, but emancipation and the spread of the commercial market economy to upcountry towns undermined the old system of long-distance factorage. As long-distance credit grew riskier than ever and merchants in upcountry towns began to buy increasing amounts of cotton, the remaining factors were forced to abandon the role of agent and become cotton buyers instead. The destruction of the antebellum financial system arguably proved the most immediate and dramatic effect of emancipation.[30]

Without slaves, landowners could offer little as security for loans. To make matters worse, many landowners owed money on pre-emancipation debts, land values plummeted following emancipation, and land sometimes could not be sold for any price in Greene County. Considering these problems, creditors showed an understandable reluctance to lend money secured by agricultural land. The nine new national banks chartered in Georgia during the late 1860s offered no real help; they were prohibited by federal law from making mortgage loans. A few factors still possessed substantial capital after the war, and others arranged northern financial backing, but they too avoided accepting land as security. In Greene County some landowners and local merchants set up mortgage loans, but it was not until the arrival of the New England Mortgage Loan Company in the late 1870s that landowners were commonly able to arrange mortgages. Even then, mortgages played a small role in financing farmers in the community, and across Georgia, as late as 1890, only about 3 percent of owner-operated farms were mortgaged. Because of the scarcity of mortgage loans, most landowners could offer only one thing as security for other kinds of loans: the future value of their anticipated crop.[31]

Securing loans with growing crops was not a new idea. Antebellum factors did this implicitly when advancing money to planters in anticipation of a crop, and landowners and tenants had sometimes given liens on their growing crops. After the war, however, planters and factors quickly realized that they needed a new system of credit. The Milledgeville *Southern Recorder* went so far as to suggest that the state aid to landowners through loans secured by growing crops. Seeing the need for a new system of finance, the Georgia legislature began work on a crop lien law.[32]

James H. McWhorter, Robert L. McWhorter's brother, represented Oglethorpe County in the Georgia House during the years 1865–66. He proposed a bill "to protect factors and commission merchants who supply farmers." This proposed bill defined the legal relationship resulting from a crop lien between a landowner and his creditors, and it provided for the automatic creation of crop liens for furnishing as well as a landlords' lien for rent against their tenants' crops. McWhorter's original version of the bill failed, but a revised bill, which gave factors and merchants who furnished landowners a lien on the expected crop, eventually emerged from the legislature as law. By law, the simple act of furnishing a farmer created a lien on the debtor's crop; creditors did not need a specific contract to secure such a debt.[33]

The legislators intended to revive the antebellum system of factorage by substituting liens on crops for liens on slaves. In practice, however, crop liens proved a far less functional basis for long-distance credit relationships than had those on slaves. Antebellum creditors could easily value a debtor's slaves, but crops that did not even exist at the time of the loan were risky. Labor problems, weather, and the typical vagaries of farming meant that the final value of a crop could vary enormously, as the crop failures of 1866 and 1867 demonstrated. Under these conditions, loans made to landowners were smaller and were lent at much higher interest rates than prewar loans. It also meant that credit became increasingly a local matter, for members of the community had the best chance to evaluate a farmer's prospects.[34]

In order to get financing, then, landowners had to grow a cash crop. Creditors secured by crop liens had little interest in food production for the farm; rather, they wanted maximum production of a readily marketable crop. Since cotton generated more cash per acre than corn, creditors preferred to extend credit to cotton planters and were unlikely to make loans secured by a corn crop. Landowners, who wished to pay off these high interest loans and make a profit, also preferred cotton for its high cash return. Just to be safe, most landowners probably planted more cotton than necessary to insure enough money to pay their loans. Rather than discouraging landowners from producing cotton, the failures of 1866 and 1867 increased landowners' need to produce a large marketable crop to pay off their debts. More than ever before, Greene County's landowners emphasized cotton production, ultimately at the expense of food production.[35]

Many in Greene County grew concerned about the increasing emphasis on cotton production. In January 1870, *Herald* editor Henry Burns pleaded for farmers to "raise corn, raise corn." But he also confessed that he did not expect anyone to heed his call, for "cotton on the brain will continue to drive this important grain from the field." Later that spring Burns rode through seven or eight miles of "the most productive and fertile section of the county, and to [my] surprise, nothing could be seen growing but cotton."[36]

The ratio of the amount of corn produced to the amount of cotton produced illustrates the increasing focus on cotton production in Greene County following the Civil War. In 1849, when the county was self-sufficient in food production, farmers grew 38.75 bushels of corn for every bale of cotton produced. In 1859 this ratio fell to 35.2 bushels, a decline of about 10 percent. During 1869 Greene County's farmers produced only 23.27 bushels of corn per bale of cotton, and in 1879 corn production fell to 15.18 bushels per bale, a decline of more than 60 percent since 1849. Total agricultural production in general declined in Greene County during the same period, but the decline in the ratio of food production to cotton production was particularly important.[37]

In 1849 the county produced a food surplus of about 212,000 bushel equivalents of corn more than the subsistence needs of the county. During 1879 the county had suffered a food shortfall of about 131,000 bushel equivalents of corn *less* than the subsistence needs of the inhabitants of

Greene County. At the same time, Greene County continued to produce about 12,000 bales of cotton in good years, meaning that as productivity and land fertility declined, greater effort and resources were devoted to growing cotton. And since they did not grow enough food to feed themselves, the farmers of Greene County had to purchase food produced outside of the county. In order to buy food, the farmers needed credit or cash, therefore increasing the need to grow more cotton.[38]

The Georgia Railroad ensured that the food needed to make up for the shortfall poured into Greene County. In 1868 the railroad joined the Green Line, a consortium of railroads that shipped western produce rapidly and inexpensively in special green boxcars to the old plantation districts of Georgia and South Carolina. The Green Line facilitated the transportation of enormous amounts of food needed to feed an increasingly dependent region. Between April 1, 1874 and April 1, 1875, for example, the railroad delivered about 60,000 bushels of grain, weighing 1,500 tons, to the Greensboro, Union Point, and Woodville depots in Greene County. Trains also brought in 809,284 pounds of bacon and 63,112 pounds of lard, for a total food value of almost 118,000 bushel equivalents of corn. This amount of food would feed more than 7,800 people for a year. In addition to food, the railroad shipped 851 tons of guano fertilizer to the county's farmers, who needed the fertilizer to maintain cotton output on lands that grew more worn every season.[39]

During the same period, from April 1874 to April 1875, Greene County's depots shipped out 11,737 bales of cotton and virtually nothing else. Thomas Janes, as the commissioner of agriculture for Georgia, estimated that the cash value of the food brought into Greene County surpassed $230,000, while the value of the cotton shipped out was about $710,000. These transactions brought about a $480,000 net gain to the people of Greene County, or an income of about $32 per year for each person in the county.[40]

Credit costs, however, ate up a substantial portion of Greene County's agricultural income. In 1875 Janes reported that 80 percent of Georgia's farmers bought their supplies on credit. That same year, statewide, the prices of agricultural supplies and provisions sold on credit averaged 44 percent higher than those sold for cash. So, for the period of 1874–75, Janes estimated an additional credit cost of $93,000 to the farmers of Greene County. This additional cost reduced the agricultural income to under $390,000, or less than $26 per person in the county. The $26 in yearly per capita income does not include the value of products made and consumed within Greene County, but it does suggest the depth of the poverty afflicting most of Greene County's citizens. And there was no improvement in sight.[41]

In 1880, 5,573 white people and 11,974 black people lived in Greene County. The per capita wealth of all people in Greene County averaged $113.14 in 1880, compared to more than $710 in 1860, giving some idea of the dramatic decline in wealth since the Civil War. This wealth, however, was not equally distributed. White people in Greene County owned an average of approximately $344 worth of taxable property per person, while black people owned an averaged of $5.67 worth of property per person. Although $5.67 represented an improvement in the per capita wealth reported to the 1870 census, the improvement largely reflected an increase in the reported value of livestock owned by black people. The median wealth for all people in Greene County remained the same as in 1870—zero. Greene County's people, especially the African Americans, were desperately poor.[42]

A variety of important factors, including the loss of wealth due to the Civil War, the search for a new labor system, and the failure of the credit system, all hurt Greene's chances of recovery after the Civil War. The one factor, however, that ensured Greene County would not recover, was its increasingly dependent position within the world market system. During the first half of the nineteenth century Greene County only partly participated in the world market system. Planters and some farmers produced cotton for the world market, but otherwise the county remained a non-market subsistence society. Aside from buying a few luxuries, most farmers and planters kept their profits from cotton sales and reinvested them in slaves, land, railroad shares, even factories. By the 1850s, however, the railroad and related influences began to transform Greene County into a commercial agricultural society. Farmers raised less food and more cotton, and as a result, some became dependent on supplies of food brought into the county by the railroad. Greenesboro itself started to become more than a mere depot for the shipment of cotton and moved toward the role of an inland market center. These changes began the process of reshaping the county's economy, but then came secession and the Civil War.[43]

The Civil War slowed the ongoing market transformation of Greene County's economy. War and the Union blockade effectively cut the county's ties to the national and international market systems. Meanwhile, Confederate government policies and the realities of the conflict with the North forced a shift from cotton to food crop production. In 1862 Greene County greatly increased its production of corn and dramatically decreased its cotton crop. Other counties of the eastern cotton belt responded similarly, and statewide, Georgia doubled its production of corn. During the war the plantation belt counties not only produced enough food to feed their inhabitants, they also contributed a substantial surplus to the southern war effort. As late as November 1864, Sherman's soldiers marveled at and feasted on the rich stores of food produced by these counties. The experience of the Civil War demonstrated that the people of Greene and other plantation counties could feed themselves and produce a significant marketable surplus.[44]

After the war, however, Greene County's landowners quickly resumed growing cotton for the market. Cotton had provided many citizens with good incomes before the war, so planting large crops seemed both natural and rational. Cotton prices were high, and landowners desperate for income expected a good return. Their hopes, however, proved hollow. As one landowner complained to the Athens *Southern Cultivator*, "ruined by the war, I had hoped to [restore] my fortune by one good cotton crop." Instead, in 1866, he harvested 20 percent of a normal crop. Labor problems, bad seed, bad weather, army worms, a lack of credit, and declining prices turned the 1866 and 1867 crops into disasters. The clear lesson, argued the *Southern Cultivator*, was that farmers should grow food first and then cotton. Depending on cotton as the primary crop would end only in bankruptcy.[45]

Yet farmers, seemingly against their own interests, persisted in planting large crops of cotton. Greensboro attorney R. R. Thurmond observed in the *Herald* that "our farmers are not in a prosperous condition." The reason, he explained, was that "for years past it has been the habit of our farmers to devote all their energies to the production of cotton. They have been compelled to buy almost all their provisions, to use large quantities of commercial manures—all bought on credit at high prices." Trapped by their need for a cash crop to secure loans, many farmers felt compelled to plant cotton at the expense of food crops. Devoting themselves to producing cotton exclusively only increased their need for cash to buy food and throughout the process exposed farmers to ruinous interest rates and to fluctuating market prices for cotton set in New York and Liverpool. Some citizens in Greene County, including farmer and businessman James B. Park, realized the danger of the growing dependence on a market they could not control for money to buy food from distant sources. Park remarked in a letter to the *Herald*, "The policy of raising all cotton and depending on the West for the staff of life has well nigh ruined this state." Recognizing the danger was one thing; escaping it, however, was something else. As Dr. John E. Walker observed, "cotton may be king in one sense, but a great tyrant in another."[46]

Escaping cotton's tyranny seemed simple to some. Dr. John E. Walker suggested in the *Herald* that farmers "raise a little cotton to buy sugar and coffee, and a few other articles we can not produce at home, but be sure [to raise enough] corn and wheat." Farmers should withdraw from the market system into partial self-sufficiency, argued Walker, just as they did during the Civil War, and there they could find prosperity. Dr. Irving Westervelt, the *Herald's* associate editor, seconded Walker's call for withdrawal from the market system. "How strange," he commented, "that we do not get out of this fatal current when we see where we are drifting. . . . The county annually becomes more and more impoverished . . . [and] excessive production of cotton to the exclusion of food crops is ruining our county and making us hewers of wood and drawers of water for other sections." Growing cotton for money to buy on credit food grown in the West seemed to be sucking the wealth out of Greene County, and both Walker and Westervelt called for farmers to stop destroying themselves.[47]

Withdrawing from the market system may have seemed simple to two town-based physicians, but they did not need credit secured by crop liens to operate their businesses. As attorney R. R. Thurmond pointed out when trying to explain why so many farmers grew so much cotton, "the effect of the lien law is to encourage the production of cotton at the expense of other crops." Most farmers could not escape the lien system if they wanted to continue farming, and by entering the credit system, they also inevitably entered the market system.[48]

Despite Walker's, Park's, and others' warnings, many found the modern market system very attractive, or at least beguiling. The market made available so many of the articles Greene County could not produce itself, which often seemed very important and practical. Few would return to wearing homespun when money might buy broadcloth or calico. Who would choose to cook in an open fireplace rather than on an iron stove, draw water from a well with a bucket when a pump worked so much better? A nascent consumerism also drew people into the market to buy items such as cooking utensils, china, canned food, kerosene lamps, and ready-made clothes. These things were not seen as luxuries any longer; they were necessities, and people needed cash or credit to buy them. Greene County's farmers were not just pushed into full participation in the market system, they were also enticed into participation.

In the years following the Civil War, Greene County's economy became more specialized as landowners focused on growing cotton. The cotton mills at Long Shoals and Scull Shoals, despite some fits and starts, ultimately failed, their owners victims of the general shortage of capital after the war. Efforts to promote crop diversification proved ineffective, so Greene County could offer the world economy only one thing: raw cotton. The established railroads, increasingly controlled by northern capital, benefited from the cotton South's growing dependency on foodstuffs and guano transported from other parts of the country. Merchants and lawyers also prospered with the growth of a cash market. Some landowners, including a few members of the old planter class, entered the commercial world as businessmen and prospered. But most farmers and farm laborers, the vast majority of people in the county, suffered in poverty because of Greene County's dependent, peripheral role in the world economy.[49]

We Have a New Class of Men
and a New Order of Things

In 1885 Thaddeus Brockett Rice visited Greene County for the first time. He was a drummer for an Atlanta drug supply company, and Greenesboro and Union Point would become regular stops on his sales route. Years later Rice remembered that first visit to Greenesboro, a town of 2,000 people in 1885. "It was midsummer," recalled Rice. "The streets were dry and dusty, [while] a number of the stores were unpainted wooden buildings with wooden awnings that extended across the [plank] sidewalks." Greenesboro resembled many inland market towns across the cotton South, and little in the town suggested prosperity. "Greenesboro had no civic improvements except a horse rack, mulberry tree, and public well," Rice continued. "Many eyesores dotted the town, and the streets were knee deep in mud when it rained. [At night] the business section was lighted by a few kerosene lamps."[1]

During his sales trips, Rice became quite familiar with local business affairs. Greenesboro had ten mercantile businesses, more than two dozen smaller shops, and three modest hotels. Union Point had six stores and one hotel. "Mr. Charles A. Davis, Sr. was the monied man of the county," Rice remembered. "His tall, erect form clothed in a frock-tailed black suit topped with a beaver hat was a familiar figure and highly respected." Charles A. Davis had indeed shown great skill in identifying opportunity, and he had focused on commerce and finance as the keys to wealth in the changing postbellum world. During the 1870s and 1880s, Davis operated as both private banker and merchant and became the most important local source of financing for Greene County's farmers. Through liens and mortgages he exercised direct power over many of his neighbors and became very influential in local politics, although he never sought office himself. By entering the commercial market economy and grasping the opportunity to provide financing to Greene County's farmers, Davis assured himself economic success in the community. By the time of his death in 1893, Davis had probably amassed the greatest fortune in Greene County's history, and some called him the "merchant prince."[2]

Charles Davis's father, Samuel Davis, built a successful plantation north of Greenesboro during the boom years of the 1820s and 1830s. Samuel's wife, Mary, bore two sons: Charles in 1820 and William in 1827. The boys grew up on the plantation and could have become successful planters, but by 1850 Charles had opened a small store in Greenesboro, and William soon joined the venture. Davis and Brother grew quickly, in part benefiting from and in part helping drive the commercial transformation that began to sweep Greene County during the 1850s. By 1860 the Davis brothers owned the largest mercantile business in Greenesboro, drawing customers from a forty-mile radius, and both had become wealthy men.[3]

Charles Davis built a new building for his business in 1860, and the "big store" not only sold dry goods and groceries but also warehoused small amounts of cotton. He also began operating as a factor, acting as an agent for local farmers selling their cotton directly to New York. This role as factor reflected the Davis brothers' financial success. In 1860 Charles Davis reported $25,000 of wealth to the census, and his brother William reported $19,000. Their father's property totaled $55,000, and together the three men owned fifty-three slaves. Interestingly, although the Davis brothers rode the 1850s commercial boom to great success, their wealth in 1860 was still not equal to that of their planter father.[4]

During the Civil War Charles Davis remained in Greenesboro and ran the business while William served with the Stephens Light Guards. By the time William and his fellow survivors surrendered at Appomattox, he and his brother owned the only operating store in Greenesboro. In June 1865 Charles Davis quickly contracted to supply the occupying Union troops and began to collect on prewar and wartime promissory notes from planters and farmers in Greene County. Debtors delayed and fought collection efforts in the courts, hoping that legislation would postpone debt collection or that sympathetic jurors would save them from these obligations. The stay laws, which postponed collections, however, proved ineffective, and jurors usually found in favor of the Davis brothers' claims. While others struggled to rebuild their fortunes as planters, Charles Davis used the commercial and legal system to exploit the opportunities existing in the wake of the Civil War. Charles A. Davis prospered because he accepted and acted within the capitalist ethic despite its effect on his neighbors, putting profit before community or personal relations.[5]

Soon after the war Charles Davis bought his brother's interest in the business. He made his son, Charles A. Davis Jr., a partner and renamed the business Davis and Son. By early 1871 Davis and Son had "an extensive retail business . . . [with a] sales average [of] $140,000 a year." In fact, while the majority of wealthy people in Greene County suffered calamitous economic setbacks between 1860 and 1870, the Davis family prospered. In 1870 Charles Davis reported $50,000 of wealth to the census, while his father's reported wealth fell to $40,000 despite an investment in the mercantile business. William died in 1869, but his widow, Ann, reported to the census in 1870 $16,000 of wealth. Charles Davis's mercantile business had made him one of the wealthiest men in Greene County by 1870, but he never allowed himself to fall into a rut. Other opportunities had always beckoned, so Davis pursued them as well.[6]

During the late 1850s Davis had entered the cotton market as a factor, but his business remained relatively small. Although the telegraph and railroad made buying and selling cotton in Greenesboro possible, most planters continued to ship their cotton to factors in Augusta, Charleston, or Savannah, with whom they already had relationships. Davis's small but growing cotton brokerage probably thrived because of the expanding production of cotton by smaller farmers during the 1850s. These producers had no established factorage relationships and for convenience dealt with a local merchant. After the Civil War, however, the collapse of long-distance credit relationships necessary to traditional factorage meant that many large producers needed local sources of credit as well as the services of a cotton broker. Many established cotton factors changed their practices and sent agents into the upcountry to buy cotton or empowered local merchants as agents to buy for the firm; but doing so allowed men like Davis to compete for the product of local growers. By 1869 Davis and Son handled almost 2,000 bales of cotton, worth more than $100,000, on top of their substantial mercantile business. Davis and Son also began providing financing to many larger landowners by offering them mortgages of up to three-quarters of the assessed taxable value of the land. The company accepted crop liens against cash loans, and the mercantile business continued to deal strictly in cash. By the early 1870s Davis and Son's "banking" business became so profitable that they leased the mercantile store to Hugh McCall and Edward Copelan and concentrated on "banking" full time.[7]

During the last third of the nineteenth century, each fall and winter, farmers began bringing their cotton into Greenesboro and selling it there rather than shipping it to factors in other towns. Cotton buyers and agents worked out of local stores or even on the streets, keeping track of prices in Atlanta, Augusta, and New York by telegraph. At the peak of the cotton-selling season, Greenesboro became quite lively. Farmers sought the best prices, buyers competed to offer them, and carload after carload of cotton rode the rails out of Greene County. Typically, a potential buyer would take a small snippet of cotton from the farmer's bales in order to grade it, so after several days of buying activity, these snippets, mixed with loose bolls of cotton, littered the streets, indicating the season as clearly as snow. While in town to sell their cotton, many farmers also sought financing for their next crop. Davis and Son, as cotton buyers, were perfectly positioned to offer this financing. Across the street from the "big store" they constructed a bank building in 1874. Like most private banks across the postbellum cotton South, Davis and Son was really an unregulated loan agency dependent on its own resources.[8]

Despite the Panic of 1873 and the deepening depression of the mid-1870s, Charles A. Davis continued to prosper. During 1874–75 he celebrated his growing wealth by building a fine new home for his family. The two-story, Italianate house contained more than 7,500 square feet of living room as well as Greenesboro's first hot and cold running water system. The veranda was more than 100 feet long, and there Davis and his family would sit in the evenings and receive visitors. Significantly, Davis had amassed a fortune during what were for most people bad times, but even more so, his new home emphasized his town's increasing ties to Atlanta and the new commercial world Atlanta seemed to represent. Davis brought in architects and contractors from Atlanta, and all the woodwork for the home was crafted there. Only the bricks in the house were made in Greenesboro, and that brickyard was owned by Davis. The Greenesboro *Herald* recognized this change in geographic economic focus when, in 1872, it began quoting Atlanta commodity prices each week instead of the Augusta prices, which it had been quoting. By the late 1870s advertisements for Atlanta businesses in the *Herald* often outnumbered adds for Augusta businesses. The postwar commercial economy increasingly directed business through Atlanta and by rail to the northeast, while produce from the West traveled by rail to Atlanta, and from there to the towns of the plantation belt. Although most Greene County cotton continued to travel by rail to Augusta and Charleston, the money earned was increasingly spent on goods and provisions shipped through the growing distribution center of Atlanta.[9]

As merchants like Charles Davis built private monuments to the new economic order, public monuments to the old order fell into decay or were destroyed. For example, across the street from Davis's new home lay the ruins of the Greensboro Female College, which during the war had served as a hospital for the Confederacy, and after the war opened as an academy for girls. On November 29, 1872, the college had burst into flames. No one was seriously injured, and townspeople managed to keep the fire from spreading to other buildings, but the brick college burned to a hollow shell. Rumors in Greensboro held that a disgruntled professor, angered by his low salary, set fire to the building. The *Herald* tried to scotch this rumor, explaining, "some have thought that the fire was the work of an incendiary, but from all that we can learn, it must have been accidental." No one had the funds—or the interest—to rebuild the school. Eventually, Alexander Seals, a successful merchant, bought the lot and built a home called Magnolia Manor there. Some years later he sold the home to attorney James B. Park Jr.[10]

Another Green County monument, Penfield's Mercer University, had officially operated throughout the Civil War, although by 1863 only twelve students were enrolled. After the war, Mercer found recovery difficult. Of the eighty-four students enrolled in 1868, one-third were disabled veterans who were attending the school free of charge. In spite of the fact that the shortage of tuition cramped operating funds, President Henry H. Tucker refused to accept the military government's offer to pay veterans' tuitions. As Tucker explained,

> General Meade informed me that we are expected to receive under this act all soldiers without reference 1st to the side on which they fought and 2nd without reference to color. If the former point be somewhat objectionable, the latter is wholly insufferable.[11]

Facing financial disaster, Mercer officials began to search for other solutions. Several committees considered the problem and concluded that Mercer needed to be moved to a city that was benefiting from commercial growth. As one trustee explained in 1870, Mercer had to train men for success in the commercial economy, and "positions in the city call for training in a city." Mercer officials announced that the university would consider moving if offered some assistance. Atlanta offered $50,000, and many trustees wanted to accept the offer. But Macon offered $125,000, six acres of prime land, and $30,000 to endow a new professorship. The citizens of Penfield, led by Robert L. McWhorter, Thomas P. Janes, and James R. Sanders, tried to block the move, correctly fearing it would destroy the town, but finally yielded in June 1871, when Mercer promised to maintain its buildings in Penfield and to support a high school there. By then the faculty and students had already moved to Macon.[12]

Academics usually show great ability to follow trends, and the faculty and leaders of Mercer were no exception. In 1873 they recommended that Mercer create a commercial department for undergraduates and a law school. In February 1874, with three new professors, the Mercer Law School began its first classes. Ironically, a school founded to train ministers and farmers turned to training businessmen and lawyers. Meanwhile, pleading continued financial problems, the university reneged on its promise to establish a high school, and its buildings in Penfield were left to decay.[13]

Concerned by Mercer University's departure and other evidence of economic decline, some citizens called for Greene County to build factories, which might have tempered the effects of economic dependency by selling finished cotton goods rather than ginned cotton. But, as attorney R. R. Thurmond explained in 1873, an almost complete "absence of capital" made building new factories impossible. The shortage of capital also eventually ensured the demise of the existing factories in Greene County. John Curtwright's Long Shoals mill, for example, had suffered some damage at the hands of Sherman's troops, and Curtwright lacked the capital needed for repairs. He searched for outside investors, and in 1876 finally found a "company of Northern capitalists" willing to buy the mill. The new owners brought in some equipment for the mill and planned for a spur line to extend from the Georgia Railroad to the factory, but these projects failed, and Long Shoals remained a ghost town.[14]

Thomas Poullain's Scull Shoals mill followed a similar path to its demise. The mill had reorganized as Fontenoy Mills after the war and continued operations as it had during the war. The mill's old equipment, however, soon needed repair and replacement, but the Poullain family lacked sufficient capital to do anything about it. In 1874 the combination of aging machinery and the financial impact of the Panic of 1873 closed the mill's doors. The Poullain family tried to raise the $150,000 needed to reopen the mill but failed to find investors for the project. Meanwhile, the family's fortunes declined since Thomas Poullain insisted on continuing plantation operations as he had before the war. In desperation Poullain's son, Antoine, sold 3,200 acres of land next to the mill to Penitentiary Company Number Three, who used leased convicts to farm the huge plantation. The $26,000 Antoine Pollain raised from the sale proved insufficient to save the mill, and in 1879 the mill, its buildings and land included, was sold under court order to satisfy taxes and debts. The Poullain family's wealth declined to a mere shadow of its former glory.[15]

The fate of the mills reflected the transformation sweeping Greene County during the 1870s and 1880s. The old mills, financed by the profits of plantation slavery, could not survive the death of the old plantation system. Meanwhile, the merchants and lawyers who began to grow wealthy in the expanding commercial economy did not accumulate sufficient capital for investment in factories until the 1890s. Outside investors, most from the north, proved understandably reluctant to invest in old mills in a rural county miles from the railroad. The decline and eventual failure of the mills left Greene County more dependent than ever on the commercial market, placing merchants and lawyers at the center of the county's economy. One worried correspondent explained in the *Herald*, "we have a new class of men, and a new order of things." The men who ran Greene County before the Civil War had faded away, and new men focused on commerce took their place. As historian Harold Woodman has explained, "although there was no industrial revolution in the South, there were significant changes in agriculture and trade, changes which supported a new class in the postwar South." This new class of businessmen and lawyers depended on the more fluid capital of a market economy for their prosperity, and land was only one of several possible investments.[16]

These "new men," however, were new only in their occupations and generation, for most came from established leading families. Edward A. Copelan's background, for example, was fairly typical. He grew up in the southwestern part of the county known as "Cracker's Neck." His father, Obadiah Copelan, owned a prosperous plantation and twenty-one slaves in 1860 when Edward was eleven years old. The war hit the Copelan family hard financially, for they lost their slaves and much of their wealth. Edward's uncle, Baldwin Copelan, lost virtually everything after the war. In 1860 he had reported owning $50,700 worth of property, including fifty-seven slaves, but in 1870 he reported owning only $500 worth of personal property and had lost all of his land. In the late 1860s, knowing his father's farm offered little opportunity and seeing the disaster that had overtaken his uncle, Edward Copelan left farming and took a position as a clerk in the Davis and Son store. By 1870 he boarded at Davis's home as well. Davis grew to trust Edward Copelan, and in 1873, at twenty-four years old, Copelan, along with Hugh McCall, leased the "big store" from Davis to operate on their own. Edward Copelan then married Charles

Davis's niece, Leila, and became a member of the family. After great success in the mercantile business, Copelan went into banking as well and in 1889 opened the Copelan Bank on Main Street. Copelan thought of himself as a self-made man, but like most of his peers, he actually came from an antebellum planter family.[17]

Although some of the older planters in Greene County managed to adapt to the changing postbellum world, more often it was their sons who were willing to make the occupational and psychological changes needed to prosper in the new South's commercial economy. Perhaps it was because most of these "new men" were young before and during the Civil War that they found it easier to function within the "new order of things," accepting the paradigm shift necessary to work successfully in the new economy. James B. Hart, for example, had used his profits as a merchant to buy a plantation and become a planter before the Civil War. After the war his sons reversed the process. James F. Hart opened a successful dry goods business in Union Point, while John C. Hart practiced law. Both men enjoyed success, and John Hart eventually became attorney general for the state of Georgia. The farm continued to operate, but as a secondary enterprise managed from a distance, just one of several investments.[18]

Robert L. McWhorter's sons followed a similar path. While Robert McWhorter lived on and managed the farm outside of Penfield, both John and Hamilton McWhorter took up law and practiced in Greenesboro. John enjoyed great success as a lawyer from 1875 until his untimely death in 1882 at only twenty-eight years old. In 1879 Hamilton moved to Oglethorpe County, where he had a long and successful career, serving as a member of the Oglethorpe County Board of Commissioners and later as superior court judge of the Northern Circuit. Hamilton ultimately became advisory counsel for the Southern Railway Company and made clear his perception of the sources of power in the "new order of things" by twice refusing appointments to the Georgia Supreme Court so that he could continue to work for the railroad and dominate affairs in eastern Georgia.[19]

Robert L. McWhorter's nephew, William Penn McWhorter, enjoyed similar success. He left his father's plantation after the war and opened a mercantile business in the railroad hamlet of Woodville. His business flourished, and by 1882 he owned the town's dry goods store, grocery store, cotton warehouse, steam-run cotton gin, saw mill, and grist mill. McWhorter built a mansion for himself on a hill overlooking the town that he owned and then successfully entered politics, being sent by the voters of Greene County to represent them in the General Assembly for several terms.[20]

Some older planters adapted only partially to the new economy, while their sons entered fully into the commercial world and found success. James B. Park, for example, left his farm soon after the war and moved to Greenesboro, where he invested in several mercantile businesses. He also continued to closely manage his farm and grist mill along the Oconee River. Though Park regretted the demise of slave plantation agriculture, he did not try to maintain the old ways on his farm. Instead, he adapted his farming and milling operations to the needs of the new sharecropping system, and he financed his workers through his own store. Still, he remained focused on agriculture and had little use for the commercial changes sweeping Greene County. Eventually, this conservatism led him into political conflict with his own son, James B. Park Jr., who had found success as a lawyer and politician in Greenesboro. James Jr. supported progressive economic causes such as the stock fencing law, an issue on which he and his father disagreed and that highlighted their different worldviews. After this political falling out, James Jr. had little to do with the family's extensive farm, but he grew wealthy as a lawyer and an investor in railroads and held several county offices. He ended his career as head of the Greene County Democratic Party and a superior court judge.[21]

Miles W. Lewis also adapted well to the new economy. A successful antebellum attorney and planter, he moved to Greenesboro and concentrated on his law practice following the Civil War. Lewis continued his leadership of the local Democratic Party and promoted the careers of his sons, Edward L., Hugh Graham, and Henry T. Lewis, all of whom practiced law in Greenesboro. Edward L. Lewis died in 1875 after a short but successful career. Hugh Graham Lewis eventually became judge of the superior court and a successful businessman. Henry T. Lewis served as mayor of Greenesboro and editor of the *Herald*. He ended his career on the Georgia Supreme Court.[22]

Men like Edward Copelan, the Hart and Lewis brothers, James B. Park Jr., and William Penn McWhorter were indeed the "new class of men" in Greene County after the war. As members of the county's leading families, these men, most of whom were young, had the resources and the opportunity to take up new professions and prosper, often expanding established family interests in commerce or law. Most leading families managed to make these kinds of shifts, and only a few individuals within the families proved unable to adapt to the new economy. Dr. Thomas P. Janes, for example, was one of Greene County's most progressive agricultural leaders, and in 1874 became head of Georgia's newly created Department of Agriculture. Janes, however, could not escape his conviction that efficient production of cotton offered the best road to wealth. Despite declining prices and increasing need for expensive fertilizers, Janes and his three sons focused on cotton production on their plantation and shunned the world of commerce or law in the years following emancipation. Forced out of the Department of Agriculture in 1879 for trying to regulate the growth of the commercial fertilizer business, Thomas Janes returned to his farm, where he died in 1885. His sons soon failed financially and drifted away, leaving the farm to tenants. The Janes family then faded into obscurity.[23]

Unlike the Janes family, who accepted the new economy and suffered for failing to adapt to it, Thomas N. Poullain's downfall was a result of his simple refusal to accept the changes in his society at all. Poullain had been one of Greene County's most progressive antebellum planters, owning and operating the Scull Shoals cotton mill. In spite of the success of the mill, Poullain's fortune still depended on his enormous plantation and control of as many as 278 slaves. After the war he continued to live and conduct his business like an antebellum planter, refusing to recognize the changes around him. Poullain, who was a leader of the secession movement in Greene County, during the 1870s sent dozens of letters to the Southern Claims Commission and to several government officials (including President Grant) professing his loyalty and demanding compensation for cotton and buildings destroyed by Sherman's raiders. All Poullain's claims were politely refused, but the increasingly desperate tone of the letters reveal Poullain's astonishment at his declining fortunes. Though a successful antebellum planter/businessman worth hundreds of thousands of dollars, Poullain continued to blame his financial plight on Sherman's troops' destruction of less than 200 bales of cotton, worth between $10,000 and $20,000. Poullain remained obsessed with this loss while his plantation and other enterprises declined into bankruptcy. When he died in 1889, Poullain owned little more than his house and the family silver.[24]

Of Poullain's children, only his son Antoine remained involved in the family business. He struggled to manage the plantation and the mill and fought to assert his business decisions over his father's. As the family fortunes declined, he sold much of the plantation in Greene County in an attempt to raise enough money to save what was left. In 1879 he presided over the forced sale of the Scull Shoals mill, the last of the family fortune in Greene County. Antoine then left for Baltimore, where he built a business of his own. Dr. Poullain's granddaughters, however, moved quickly into the circle of successful "new men" in Greensboro. In 1880 Harriette Byron Poullain married lawyer Henry T. Lewis, and Anna Maria Poullain married lawyer James B. Park Jr., conferring the social mantel of the old elite onto the leaders of the new.[25]

Lawyers benefited enormously from the expanding commercial market economy. The growth of long-distance trade in provisions and goods, the increasing number of mortgages, crop liens, and business and labor contracts, all allowed lawyers to play a central role in the new economy. The effect of the market transformation can be seen most clearly in the civil cases before Greene County's superior court. In the three-year period before emancipation, from 1859 to 1861, 80 percent of the civil cases before the superior court were a variety of suits for debt, usually based on accounts or promissory notes. From 1883 to 1885 such debt collection made up only 20 percent of the superior court's civil cases, while suits involving contract enforcement made up more than 21 percent of cases before the court. Most of these involved foreclosure of mortgage contracts, but 15 percent of the contract cases involved lawsuits for specific performance of commercial contracts. In contrast, from 1859 to 1861 the superior court handled no mortgage foreclosure cases and only two contract cases. The increased number of mortgage and contract cases mirrored the increasing importance of commerce and finance in Greene County. In 1888 General E. P. Alexander, president of the Central of Georgia Railroad, explained in an essay on business management what the central component of successful business was in the commercial economy of late-nineteenth-century Georgia. Keep lawyers on retainer, he argued, for prudent businessmen recognized that "every contract or agreement should pass under scrutiny of counsel."[26]

Not only did lawyers have more commercial work, they also had more criminal cases to prosecute or defend. Moving the discipline and control of black laborers from the private sphere of slavery to the public sphere of the county and superior courts gave lawyers and judges a central role in managing Greene County's labor force. Edward Ayers's study of criminal cases before the Greene County Superior Court during the late nineteenth century revealed a remarkable increase in the number of indictments for property crime following emancipation, the increase in part reflecting attempts to control the freed slaves through legislation and the courts. Ayers only looked at superior court records, but had he been able to systematically study the county courts, the legal system's focus on labor control would have been even clearer. The increasing prosecution of property crimes, however, reflected not only the attempts of county officials to control laborers but also the ideological impact of the growing commercial market economy. Property crimes threatened the basis of commercial power in postbellum Greene County, so they drew a draconian response.[27]

The control of laborers, however, did not always follow current legal forms. In June 1884 a black man named Carey Thomas worked on Colonel James Brown's plantation in Greene County. One Saturday Colonel Brown's little boy so harassed Thomas that the black man gave the child a spanking. The sheriff arrested Thomas that night and jailed him on charges of assault. While he was in jail awaiting arraignment, Thomas apparently became frightened by the prospect of serving time on the county chain gang, the usual fate of blacks convicted of minor crimes by the county court. In 1884 the firm of Powell and Davenport leased most of the county convicts for work on an enormous farm in the fork region of Greene County, where prisoners suffered in appropriate misery. At his hearing, Thomas begged "Col. Brown to abandon the prosecution and take him out and settle the matter in the old *'ante bellum'* style." The court dismissed the charges, and Carey Thomas submitted to a whipping administered by Colonel Brown outside the courthouse.[28]

The whipping was not a typical event, but it reflected the legal profession's willingness to step outside the boundaries of formal law in cases involving the discipline and control of black workers. In Cary Thomas's case, the antagonists, James Brown, County Court Judge Henry C. Weaver, and the editor of the *Herald*, Henry T. Lewis, who approvingly recounted the story, were all attorneys. In fact, the younger attorneys who came to dominate the legal profession in Greene County during the 1880s were far less tolerant of black workers' "crimes" than their fathers. The paternalistic amusement characteristic of the old planters' approach to the perceived failings of black workers was replaced by a legalistic and intolerant approach, or sometimes simple hate. Future Supreme Court Justice Henry T. Lewis expressed his hate in several articles explaining that although lynching was wrong, it was inevitable when black criminals outraged the good people of a community. "Every one who is acquainted with the fiendish sensuality of the negro," wrote Lewis in 1884 after the lynching of two black men for rape, "knows that nothing can prevent a frequent repetition of [such] horrible outrages but the prompt and summary visitation of punishment." Lynching could only be prevented, he argued, if courts tried and executed black rapists as swiftly as lynch mobs did their work. Having become the enforcers of labor control through criminal law, many lawyers, like Lewis, came to believe that black people were criminal by nature and deserving only of swift and violent punishment when caught.[29]

The growing prosperity of lawyers and merchants also began to transform power relations among the elite in Greene County. During the 1850s the county inferior court was the most important local governing body in Greene County. During that decade, only one-fifth of the men who served on the court were merchants, and no lawyers at all won election to the court. By the late 1870s and the 1880s this situation had changed. The Georgia Constitution of 1868 eliminated the inferior court, but in 1876 the legislature created a county commission for Greene County, which had virtually the same powers as the old inferior court. This commission consisted of three men elected by the grand jury for four-year terms, and it controlled all county finances and other local affairs. Wealthy planters dominated the inferior court, but of the nine men who served on the county commission from 1876 through 1888, only four were active farmers. Four other commissioners were lawyers or merchants, and at least two commissioners, Baldwin Copelan and Charles Davis Jr., were sponsored by and under the influence of the "merchant prince," Charles A. Davis Sr. The ninth man to serve on the county commission was John B. Y. Warner, a carpetbagger from Rochester, New York, who bought and managed the enormous Early plantation along the Oconee River and acted as an agent for several New York cotton buyers. Despite his large, active farm, Warner clearly shared the commercial orientation of the lawyers and merchants of Greene County. Thus, the most important organ of local government went from an inferior court dominated by planters to a county commission controlled by men committed to the expanding commercial market economy in Greene County.[30]

In turn, progressive representatives of the "new order" gained control of the local Democratic Party in the late 1870s. In 1878 Miles W. Lewis, James L. Brown, and Charles A. Davis Jr. led Greene County's Democratic Party. When Miles Lewis died in 1880, his son, attorney Henry T. Lewis, took his place as a Democratic leader, and when James L. Brown retired from politics in 1885, attorney James B. Park Jr. took his place. These men all worked within the tradition of the "New Departure Democrats," business-oriented Democratic leaders who in the late 1860s decided to accept Reconstruction in hopes of regaining local self-rule and promoting commercial development. They did not win political power without a fight; they faced great resistance in Greene County from older planters as well as smaller farmers and black workers, who suffered under the new economy. Progressive Democrats did not successfully consolidate their power until the early 1880s.[31]

Lawyers also gained control of the most important source of information in Greene County, the *Greensboro Herald*, and through it promoted the spread of market relations among the county's inhabitants. In 1872 attorney R. R. Thurmond purchased the paper from Henry Burns, and for the rest of the 1870s and 1880s, lawyers owned and edited the *Herald*. Though not completely consistent in their support for the changes sweeping Greene County's economy, the editors presented a worldview shaped by law and commerce, not plantation agriculture.[32]

As lawyers and merchants struggled to displace the older planter leaders in Greene County and eventually prospered, small white farmers suffered quite a different fate. A hint of this fate could be seen as early as February 1866 in a contract made by E. F. M. Calloway with his workers. This sharecropping contract was signed by eight freedpeople and a ninth man, Albert O'Neal, who was white. Despite his race, O'Neal worked within the same formal structure of sharecropping as the freedmen. Over time in Greene County, the same economic needs and legal structures that helped reduce the freed laborers to a new dependency also worked to reduce landless white people to similar dependency.[33]

Small landowners also suffered in the changing economy. Most of them lived around Siloam and White Plains in southern Greene County. These areas had grey, ashen, or white sandy soil that antebellum planters avoided in favor of the brown loam and red clay of Prosperity Ridge and the Oconee bottomlands north and west of Greensboro. The "grey lands" were farmed by men who on the average owned less than 200 acres of land. Most of these farms were self-sufficient and depended on family labor and perhaps a few slaves. Before 1860 most "grey land" farmers produced only small amounts of cotton for the market.[34] After emancipation the "grey land" farmers began producing much more cotton, and by 1881, 3,000 bales of cotton passed through White Plains alone. At first, growing cotton seemed to offer these small landowners a window of opportunity, for after the war, cotton production declined dramatically in other parts of the county while prices promised to stay high. Some farmers prospered and gladly promoted the extension of market relations throughout the "grey lands." But during the late 1870s and the 1880s, prices fell, and many farmers who had borrowed money to plant cotton found themselves deep in debt. In order to pay the debt, they needed cash, and cotton offered the greatest return. Many farmers had to plant cotton or face bankruptcy. Some lost their land to mortgages or debts, while most managed to hang onto their farms, producing increasing amounts of cotton and growing more dependent on credit and provisions from local merchants' stores. Younger men had little prospect of acquiring farms of their own as their parents struggled to hang onto their own small places, so many of the young men became tenants, sometimes for their family, but more often working for larger landowners. Ironically, local merchants and landowners benefited from their plight. The Tappan brothers of White Plains were one such example.[35]

Alexander and Theo Tappan came to Greene County from New Jersey before the Civil War and in 1860 owned small businesses in White Plains. Alexander Tappan ran a blacksmith shop and built wagons, while Theo Tappan owned a store and a small farm with seven slaves. After the war the Tappan brothers expanded their businesses and financed many local farmers who began to grow cotton. The business was lucrative enough to attract two more Tappans to the area in 1871, and by 1885 the Tappan family owned the large general store, carriage works, grist mill, and saw mill in White Plains. Alexander Tappan had accumulated more than $10,000 worth of real estate through mortgage foreclosure and purchase, and in an 1886 directory of Georgia planters he was listed as the wealthiest of four farmers living in the White Plains area.[36]

As Thomas P. Janes discovered in his survey of farmers in 1874, most landowners preferred black laborers and sharecroppers to white workers. As Janes explained in a Department of Agriculture circular, white workers "do not render as efficient labor as the negroes, being less tractable as employees." White tenants were more independent than black sharecroppers, less obligated to their landlords, and had all the problematic rights of tenancy to the land they occupied. Because of these inconveniences, during the 1870s and 1880s landowners in the "grey lands" began to bring in black sharecroppers to replace or augment their white tenants and laborers. As a result, great tension arose between the growing numbers of black workers moving into the "grey lands" and the hard-pressed white small landowners and tenants. Throughout the 1880s and into the next century the "grey lands" were the center of lynchings and other racially motivated crimes against blacks, a legacy of economic "development" in the area.[37]

Even though the situation for most white farmers worsened, the lives of black farmers improved very little. In 1885 only forty-three blacks owned land, and nine of them owned less than twenty acres. The vast majority of black people owned little property of any kind and continued to face virtually inescapable poverty. During the 1880s black and white workers, sharecroppers, and tenants began to leave Greene County. Between 1880 and 1890 the white population declined by 241 persons, and the black population declined by 496. Despite the natural increase of families in Greene County the population declined by almost 5 percent between 1880 and 1890. These hundreds of emigrants sought opportunity in western land, or more commonly, in southern cities, especially Atlanta. There, at least, they had some hope of escaping the poverty that plagued them in Greene County.[38]

By 1885 the transformation of Greene County's economy had left many farmers in dire poverty, and they blamed their problems on the merchants and lawyers in their own community, "capitalists" in New York, and in some cases the market system itself. But were these legitimate allegations? Small farmers may have had played a part in their downfall. In fact, during the late 1870s and early 1880s, small farmers had failed to join in Greene County's Independent political movement, an alliance between traditional planters and black voters to resist new legislation such as the Constitution of 1877 and the imposition of new laws requiring the fencing of livestock. The independents did enjoy some success. The leaders of the movement, Robert L. McWhorter and James B. Park Sr., for example, had won election to the Georgia House. But the alliance between old planters and black laborers proved unstable, and without the support of small landowners, the Independent movement soon fell apart. By the late 1880s, however, Greene County's small farmers had joined with many other like-minded farmers in the Farmer's Alliance, and through a mixture of self-help and politics, they tried to remake elements of their society. The goals of the Alliance in Greene County included limiting the exploitative system of debt while promoting higher prices for cotton and other agricultural products. But the effort came far too late. By then the Alliance and its political wing, the Populists, had little hope of rewriting Greene County history.[39]

In 1850 commercial market capitalism was not a part of everyday life for most people in Greene County, Georgia, but by 1885 it was. The Civil War, Reconstruction, and the market transformation did not "modernize" the economy of Greene County. If anything it did the opposite, replacing the carefully managed, centralized, factorylike slave plantations with decentralized, family-based production. In the process, the white people of Greene County became poorer, and the freed slaves found little opportunity for economic advancement. The population became almost completely dependent on the world market economy for the very meat and bread of life. To some degree this dependency may have been the cost of escaping the terrible legacy of slavery. But the remnants of slavery, the exploitative racism of southerners after Reconstruction, only further impoverished their region.

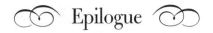 Epilogue

"Thy brother came with subtlety,
and hath taken away thy blessing."

Genesis 27:35

Today a drive south through Greene County from Penfield to White Plains reveals a changed landscape. Where once farms and plantations prospered, only a few families continue to work the soil. For the most part pulpwood forests cover the land and the people are gone. The tenants and sharecroppers that began to leave Greene County during the 1880s grew in number until the exodus became a flood during the 1930s. The federal government helped push the fleeing laborers off the land by buying tens of thousands of acres for the Oconee National Forest. Paper companies joined in the buying spree, and some landowners who had faced bankruptcy were saved from the final embarrassment. Corporations replaced landlords, timber replaced cotton, and the very land itself changed.

The Oconee River, once brisk and clear, meanders downstream at Scull Shoals, sluggish with topsoil washed from the land along its banks. A few miles south of Scull Shoals the river empties into a new man-made lake. There, exclusive communities line the shore like colonial outposts, providing a playground for wealthy urban refugees. Gates and security guards insure that only a few worthy locals, maids, and gardeners from Greene County ever enter these places of progress. Ironically, as developers struggle to create a historical cachet for their "plantations," the lake itself has covered Park's Mill, Long Shoals, Willis Ferry, and several large Indian mounds. Apparently, the developers would rather fabricate moonlight and magnolias than engage the real history that surrounds their properties.

Yet, for all the alterations in the land since the mass exodus of the 1930s, little has changed for the people of Greene County. Most are poor, and they live in the same segregated communities that existed more than a century ago. In Greensboro the majority of black people still live in Canaan. The impressive red brick edifice of the Springfield Baptist Church physically dominates the community of small bungalows. Springfield Baptist and nearby Ebenezer A.M.E. Church brim with history, and at homecoming each year, members of the black community return to remember their past and talk about their present. Across the highway from Ebenezer Church stands a low brick housing project that looks much like small-town projects anywhere. For the casual visitor to Canaan today, these projects, symbols of poverty and hopelessness, are far more likely to define the community than the old churches, symbols of trust and faith.

A short drive from Canaan leads to Main Street, which is lined with impressive antebellum homes. Some white families still occupy homes built by their ancestors, and many of the names are familiar: Robinson, Marchman, Armor, Boswell, and Lewis. Some of them have struggled to keep the county's past alive through family and community history and have built a small but active historical society and museum. Sadly, even as the white families have managed to preserve their history, the black people of Greene County have lost much of theirs. Some elements of oral history recall slavery and Reconstruction, but they usually reflect the interpretations of textbooks used in the schools. Among black people the story of the freedpeople's struggle for political power, the triumph and disappointment of political victory, and the courage of men such as Abram Colby have all been forgotten. The failure of Reconstruction cost the black people of Greene County not just their future, but much of their history as well.

A glimpse of Canaan or the countryside reveals appalling poverty. In a "county where plenty should abound and all should prosper" very few are prosperous. White people still control politics in Greene County, and white families still own most everything of value, so poverty hits hardest among Greene County's black people. Visiting one shack after another one struggles not to wince at the living conditions of the poor, and especially the elderly. The old people tell marvelous tales of struggle and suffering that occurred in the twentieth century, but the stories only reflect the tragic failure of Reconstruction in the nineteenth century. The white leaders of Greene County cheated these people of their birthright and by fraud and trickery stole from them the blessings and rights of citizenship promised in the United States Constitution. The results show in faces and hands of the older black folk.[1]

In black households one often finds hostility, anger, and hate. These people know that white people cheated the black folk of Greene County; their dream of prosperity has been deferred too long, and they are ready to explode. In white households by contrast, anxiety characterizes any discussion of the black community. Just as Jacob feared the wrath of his brother Esau, from whom he had stolen their father's blessing, so the white people of Greene County fear the potential reckoning with their county's black people.

One descendent of Greene County sharecroppers and slaves pointed to a reckoning that did not require a violent confrontation. In the early 1860s Adam Daniel Williams, the son of Shiloh Baptist Church leader Willis Williams, was born into slavery near Penfield. He grew up helping his father sharecrop in northern Greene County, but in 1893 joined the exodus of black workers hoping to find opportunity in Atlanta. In 1894, A. D. Williams became pastor of the Ebenezer Baptist Church in Atlanta and led his congregation for more than thirty years. He lived to see the birth of his grandson, Martin Luther King Jr.[2]

For all his human frailties, failures, and mistakes, Martin Luther King Jr. stood for the hope of reconciliation between white and black Americans. He would surely have recommended the example of Jacob and Esau's reconciliation to the people of Greene County. Jacob had grown prosperous. He could have remained in another country and avoided his brother's wrath but instead decided to return home and seek forgiveness, regardless of the cost. Hearing that Esau approached with 400 men, Jacob expected the worst. But Esau was not choosing the path of vengeance and justice but the path of love and forgiveness: "Esau ran to meet him, and embraced him, and fell upon his neck and kissed him, and they wept." Once again they lived as brothers, and the violence and destruction that could have ensued was avoided. Reconciliation, like Jacob and Esau's, between the black and white citizens of Greene County may only be a naive dream, but perhaps it can provide Americans with an agenda for the future.[3]

 Appendix

Table 1. Greene County Inferior Court Justices, 1851–1861

Name	Age in 1860	Occupation	Value of Real Property/ Personal Property	Slaves
Stewart Anderson	66	farmer	$10,000/13,500	40
James Burke	60	farmer	3,500/8,500	14
James A. Davidson	51	farmer	15,000/20,000	24
James W. Godkin	60	magistrate	1,100/1,4000	6
Sterling Gresham	32	farmer	5,000/12,000	35
John G. Holtzclaw	56	farmer	1,200/18,000	21
Little Berry Jackson	43	farmer	11,950/18,150	38
Wiley G. Johnson	41	merchant	5,500/4,500	5
Henry C. Weaver	26	merchant	800/0	0
William W. D. Weaver	61	farmer	14,560/52,000	79
Isaac A. Williams	49	farmer	5,150/82,940	6
Alfred L. Willis	32	farmer	4,000/12,000	17
Matthew Winfield	66	farmer	4,750/41,000	11
John F. Zimmerman	51	merchant	5,600/13,500	12
Isaac R. Hall	60	clerk superior court	dependent of John F. Zimmerman	
John Copeland	deceased (estate in 1860)		0/23,000	23

Source: Inferior Court Minutes, 1850–61, Greene County Courthouse; Population and Slave schedules, 1860 Manuscript Census Returns, Georgia Department of Archives and History.

Table 2. Quartiles of Household Wealth in Greene County, 1860

Quartile	Wealth	Number
Poor	less than $200	212
Lower middle	$200–2,499	187
Upper middle	$2,500–12,999	204
Wealthy	$13,000 or more	194

Source: Population and Slave schedules, 1860 Manuscript Census Returns, Georgia Department of Archives and History.

Table 3. Greene County Lawyers, 1860

Name	Age in 1860	Total Wealth	Slaves	Notes
James L. Brown	41	$28,000	19	
George O. Dawson	36	5,000	0	lived at William W. Weaver's
William A. Florence	23	5,000	1	
Frederick C. Fuller	35	6,200	1	lived at Ann Nickelson's
Columbus Heard	26	0	0	lived at Margaret Wade's
Yelverton P. King	66	14,000	7	
Miles W. Lewis	40	10,500	26	listed as farmer/lawyer
Philip B. Robinson[a]	29	33,600	24	
John C. Reid	24	0	0	lived at Ruben Dawson's
Rolin W. Stephens	25	10,000	6	lived at Nancy Jackson's

Source: Population and Slave schedules, 1860 Manuscript Census Returns, Georgia Department of Archives and History.
[a]Philip B. Robinson also controlled his stepchildren's trust consisting of property worth $150,029, including 94 slaves.

Table 4. Greenesboro City Officials, 1860

Name	Age	Occupation	Property Value	Slaves
James L. Brown (mayor)	41	lawyer	$28,000	19
William S. Davis	30	merchant	17,000	11
Frederick C. Fuller	35	lawyer	6,200	1
David Howell	41	merchant	13,500	0
Wiley G. Johnson	41	merchant	10,000	5

Source: Greenesboro *Planters' Weekly*, March 28, 1860; Population and Slave schedules, 1860 Manuscript Census Returns, Georgia Department of Archives and History.

Table 5. Secession Committee Members at Public Meeting in Greenesboro, November 16, 1860

Name	Occupation	Slaves
James N. Armor	farmer	69
James B. Hart	farmer	30
Archibald Perkins	farmer	22
Philip B. Robinson	lawyer	24[a]
David S. Terrill	farmer	30
Henry H. Tucker[b]	professor	0
William W. Weaver	farmer	79

Source: Population and Slave schedules, 1860 Manuscript Census Returns, Georgia Department of Archives and History; Greenesboro *Planters' Weekly*, November 21, 1860.

[a] Philip B. Robinson also controlled the 94 slaves inherited by his wife's three children from a former marriage.

[b] Henry H. Tucker came from a very wealthy planter family in Warren County, Georgia.

Table 6. Farm Value and Agricultural Production,
Greene County, 1849 and 1859

	1849	1859	Change
Total farm acres	253,643	281,877	+11%
Value of farmland	$1,767,288	$1,855,185	+5%
Value per acre	$ 6.97	$ 6.58	−5%
Wheat produced	13,882 bu.	35,036 bu.	+252%
Corn produced	480,326 bu.	302,205 bu.	−37%
Oats produced	96,787 bu.	24,442 bu.	−75%
Cotton produced	12,600 bales	8,643 bales	−31%

Source: U.S. Census Bureau, *Appendix of the Seventh Census of the United States, 1850*, pp. 377–81, and *Agriculture of the United States in 1860*, pp. 22–25.

Table 7. Number and Value of Slaves, Greene County, 1858–1860

	1858	1859	1860	Change, 1858–60
Number of slaves	8,306	8,251	8,218	−1%
Value of all slaves	$4,136,966	$5,008,532	$5,342,562	+29%
Value per capita	$498.07	$607.02	$650.10	+30%

Source: Greenesboro *Planters' Weekly*, September 5, 1860.

Table 8. Farm Value and Agricultural Production, Greene County, 1849–1879

	1849	1869	Change, 1849–69	1879	Change, 1869–79	Change, 1849–79
Value of farmland	$1,767,288	$1,059,700	−40%	$1,656,662	+56%	−6%
Number of cattle	10,696	4,035	−62%	6,488	+61%	−39%
Number of swine	30,323	5,100	−83%	12,819	+151%	−58%
Value of livestock	392,975	215,703	−45%	285,727	+32%	−27%
Wheat produced	13,882 bu.	24,651 bu.	+78%	44,581 bu.	+81%	+221%
Oats produced	96,787 bu.	9,735 bu.	−90%	77,269 bu.	+694%	−20%
Corn produced	480,326 bu.	132,635 bu.	−72%	188,909 bu.	+42%	−61%
Cotton produced	12,600 bales	5,699 bales	−55%	12,448 bales	+118%	−1%[a]
Ratio of corn to cotton	38.12	23.27	−39%	15.18	−35%	−60%[b]

Source: U.S. Census Bureau, *Appendix of the Seventh Census of the United States, 1850*, pp. 377–81; *A Compendium of the Ninth Census, 1870*, pp. 722–23; *Report on the Cotton Production of the State of Georgia, 1880*, p. 6; *Compendium of the Tenth Census, 1880, Part I*, pp. 694, 757.

[a] In 1880 a bale of cotton supposedly weighed an average of 475 pounds, while in 1850 a bale supposedly weighed an average of only 400 pounds. If this was really the case, then the 1849 crop weighed 5,040,000 pounds and the 1879 crop weighed 5,912,800 pounds, an increase of 17 percent. In actual practice farmers apparently assumed a "bale is a bale," and bale weights recorded by merchants vary enormously. The best guess would be to say that the size of the cotton crop in 1879 was about equal to that in 1849.

[b] Assuming that in 1879 a bale weighed 475 pounds, the number of bales of cotton produced in 1879 adjusted to 400-pound bales was about 14,782, giving a ratio of corn to cotton of 12.78 bushels. The percentage decline in the ratio from 1849 to 1879 in this case would equal 67 percent.

Table 9. Quartiles of Household Wealth among
Whites in Greene County, 1870

Quartile	Wealth	Number
Poor	no property	246
Lower middle	$0–499	247
Upper middle	$500–3,199	247
Wealthy	$3,200 or more	246

Source: Population schedule, 1870 Manuscript Census Returns, Georgia Department of Archives and History.

Table 10. Greene County Commissioners, 1876–1888

Name	Occupation in 1870	Wealth in 1870
James B. Park Sr.	farmer	$25,000
Baldwin Copelan	farmer	500
Peter W. Printup	merchant	15,000
John F. Zimmerman	merchant	9,000
James M. Griffin	farmer	4,210
William W. Moore	farmer	2,500
Charles A. Davis Jr.	merchant	5,500
William H. Branch	lawyer	2,500
J. B. Y. Warner	none recorded	20,500

Source: Grand Jury Presentments, Superior Court Proceedings, March Terms, 1876, 1880, 1884, September Term, 1884; Population schedule, 1870 Manuscript Census Returns, Georgia Department of Archives and History.

⟳ Notes ⟲

Prologue

1. See Bryant, "Race, Class, and Law in Bourbon Georgia" and "A Dangerous Venture," pp. 1–59. For an explanation of the concept of living law, see Ehrlich, *Fundamental Principles of the Sociology of Law*.

2. Raper, *Tenants of the Almighty*.

Introduction

1. Greensboro *Herald*, August 7, 1885. Hereafter cited as *Herald*.

2. Population schedule, 1860 Manuscript Census Returns, Georgia Department of Archives and History (hereafter cited as GDAH). In 1860 only twenty-five free African Americans resided in Greene County. See U.S. Census Bureau, *Population of the United States in 1860*, p. 72. See Chapter 1 for detailed wealth comparisons and sources.

3. Population schedule, 1870 Manuscript Census Returns, GDAH; *Herald*, March 30, 1871.

4. *Herald*, March 30, 1871.

5. Ibid., December 9, 1875; O'Brien, in *The Legal Fraternity and the Making of a New South Community, 1848–1882*, deals with the rise to power of lawyers in Guilford County, North Carolina. While several studies have focused on the rise of merchants, only O'Brien's directly engages the rising power of southern lawyers in the nineteenth century.

6. *Herald*, December 9, 1875.

7. "Reconstruction" is usually used to mean the abortive political attempt to change the South following the Civil War. Here, however, the term "reconstructed" is used to mean the transformation of the structural components of this community. See Bender, *Community and Social Change in America*, pp. 86–120.

Chapter One

1. Inferior Court Records, March 23, 1848, Greene County Courthouse; Rice and Williams, *History of Greene County, Georgia*, p. 85. The inferior court added the third floor for the Masons after they offered to pay for it. The result was a more balanced building.

2. Rice and Williams, *History of Greene County, Georgia*, pp. 213–18; Dowell, *A History of Mercer University, 1833–1945*, pp. 64–66.

3. Rice and Williams, *History of Greene County, Georgia*, p. 85; Penfield Baptist Church Papers, 1839–85, Microfilm Publication 260, Southern Baptist Historical Commission (Nashville), January 1, February 4, 1849, GDAH.

4. Debo, *Road to Disappearance*, pp. 37–40. An excellent account of the Revolution on the Georgia frontier and the negotiations with the Creeks can be found in Edward J. Cashin, *The King's Ranger*, pp. 17–173.

5. Debo, *Road to Disappearance*, pp. 40–48; Shivers, in *The Land Between*, pp. 7–45, tells the story of this war. The ceded lands included the future site of the University of Georgia, created in 1785.

6. Raper, *Tenants of the Almighty*, pp. 12–15; Hodler and Schretter, *The Atlas of Georgia*, pp. 72, 254. Greene County's seat has had three spellings over the past two centuries. Originally "Greenesborough," it was changed in about 1850 to "Greenesboro," which prevailed until about 1900, when the U.S. Post Office Department changed the spelling to "Greensboro." Some older inhabitants of Greene County insist that the latter spelling is incorrect and have not forgiven the Post Office. Throughout this work the spelling "Greenesboro" will be used.

7. United States, *American State Papers, Indian Affairs*, 1:23; Raper, *Tenants of the Almighty*, pp. 12–15.

8. U.S. Census Bureau, *Aggregate Amount of Each Description of Persons*, pp. 83–85; Garnett Andrews, *Reminiscences of an Old Georgia Lawyer*, p. 15. Determining the number of Native Americans who might still have lived in Greene County proved impossible. Most likely, the ongoing low-level war along the borders of the county ensured that Native Americans were not welcome there, preventing the creation of any sort of triracial community.

9. United States Census figures for 1790, 1800, and 1810, from Raper, *Tenants of the Almighty*, p. 366. The original Greene County included land that would become parts of Hancock, Oglethorpe, Clarke, and Taliaferro Counties. By 1826 the legislature had reduced Greene County to its present size of approximately 400 square miles.

10. United States Census figures for 1790, 1800, and 1810, from Raper, *Tenants of the Almighty*, p. 366. Greene County Tax Digest, 1810, GDAH. African Americans had made up a majority of Greene's population until the 1990 census.

11. Raper, *Tenants of the Almighty*, pp. 33–35; Coleman, *A History of Georgia*, p. 111. See Woodman, *King Cotton and His Retainers*, pp. 3–71, for a superb account of the cotton revolution. The value of all American tobacco exports remained flat during this period, totaling about $8 million in 1815 and $10 million in 1840. By contrast, American cotton exports totaled $17.5 million in 1815 and rose to $64 million in 1840. See Chandler, *The Visible Hand*, p. 20.

12. Rice and Williams, *History of Greene County, Georgia*, p. 347; Raper, *Tenants of the Almighty*, pp. 33–35; Coulter, "Scull Shoals"; White, *Statistics of the State of Georgia*, p. 291; Griffin, "The Textile Industry in Greene County, Georgia, before 1860," pp. 81–84. These three mills actually processed cotton from Greene County and the neighboring counties of Clarke, Morgan, Putnam, and Hancock, so they processed far less than half of Greene County's cotton. The

profits, however, did go to owners in Greene County. The cotton boom did not result from high cotton prices so much as it resulted from the availability of inexpensive fertile land. Though the cotton boom ended during the early 1830s in Greene and surrounding counties, it continued to spread westward to southwest Georgia, Alabama, and ultimately, Texas. See Morris, *Becoming Southern*, for a detailed account of the rise of a cotton plantation economy in Mississippi.

13. Phillips, *A History of Transportation in the Eastern Cotton Belt to 1860*, pp. 221–51; Raper, *Tenants of the Almighty*, pp. 34–35. For the use of eminent domain power to advantage private enterprises like railroads, see Horwitz, *The Transformation of American Law, 1780–1860*. The classic debate on the economic impact of railroads can be found in Fogel, *Railroads and American Economic Growth*, and Fishlow, *American Railroads and the Transformation of the Antebellum Economy*. Allison was not alone in refusing to welcome the railroad. The entire town of Lexington, in Oglethorpe County, refused to let the railroad pass through. The railroad decided simply to bypass the town.

14. Surprisingly, J. William Harris's *Plain Folk and Gentry in a Slave Society* does not adequately deal with this development. One has to return to Ulrich B. Phillips, *A History of Transportation in the Eastern Cotton Belt to 1860*, published in 1908, to gain an adequate consideration of the impact of the railroad on the communities of east Georgia. The transportation problems were one force behind the creation of early cotton mills in Greene County, for yarn and cloth were easier to transport and had higher value than ginned cotton.

15. Phillips, *A History of Transportation in the Eastern Cotton Belt to 1860*, pp. 122–31, 244–45; Jones and Dutcher, *Memorial History of Augusta, Georgia*, pp. 161–91; Greensboro *Planters' Weekly*, September 12, 1860.

16. Raper, *Tenants of the Almighty*, pp. 32–36; Cumming, *Georgia Railroad and Banking Company, 1833–1945*, pp. 22–24.

17. Rawick, *The American Slave*, 13:340–41.

18. Gavin Wright, *The Political Economy of the Cotton South*, pp. 55–74. Greene County figures derived from Population, Agriculture, and Slave schedules, 1860 Manuscript Census Returns, GDAH. East Georgia figures are from Harris, *Plain Folk and Gentry in a Slave Society*, p. 25. The food production calculations were made using the method explained in Ransom and Sutch, *One Kind of Freedom*, pp. 244–53. By this method it was determined that in 1849 Greene County produced the food equivalent of more than 600,000 bushels of corn, while it produced less than 400,000 bushel equivalents in 1859.

19. Harris, *Plain Folk and Gentry in a Slave Society*, p. 25; Gavin Wright, *The Political Economy of the Cotton South*, pp. 55–74.

20. Georgia Department of Agriculture, Henderson, *The Commonwealth of Georgia*, pp. 357–70; Wright, *The Political Economy of the Cotton South*, pp. 55–74.

21. Wright, *The Political Economy of the Cotton South*, pp. 55–74; Phillips, *A History of Transportation in the Eastern Cotton Belt to 1860*, pp. 244–45; Crawford, "Cotton, Land, and Sustenance"; Augusta *Daily Chronicle and Sentinel*, April 15, 1849. On December 1, 1849, the first train ran between Atlanta and

Chattanooga, completing the Western and Atlantic's link to the food-producing regions of east and middle Tennessee. See *Southern Banner*, December 13, 1849.

22. "Colonel R. H. Ward's Address to the Greene County Agricultural Society," Augusta *Daily Chronicle and Sentinel*, February 12, 1851; *Transactions of the Southern Central Agricultural Society*, pp. 1–26.

23. Penfield *Temperance Banner*, May 22, June 26, September 4, 1852.

24. Adam Smith, *An Inquiry into the Nature and Causes of the Wealth of Nations*, pp. 20–23.

25. Appleby, *Capitalism and a New Social Order*, pp. 25–50, provides one of the best and most concise discussions of the market transformation and its impact on society.

26. Dowell, *A History of Mercer University, 1833–1953*, pp. 34–63; Raper, *Tenants of the Almighty*, pp. 35–37. The census did not collect population figures for the town of Penfield itself, but in 1860, 85 households with a total population of 485 free persons and 717 slaves were listed under the Penfield post office, which was shown with a total of 1,202 persons.

27. Greensboro *Weekly Gazette*, December 14, 1859; Greensboro *Planters' Weekly*, October 10, 1860; Rice and Williams, *History of Greene County, Georgia*, pp. 348–49; Phillips, *A History of Transportation in the Eastern Cotton Belt to 1860*, pp. 221–51; Population schedule, 1860 Manuscript Census Returns, GDAH; *The State v. Hope H. Mattox*, Superior Court Proceedings, September Term, 1860, Greene County Courthouse.

28. Rice and Williams, *History of Greene County, Georgia*, pp. 214–16; Greensboro *Weekly Gazette*, February 16, March 2, April 6, 1859; Raper, *Tenants of the Almighty*, p. 37. Whether young Woodrow Wilson accompanied his father to the commencement is unknown, but he later married Ellen Axson, the daughter of Dr. I. S. K. Axson, who was president of the Female College. Romantic tradition in Greene County holds that this was the first meeting between Ellen and Woodrow, despite the fact that Ellen was not born until 1860, two years after the 1858 commencement.

29. Population and Slave schedules, 1860 Manuscript Census Returns, GDAH; U.S. Census Bureau, *Statistics of the United States in 1860*, pp. xx, 294–98; Greensboro *Planters' Weekly*, September 5, 1860, October 10, 1860; U.S. Census Bureau, *Agriculture of the United States in 1860*, pp. 22–25; Hobsbawm, *The Age of Capital, 1848–1875*, pp. 28–29. If one includes slaves in the calculation of Greene County's per capita wealth, the result is well over $700, twice the national average. Greene County was by no means the wealthiest county in Georgia. The per capita wealth of free people in Dougherty County exceeded $4,000.

30. Population and Slave schedules, 1860 Manuscript Census Returns, GDAH; U.S. Census Bureau, *Statistics of the United States in 1860*, xx, 294–98; Greensboro *Planters' Weekly*, September 5, 1860; Ayers, *Vengeance and Justice*, p. 107. Providentially, since such information has otherwise been lost, the Greensboro *Planters' Weekly* printed an accounting of the taxable value of slaves for 1858, 1859, and 1860 in its September 5, 1860, issue. These numbers

showed a rapid increase in the average taxable value of slaves to $650 in 1860. I have assumed that this number is generally valid when used along with the census data of 1860, which would yield a total slave value of $5,458,700 and a total property value in Greene County of $8,983,696 in 1860, resulting in the figure of 60 percent of wealth in the county representing the value of slaves. Similar numbers can be generated from the 1859 tax returns reported in the Greensboro *Weekly Gazette*, August 17, 1859. There, returns reported a taxable value of $5,002,532 for slaves in Greene County and a total taxable property value of $8,895,570; thus slaves made up about 56 percent of all taxable wealth in that year. Interestingly, the taxable value of farmland in 1859 was $1,858,466, or only 37 percent of the value of slaves in the county. Clearly, the wealth of Greene County depended on slaves.

31. U.S. Census Bureau, *The Seventh Census of the United States, 1850*, p. 377; U.S. Census Bureau, *Agriculture of the United States in 1860*, p. 22; Population and Agriculture schedules, 1860 Manuscript Census Returns, GDAH; Penfield *Temperance Banner*, November 12, 1853; Greenesboro *Planters' Weekly*, March 21, 1860.

32. U.S. Census Bureau, *The Seventh Census of the United States, 1850: An Appendix*, p. 377; U.S. Census Bureau, *Agriculture of the United States in 1860*, p. 22; Population, Slave, and Agriculture schedules, 1860 Manuscript Census Returns, GDAH. Bode and Ginter, in *Farm Tenancy and the Census in Antebellum Georgia*, powerfully argue that scholars have underestimated the extent of antebellum farm tenancy. They suggest that tenants made up between 7.6 and 17.2 percent of farm operators in Greene County in 1860. Wiebe, *The Search for Order, 1877–1920*, pp. 3–4, made powerful use of the "island community" metaphor.

33. Social Statistics, 1860 Manuscript Census Returns, GDAH; Greenesboro *Weekly Gazette*, March 2, September 21, 1859.

Chapter Two

1. Abigail Colby Headstone, Greensboro City Graveyard, Greensboro, Georgia; *Herald*, February 6, 1885; "John Colby's Will," Will Book G, pp. 94–95, Greene County Courthouse; U.S. Congress, *Report of the Joint Select Committee on the Condition of Affairs in the Late Insurrectionary States*, 1:696. Hereafter cited as *KKK Testimony*.

2. "John Colby's Will," Will Book G, p. 95, Greene County Courthouse; Population, Slave, and Agriculture schedules, 1850 Manuscript Census Returns, GDAH. Abram Colby believed that his father had freed him and insisted this was true in 1871, suggesting that his legal status as a slave after 1850 had little tangible effect on his life. See *KKK Testimony*, 1:696.

3. *KKK Testimony*, 1:696, 702, 706.

4. Rawick, *The American Slave*, 12:104–5, 107–9. Samuel Davis was the father of William and Charles Davis, who became two of Greene County's leading merchants.

5. Rawick, *The American Slave*, 12:104–14.

6. Raper, *Tenants of the Almighty*, p. 59; Social Statistics, 1860 Manuscript Census Returns, GDAH; Rawick, *The American Slave*, 13:96; U.S. Census Bureau, *Statistics of the United States in 1860*, p. 341. The three nonworking members of families could be children or elderly persons, though as slaves they would perform some small duties, increasing the total return per family group over this estimate. Fogel and Engerman argue that the annual average maintenance cost of $48 per slave allowed a relatively prosperous existence. That a laborer's cost for one year's food and shelter in Greene County averaged $104 belies that argument, as does the testimony of many slaves. See Fogel and Engerman, *Time on the Cross*, p. 151. Roger L. Ransom and Richard Sutch argue that masters spent far less on the maintenance of their slaves, calculating an average of about $29 per slave. See Ransom and Sutch, *One Kind of Freedom*, pp. 203–14.

7. Douglass, *My Bondage and My Freedom*, p. 64; Rawick, *The American Slave*, 13:59. Seven Georgia narratives, one Arkansas narrative, and one Florida narrative in Rawick's collections were by former slaves from Greene County.

8. Rawick, *The American Slave*, 12:49, 317, 13:93. By far the most convincing treatment of slave marriages can be found in Gutman, *The Black Family in Slavery and Freedom, 1750 to 1925*.

9. Rawick, *The American Slave*, 12:53, 106, 318, 17:23; Rice and Williams, *History of Greene County, Georgia*, p. 149.

10. Georgia, *The Code of the State of Georgia*, 1845, title 2, chap. 32, art. 2, and 1861, pt. 1, title 15, chap. 5, art. 1 (hereafter cited as *Ga. Code*); Greensboro *Planters' Weekly*, September 12, 19, 1860; See list of patrol commissioners for 1859 in Rice and Williams, *History of Greene County, Georgia*, p. 448; Population and Slave schedules, 1860 Manuscript Census Returns, GDAH. About two-thirds of Greene County's slaves in 1860 lived on plantations with twenty or more slaves, but less than one-fourth lived on plantations with more than fifty slaves. Twenty slaves represents about four families—too small a number to really function as a community, so slaves built a community network between several farms and plantations.

11. Greene County Superior Court Proceedings, September Term, 1853, March Term, 1854, September Term, 1860, Greene County Courthouse; Greensboro *Planters' Weekly*, September 12, 19, 1860.

12. Rawick, *The American Slave*, 12:235, 13:34. The slave community is described in detail in several works, the most accessible of which are Genovese, *Roll, Jordan, Roll*, and Blassingame, *The Slave Community*.

13. Bryant, "'My Soul An't Yours, Mas'r," pp. 401–12.

14. Ibid.; Carson, Luker, and Russell, *Called to Serve, January 1929–June 1951*, pp. 1–4.

15. Conference Minutes of Bethesda Baptist Church, April 14, 1849, July 9, August 15, 1856, July 17, 1858, Greene County Historical Society Museum.

16. Rawick, *The American Slave*, 12:51, 57, 109, 13:97–98; *Transactions of the Southern Central Agricultural Society*, pp. 195–201; Greensboro *Planters' Weekly*, March 28, 1860.

17. Rawick, *The American Slave*, 12:51, 57, 109, 13:97–98.

18. Ibid.; Agriculture schedule, 1860 Manuscript Census Returns, GDAH; Greensboro *Weekly Gazette*, January 5, May 18, 1859.

19. Rawick, *The American Slave*, 12:49, 13:97–99.

20. Some apologists for slavery argued that slaves were not "things" but that they were men who had simply surrendered their labor for life. At law, slaves were sometimes treated as chattels, sometimes not. See Jenkins, *Pro-Slavery Thought in the Old South*, pp. 108–16.

21. Superior Court Proceedings, September Terms, 1859, 1861, Greene County Courthouse. Perhaps the masters in each case made some sort of restitution to the slaves involved, but this possibility only emphasizes the horrible arbitrariness of the slave system.

22. Superior Court Proceedings, September Term, 1860, Greene County Courthouse. Greensboro *Planters' Weekly*, September 19, 1860.

23. Superior Court Proceedings, March and September Terms, 1859, 1860, 1861, and Inferior Court Minutes, 1859, 1860, 1861, all in Greene County Courthouse; Penfield Baptist Church Papers, January 8, 1860; Raper, *Tenants of the Almighty*, p. 52. Earlier in the nineteenth century the inferior court had jurisdiction over all criminal cases involving slaves, but after 1850, the superior court held jurisdiction in all capital cases.

24. Greensboro *Planters' Weekly*, June 13, 1860; Mohr, *On the Threshold of Freedom*, pp. 10–11.

25. Tushnet, *The American Law of Slavery, 1820–1860*, pp. 11–27, properly warns historians against misusing legal cases as evidence of common experience or sentiment. However, with care and an understanding of the ideological and social context, one can use cases as points of insight into the slave society.

26. Greensboro *Weekly Gazette*, December 29, 1859; *The State v. Tom (a slave)*, Superior Court Proceedings, March Term, 1860, Greene County Courthouse.

27. Population and Agriculture schedules, 1860 Manuscript Census Records, GDAH; Greensboro *Weekly Gazette*, March 7, 1860. Tom's master, John Cartright, also styled himself as Dr. John Curtwright. In 1860 John Curtwright owned the Long Shoals Cotton Mill, making him one of Greene County's most powerful men.

28. *The State v. Tom (a slave)*, Superior Court Proceedings, March Term, 1860, Greene County Courthouse. Greene County's clerk of superior court, Isaac R. Hall, often included in his "Proceedings" detailed information about particular cases. Hall's notes in the "Proceedings" allow a greater understanding of events in court than would normally be the case. Note that the dispute between the lawyers centered on language, particularly the meaning of the term murder.

29. *The State v. Tom (a slave)*, Superior Court Proceedings, March Term, 1860, Greene County Courthouse.

30. Population and Slave schedules, 1860 Manuscript Census Returns, GDAH; Greensboro *Planters' Weekly*, April 4, 1860; Augusta *Daily Chronicle*

and Sentinel, March 31, 1860; *Savannah Morning News*, April 2, 1860; Raper, *Tenants of the Almighty*, p. 52.

31. Greensboro *Planters' Weekly*, April 4, 1860; Augusta *Daily Chronicle and Sentinel*, March 31, 1860; *Savannah Morning News*, April 2, 1860.

32. Greensboro *Planters' Weekly*, April 4, 1860; Augusta *Daily Chronicle and Sentinel*, March 31, 1860; *Savannah Morning News*, April 2, 1860. For a fictional account of why a slave mother might kill her own child, see Morrison, *Beloved: A Novel*.

33. Greensboro *Planters' Weekly*, March 28, 1860; Augusta *Daily Chronicle and Sentinel*, March 27, April 1, 1860.

34. *The State v. Becky (a slave)*, Superior Court Proceedings, September Term, 1860, Greene County Courthouse. Unlike some states, Georgia did not compensate the owners of slaves executed for capital crimes.

35. *Savannah Morning News*, April 2, 1860; *The State v. Becky (a slave)*, Superior Court Proceedings, September Term, 1860, Greene County Courthouse.

36. See Flanigan, "Criminal Procedure in Slave Trials in the Antebellum South"; Hindus, "Black Justice Under White Law." Mark Tushnet argues that protecting slave property did *not* influence the procedural treatment of slaves in court. For his view, see Tushnet, *The American Law of Slavery, 1820–1860*, p. 122.

37. See Ayers, *Vengeance and Justice*, p. 134, n. 67.

Chapter Three

1. Florie Carter Smith, *The History of Oglethorpe County, Georgia*, pp. 167–70; Georgia, St. Clair–Abrams, *Manual and Biographic Register of the State of Georgia, 1871–72*, pp. 22–23, 70–71; Georgia General Assembly, *Georgia's General Assembly, 1880–81*, pp. 77–80; Northen, *Men of Mark in Georgia*, 8:397–400; McWhorter Family File, GDAH.

2. Florie Carter Smith, *The History of Oglethorpe County, Georgia*, pp. 167–70; St. Clair–Abrams, *Manual and Biographic Register of the State of Georgia, 1871–72*, pp. 22–23, 70–71; Georgia General Assembly, *Georgia's General Assembly, 1880–81*, pp. 77–80; Northen, *Men of Mark in Georgia*, 8:397–400; McWhorter Family File, GDAH; *History of the Baptist Denomination in Georgia*, pp. 290–91.

3. St. Clair–Abrams, *Manual and Biographic Register of the State of Georgia, 1871–72*, pp. 22–23, 70–71; Georgia General Assembly, *Georgia's General Assembly, 1880–81*, pp. 77–80; McWhorter Family File, GDAH; *History of the Baptist Denomination in Georgia*, pp. 290–91.

4. St. Clair–Abrams, *Manual and Biographic Register of the State of Georgia, 1871–72*, pp. 22–23, 70–71; Georgia General Assembly, *Georgia's General Assembly, 1880–81*, pp. 77–80; Northen, *Men of Mark in Georgia*, 8:397–400; McWhorter Family File, GDAH; Formwalt, "Antebellum Planter Persistence," p. 416; *Greensboro Herald Journal*, February 24, 1899. Whether Nancy Thurmond brought a dowry to the marriage is unknown, but the timing of the

plantation purchase suggests McWhorter used funds he obtained through the marriage.

5. St. Clair–Abrams, *Manual and Biographic Register of the State of Georgia, 1871–72*, pp. 22–23, 70–71; Georgia General Assembly, *Georgia's General Assembly, 1880–81*, pp. 77–80; Northen, *Men of Mark in Georgia*, 8:397–400; *Herald Journal*, February 24, 1899. Throughout his political career, McWhorter enjoyed the role of the "opposition." His membership in the American Party did not so much result from agreement with their platform as the fact that it was the only organized alternative to the Democrats. McWhorter would later participate in the Republican Party and the Greenback Party and toyed with the People's Party near the end of his life.

6. St. Clair–Abrams, *Manual and Biographic Register of the State of Georgia, 1871–72*, pp. 22–23; Florie Carter Smith, *The History of Oglethorpe County, Georgia*, pp. 167–70; McWhorter Family File, GDAH.

7. Burton, *In My Father's House Are Many Mansions*, provides a detailed study of the family power structure of a county in South Carolina. Most planter/businessmen identified themselves in the census as farmers or planters.

8. Wrong, *Power*, p. 2; Max Weber's definition of power as the "possibility of imposing one's will on the behavior of other persons" fails to account for power that does not influence behavior but otherwise exists. See Weber, *Law in Economy and Society*, p. 323.

9. The first approach is most commonly identified with Marxism, though it has many variations. Charles A. Beard produced some of the earliest and best of such work. Traditional political history and political science have often taken the second approach, a fine example of which is the work of V. O. Key. Anthropological approaches that consider the cultural components of power in society usually build on the work of Clifford Geertz. The focus on language owes much to Ludwig Wittgenstein's work and to the work of more recent French theorists such as Michel Foucault. Finally, one branch of the deconstructionist movement seems to have moved toward a nihilistic theory of society. See Sampford, *The Disorder of Law*. This sort of nihilism must be distinguished from Chaos Theory, which is a form of "structurism"; see Reisch, "Chaos, History, and Narrative," pp. 1–20, and McCloskey, "History, Differential Equations, and the Problem of Narration."

10. Lloyd, "The Methodologies of Social History." Lloyd uses the term "structurism" to distinguish this approach from deterministic Althusserian structuralism. See also McKinney and Thompson, *The South in Continuity and Change*, pp. 3–33. By language structures I mean the linguistic coordinate system of a culture. See Habermas, *Reason and Rationalization of Society*.

11. Lloyd, "The Methodologies of Social History"; Lears, "The Concept of Cultural Hegemony."

12. Some of the finest studies of power in communities have used similar methods. Robert A. Dahl, in *Who Governs? Democracy and Power in an American City*, focused on the decision-making power of politicians in a community and engaged the impact of democratic rituals on that power. In his masterful

Community Power Structures, Floyd Hunter interviewed numerous community leaders, asking them to identify the powerful in their community. As historians can hardly conduct interviews of nineteenth-century leaders, Gail Williams O'Brien, in *The Legal Fraternity and the Making of a New South Community*, built on Hunter's ideas a fascinating system of quantifying individuals' power by tracing their participation in local economic, social, cultural, and political events. Though her ideas and conclusions are sound, attempting to quantify power numerically has been rejected here as too problematic. Of note is the fact that all three approaches essentially take the members of a community at their word when they identify individuals as powerful. Historians, however, have the added advantage of identifying power holders through the course of events.

13. Wooster, *The People in Power*, pp. 66, 94; Georgia Executive Department Commissions, Justices of the Inferior Court, 1813–1861, GDAH. Floyd Hunter used four categories of leaders, a model followed here. These categories were governmental leaders, business leaders, civic leaders, and status leaders. See Hunter, *Community Power Structure*, pp. 262–71. Community is used here to mean the relatively self-sufficient social and cultural world of people within Greene County.

14. Wooster, *The People in Power*, pp. 97–103.

15. Georgia Executive Department Commissions, Justices of the Inferior Court, 1813–61, and Population and Slave schedules, 1860 Manuscript Census Returns, both in GDAH. The two men who did not own slaves in 1860 were Henry C. Weaver and Isaac R. Hall. Henry C. Weaver was the youngest man to serve on the inferior court during this period. Weaver, a merchant, was the son of William W. D. Weaver, a wealthy planter who also served on the inferior court. The other man, Isaac Hall, was also the only man who did not own realty in 1860. A hunchbacked dwarf, Hall served as clerk of the Greene County Superior Court for many years and was related to the wealthy Hall family of southwestern Greene County. Hall may have misrepresented his wealth, for he was a partner in the Davis and Barber clockmaking firm and owned the building that served as the firm's factory. See Rice and Williams, *History of Greene County*, pp. 158–59, 163, 449.

16. Population, Agriculture, and Slave schedules, 1860 Manuscript Census Returns, and Population schedule, 1850 Manuscript Census Returns, all in GDAH. Local officials' names were culled from various issues of the Greensboro *Weekly Gazette* and the Greensboro *Planters' Weekly*. Cases involving King and Lewis fill the Greene County Superior Court Proceedings for 1859 and 1860, suggesting a very active practice.

17. Population, Agriculture, and Slave schedules, 1860 Manuscript Census Returns, Population schedule, 1850 Manuscript Census Returns, GDAH. Local officials' names were culled from various issues of the Greensboro *Weekly Gazette* and the Greensboro *Planters' Weekly*.

18. Wooster, *The People in Power*, pp. 35–40.

19. Population and Slave schedules, 1860 Census, GDAH. Representatives' names were drawn from Georgia General Assembly, *Journal of the House of*

Representatives of the State of Georgia, 1851, 1853, 1855, 1857, 1859; hereafter cited as *Georgia House Journal*. Senators' names were drawn from Georgia General Assembly, *Journal of the Senate of the State of Georgia*, 1853, 1855, 1857, 1859; hereafter cited as *Georgia Senate Journal*. The men who represented Greene County during the 1850s were Judge Francis Cone, George O. Dawson, a lawyer (and the son of Senator William Dawson), and John Armstrong, Jesse Champion, Rowan Ward, and Robert L. McWhorter, who were all planters. Miles Lewis planted and practiced law. Several of these men died before the 1860 census, making conclusive calculations of wealth impossible. All seven men owned twenty or more slaves according to the 1854 Greene County Tax Digest, Microfilm of Greene County Records, GDAH.

20. Greensboro *Weekly Gazette*, April 6, 1859; Greensboro *Planters' Weekly*, March 28, 1860; Population and Slave schedules, 1860 Manuscript Census Returns, GDAH.

21. Coulter, "Scull Shoals," p. 33; Poullain Family File, Greene County Historical Society Museum; Rice and Williams, *History of Greene County, Georgia*, pp. 144–52, 270; Northen, *Men of Mark in Georgia*, 8:153–56; Park Family File, GDAH; Park Mill Collection, Greene County Historical Society Museum; Population schedule, 1860 Manuscript Census Returns, GDAH.

22. Raper, *Tenants of the Almighty*, pp. 33–35; Rice and Williams, *History of Greene County, Georgia*, pp. 148, 158–60, 282–83.

23. *Henry Atwood v. The Greensboro Manufacturing Co.*, Superior Court Proceedings, March Term, 1859, March and September Terms, 1860, Greene County Courthouse; Rice and Williams, *History of Greene County, Georgia*, pp. 456–59; Clayton Papers, Perkins Library, Special Collections, Duke University.

24. Rice and Williams, *History of Greene County, Georgia*, p. 191; Leaders' names are from *Transactions of the Southern Central Agricultural Society*. The term "organizational" leader seems more appropriate than the term "civic" leader in this study.

25. Greensboro *Weekly Gazette*, July 13, August 3, September 21, 1959; Greensboro *Planters' Weekly*, July 4, 1860.

26. Saye, *A Constitutional History of Georgia, 1732–1945*, pp. 474–75; *Ga. Code*, 1861, pt. 3, title 11, chap. 1, arts. 1 and 2, pp. 735–37.

27. Superior Court Proceedings, March and September Terms, 1860, Greene County Courthouse; Population and Slave schedules, 1860 Manuscript Census Returns, GDAH. The grand jury lists are the closest thing to Hunter's questionnaires about community leaders. See Hunter, *Community Power Structures*, pp. 262–71.

28. Population and Slave schedules, 1860 Manuscript Census Returns, GDAH. Fields, "The Nineteenth-Century American South," pp. 7–27, and Hahn, *The Roots of Southern Populism*, pp. 137–69, do an excellent job explaining the impact of market forces on the plantation South.

29. Woodward, *Tom Watson*, p. 110.

30. Woodman, *King Cotton and His Retainers*, pp. 32–42, 76–83, 132–75; Harris, *Plain Folk and Gentry in a Slave Society*, pp. 95–100.

31. Wyatt-Brown, *Southern Honor*, p. 345; Penfield *Temperance Banner*, April 21, 1855.

32. Population and Slave schedules, 1860 Manuscript Census Returns, GDAH. Interestingly, this ratio of 425 free people per lawyer is not much different from the 1990 ratio of about 385 people per lawyer in the United States. See Gerber, "Of Lawyers and Lawsuits," p. 33. Several men, including Dell Mann, who was the former editor of the Greensboro *Weekly Gazette*, James B. Park, and Professor Henry H. Tucker, were members of the bar but not actively practicing in 1860. William H. McWhorter practiced law in 1860, but he reported his occupation to the census as farmer. Tucker, Park, Mann, and McWhorter were not counted as part of the sample of lawyers.

33. Grice, *The Development of Georgia's Judicial System*, p. 350; Schott, *Alexander H. Stephens of Georgia*, pp. 24–27; John Paul Frank, *Lincoln as a Lawyer*, pp. 7–34.

34. Custer, "The Good Time is Coming," pp. 31–40; Schott, *Alexander H. Stephens of Georgia*, pp. 24–27.

35. Custer, "The Good Time is Coming," pp. 31–40; Boyd, *A Family History*, pp. 262–63, 310–12; *History of the Baptist Denomination in Georgia*, pp. 451–52.

36. Superior Court Proceedings, March and September Terms, 1859, 1860, 1861, Greene County Courthouse; Population schedule, 1860 Manuscript Census Returns, GDAH. Only six of these lawsuits were actual actions for "Debt," which required a sum certain could be proven from documentary evidence. These six cases involved promissory notes or bills. Most claims were simple "Complaints," reflecting the transitional nature of pleading at the time between formal common-law pleadings and code-influenced pleadings. These "Complaint" pleadings merely claimed damages as a result of the defendant's actions. Finally, more than a third of the cases were pled in "Assumpsit," based on oral or implied promises to pay. No formal contract existed in these cases, nor did the plaintiffs claim a sum certain. Rather, the jury determined the amount owed. The nature of the pleadings in these cases emphasizes the personal and informal nature of business relationships in the antebellum community.

37. Superior Court Proceedings, September Term, 1861, Greene County Courthouse; Greensboro *Weekly Gazette*, January 3, 1860. The case involving the slave, Kit, is the same case mentioned above in Chapter 2.

38. Wyatt-Brown, *Southern Honor*, pp. 345–46; Gordon S. Wood, *The Radicalism of the American Revolution*, pp. 67–68. Polanyi, in *The Great Transformation*, discusses the similar effects of the change to an industrial market economy, focusing on Great Britain. In his early work, Eugene Genovese characterized the slave South as "pre-capitalist." See Genovese, *The Political Economy of Slavery*, pp. 19–23. Planters and farmers, however, were very much capitalists, intent on reinvesting their profits in the means of production, slaves, and land. The terms "precommercial" or "undeveloped" are far more useful than "precapitalist" in describing the antebellum cotton South. The choice of action in

suits to collect debts, as discussed in note 36 above, reflects the precommercial nature of the economy.

39. Morris, in *Becoming Southern*, p. 19, argues that courts formalized what otherwise could be seen as an attack on personal honor; thus, honor was not involved in the collection of business debts. See also William C. Preston to George Ticknor, March 2, 1824, quoted in Burton, *In My Father's House are Many Mansions*, p. 21.

40. Goodrich, "Law and Language," pp. 173–206. See also Milovanovic, *A Primer in the Sociology of Law*, pp. 125–40.

41. Hurst, *The Growth of American Law*, and Horwitz, *The Transformation of American Law, 1780–1860*, both contain clear discussions of the impact of contract law on the American economy and legal profession. See also Gabel and Feinman, "Contract Law as Ideology," in David Kairy's *The Politics of Law*, pp. 172–84.

Chapter Four

1. Penfield *Temperance Banner*, March 24, 1855; Raper, *Tenants of the Almighty*, pp. 56–57. Riding Webster on the rail was not just harmless fun but caused great pain and could cause severe injury. The same is true of blacking with tar, which was hot and could burn the victim.

2. Darnton, *The Great Cat Massacre and Other Episodes in French Cultural History*; Geertz, *The Interpretation of Cultures*, pp. 412–53; Wyatt-Brown, *Southern Honor*, pp. 435–93. Perhaps the finest recent survey of literature on mob violence in the South can be found in Brundage, "Mob Violence, North and South, 1865–1940," and though focused on a later period, one of the best treatments of the subject is Brundage's superb *Lynching in the New South*.

3. Penfield *Temperance Banner*, March 24, 1855.

4. Greenesboro *Weekly Gazette*, November 23, 1859.

5. Greenesboro *Weekly Gazette*, November 23, 1859.

6. Penfield *Temperance Banner*, March 24, 1855; Raper, *Tenants of the Almighty*, pp. 56–57. See also Wyatt-Brown, *Southern Honor*, pp. 435–61. Channing, in *Crisis of Fear*, argues that South Carolina withdrew from the Union in the midst of growing fear about the effects of the events leading up to and including Lincoln's election, and this fear grew out of very real threats. Channing more accurately describes the responses of Greene County's leaders in the fall of 1860 than does Johnson, in *Toward a Patriarchal Republic*, who argues that secession also reflected an attempt by slaveholders to control a growing conflict with nonslaveowners in Georgia. Perhaps Johnson is right about the new state constitution that resulted from the succession movement, but such concerns were not apparent in Greene County before secession.

7. Edmund Ruffin, quoted in Wyatt-Brown, *Southern Honor*, p. 405; Thomas R. R. Cobb, *An Inquiry into the Law of Slavery in the United States of America*, pp. 82–85; Genovese, *Roll, Jordan, Roll*, pp. 587–657.

8. Oates, *To Purge This Land with Blood*, pp. 287–314; Greensboro *Weekly Gazette*, December 14, 1859.

9. Greensboro *Weekly Gazette*, November 2, 9, 16, 23, December 7, 1859; Grand Jury Presentments, Superior Court Proceedings, September Term 1860, Greene County Courthouse.

10. Greensboro *Weekly Gazette*, November 7, December 7, 14, 1859; Foner, *Free Soil, Free Labor, Free Men*.

11. Paludan, *A People's Contest*, pp. xiii–31; Foner, *Politics and Ideology in the Age of the Civil War*, pp. 3–93.

12. Shelton P. Sanford Papers, Woodruff Library, Special Collections, Emory University.

13. Greensboro *Planters' Weekly*, November 7, 14, 1860. Greene's voters cast 528 votes for Bell, 145 votes for Douglas, and 108 votes for Breckenridge.

14. Greensboro *Planters' Weekly*, November 7, 14, 21, 1860; Shelton P. Sanford Papers, Woodruff Library, Special Collections, Emory University. At the same time, Georgia's legislature was caught up in debate over the issue of secession. See Freehling and Simpson, *Secession Debated*, for the main arguments made in the legislature.

15. Greensboro *Planters' Weekly*, November 21, 1860.

16. Ibid.; Shelton P. Sanford, Woodruff Library, Special Collections, Emory University. See Harris, *Plain Folk and Gentry in a Slave Society*, for an analysis of the ritualistic symbolism of "mass meetings," especially pp. 112–22.

17. Greensboro *Planters' Weekly*, November 28, December 12, 19, 1860; Georgia General Assembly, *Georgia House Journal*, 1860, pp. 106–7. Freehling and Simpson, *Secession Debated*, contains the full text of the speeches and public letters of the legislative debate in November 1860 that led to the calling of the Secession Convention, materials that are not part of the *House Journal*.

18. Bensel, *Yankee Leviathan*, p. 11; Greensboro *Planters' Weekly*, March 21, 1860; Freehling and Simpson, *Secession Debated*, p. 40.

19. U.S. Census Bureau, *Seventh Census of the United States, 1850*, pp. 377–81; U.S. Census Bureau, *Agriculture of the United States in 1860*, pp. 22–25.

20. U.S. Census Bureau, *Statistics of the United States in 1860*, p. 298; U.S. Census Bureau, *Agriculture of the United States in 1860*, p. 22; Greensboro *Planters' Weekly*, September 5, 1860; Wright, *The Political Economy of the Cotton South*, p.35.

21. Population and Slave schedules, 1860 Manuscript Census Returns, GDAH; Greensboro *Weekly Gazette*, December 7, 1859, March 7, 1860; Greensboro *Planters' Weekly*, April 11, September 5, 1860.

22. The best analysis of this argument can be found in Wright, *The Political Economy of the Cotton South*, pp. 128–57.

23. Greensboro *Planters' Weekly*, April 18, November 21, December 12, 1860. The correspondent probably based his argument on an article in the *Charleston Mercury*, October 11, 1860.

24. See Wyatt-Brown, *Southern Honor*, and Fox-Genovese, *Within the Plantation Household*, especially pp. 37–145.

25. Greenesboro *Planters' Weekly*, December 12, 1860. See Chapter 1 on the ideological structures of the slave society. Also see Genovese, *The Political Economy of Slavery*, especially pp. 243 – 320.

26. Greenesboro *Planters' Weekly*, December 19, 1860; Population, Slave, and Agricultural schedules, 1860 Manuscript Census Returns, GDAH. Delegates to the Secession Convention felt a similar need for unity, so even those who opposed secession signed the ordinance.

27. Shelton P. Sanford Papers, Woodruff Library, Special Collections, Emory University. The Dawson Grays honored William C. Dawson (1798 – 1856), a leading lawyer, judge, and U.S. senator from Greene County.

28. Shelton P. Sanford Papers, Woodruff Library, Special Collections, Emory University; Rawick, *The American Slave* 12: 49 – 59, 252 – 64.

29. Shelton P. Sanford Papers, Woodruff Library, Special Collections, Emory University; Greenesboro *Planters' Weekly*, January 9, 1861.

30. Wooster, "The Georgia Secession Convention," pp. 28, 29; Phillips, in *Georgia and State Rights*, and Johnson, in *Toward a Patriarchal Republic*, both present excellent discussions of these factions at the convention. Of course, there was little chance the Lincoln administration would accept these demands.

31. Wooster, "The Georgia Secession Convention," p. 45.

32. Shelton P. Sanford Papers, Woodruff Library, Special Collections, Emory University.

33. Captain Shelton P. Sanford to Governor Joseph Brown, March 27, 1861, Governors' Incoming Correspondence, GDAH; Rice and Williams, *History of Greene County, Georgia*, pp. 400 – 405; Inferior Court Minutes, April 26, 1861, Greene County Courthouse. Sanford clearly had a public and a private side. While the public side required him to prepare the young men under his charge for war, the private side feared what that war would mean.

34. Shelton P. Sanford Papers, Woodruff Library, Special Collections, Emory University. The best treatment of the growth of Confederate nationalism can be found in Thomas, *The Confederate Nation, 1861 – 1865*.

35. Shelton P. Sanford Papers, Woodruff Library, Special Collections, Emory University; Shelton P. Sanford and J. E. Willet to Gov. Brown, October 10, 1861, Governors' Incoming Correspondence, GDAH.

36. Shelton P. Sanford Papers, Woodruff Library, Special Collections, Emory University; E. P. Thompson, *The Making of the English Working Class*, Thomas, *The Confederate Nation, 1861 – 1865*, and Faust, *The Creation of Confederate Nationalism* best discuss the formation of class and national identities.

37. Shelton P. Sanford Papers, Woodruff Library, Special Collections, Emory University; R. H. L. Clack to James J. Clack, April 16, 1861, quoted in King, *Sound of Drums*, p. 400; Augusta *Daily Chronicle and Sentinel*, October 16, 1861.

38. Shelton P. Sanford Papers, Woodruff Library, Special Collections, Emory University.

39. Greenesboro *Planters' Weekly*, June 5, 1861. The Stephens Light Guards were named for Alexander Stephens, the vice president of the Confederacy.

40. Greenesboro *Planters' Weekly*, June 5, 1861; Shelton P. Sanford Papers, Woodruff Library, Special Collections, Emory University.

41. Greenesboro *Planters' Weekly*, June 5, 1861; Shelton P. Sanford Papers, Woodruff Library, Special Collections, Emory University. Annotated Muster Role of the Greene Rifles, Civil War Collection, Greene County Historical Society Museum; Henderson, *Roster of the Confederate Soldiers of Georgia, 1861–1865*, 4:837.

42. Raper, *Tenants of the Almighty*, p. 68; Augusta *Weekly Chronicle and Sentinel*, October 16, 1861.

43. Reed Collection, Alabama Department of Archives; G. C. Butler to My Dear Sister, July 28, 1861, quoted in Raper, *Tenants of the Almighty*, p. 65. John C. Reid changed the spelling of his name to "Reed" when he moved to Atlanta in 1882, and he wrote under the second spelling.

44. Reed Collection, Alabama Department of Archives; Shelton P. Sanford Papers, Woodruff Library, Special Collections, Emory University; Augusta *Weekly Chronicle and Sentinel*, October 16, 1861.

Chapter Five

1. Carole E. Scott, "Coping with Inflation," pp. 537, 541; Augusta *Daily Chronicle and Sentinel*, April 4, 1863; Jean E. Friedman, *The Enclosed Garden*, p. 103.

2. Augusta *Daily Chronicle and Sentinel*, April 4, 1863.

3. The best account of this process can be found in Thomas, *The Confederate Nation, 1861–1865*. See also McPherson, *Battle Cry of Freedom*, pp. 428–42, and Beringer, Hattaway, Jones, and Still, *Why the South Lost the Civil War*, pp. 4–63, 203–35.

4. McPherson, *Battle Cry of Freedom*, pp. 437–53; Todd, *Confederate Finance*.

5. Grand Jury Presentments and *The State v. Walter Buckner et al.*, Superior Court Proceedings, September Term, 1861, Greene County Courthouse; Shelton P. Sanford Papers, Woodruff Library, Special Collections, Emory University.

6. Shelton P. Sanford Papers, Woodruff Library, Special Collections, Emory University.

7. Grand Jury Presentments, *The State v. Thomas N. Poullain*, and *The State v. Henry Atwood and Jacob Rokenbaugh*, Superior Court Proceedings, March Term, 1862, Greene County Courthouse; 1860 Manuscript Census Returns, GDAH. The grand jury's indictment also reflected precommercial assumptions about the nature of contractual relations. See Horwitz, *Transformation of American Law, 1780–1860*, and Hall, *The Magic Mirror*, pp. 119–23.

8. Superior Court Proceedings, September Term, 1862, Greene County Courthouse.

9. Grand Jury Presentments, Superior Court Proceedings, September Term, 1862, and Superior Court Minutes, March Term, 1863, Greene County Courthouse; Population schedules, 1860 Manuscript Census Returns, GDAH.

10. Augusta *Daily Chronicle and Sentinel*, December 7, 1861, April 20, 1862; Augusta *Constitutionalist*, December 8, 1861.

11. Athens *Southern Cultivator* 19 (July 1861), p. 201, and (August 1861), p. 242.

12. "Public Meeting in Greenesboro. All Corn—No Cotton to be Planted," handbill, March 15, 1862, Civil War Collection, Greene County Historical Society Museum; Augusta *Constitutionalist*, March 19, 1862.

13. "Public Meeting in Greenesboro. All Corn—No Cotton to be Planted," handbill, March 15, 1862, Civil War Collection, Greene County Historical Society Museum; Augusta *Constitutionalist*, March 19, 1862.

14. Coulter, "The Movement for Agricultural Reorganization in the Cotton South During the Civil War," pp. 3–5; Robertson, *The Diary of Dolly Lunt Burge*, May 6, 1862; Georgia Comptroller General, *Annual Report*, 1862, pp. 23–35.

15. Athens *Southern Cultivator* 19 (September 1861), p. 264.

16. Georgia, *Confederate Records of the State of Georgia*, 2:267–69, 367–70, 505–7; Thomas, *Confederate Nation, 1861–1865*, pp. 150–54, 196–98; Augusta *Constitutionalist*, October 23, 1863.

17. Thomas, *Confederate Nation, 1861–1865*, pp. 208–16; Sellers and Smith, *American Percussion Revolvers*, pp. 43–44.

18. Augusta *Daily Chronicle and Sentinel*, July 31, 1863; Tax Statement, December 6, 1864, Barrow Papers, Hargrett Library, University of Georgia Libraries; Joseph J. Printup to Dear Brother, February 14, 1864, Printup Papers, Perkins Library, Special Collections, Duke University.

19. Augusta *Weekly Chronicle and Sentinel*, October 16, 1861.

20. Ibid., October 16, 1861, January 1, 1863; 1860 Manuscript Census Returns, GDAH; Raper, *Tenants of the Almighty*, p. 67; Rice and Williams, *History of Greene County, Georgia*, pp. 415–17.

21. Augusta *Weekly Chronicle and Sentinel*, October 16, 1861; Nep to Shep, October 14, 1861, Shep to Nep, November 19, 1861, March 28, 1862, Pryor Collection, Hargrett Library, University of Georgia Libraries. The Pryors farmed in Sumter County, Georgia, but men and women across the state struggled with similar problems. Anne Scott, in *The Southern Lady*, pp. 80–133, argues that women's new responsibilities changed their role in southern society. Jean E. Friedman, in *The Enclosed Garden*, pp. 92–130, however, has argued convincingly that although women took up new activities during the war, basically unchanged family, church, and community structures pushed women back into their former roles after the war.

22. Rice and Williams, *History of Greene County, Georgia*, p. 445.

23. Raper, *Tenants of the Almighty*, pp. 66–68; Wayside Home Register, Southern Historical Collection, University of North Carolina.

24. Augusta *Daily Chronicle and Sentinel*, January 1, 1863.

25. Ibid., January 1, 1863, February 18, April 1, 1863; Royster, *The Destructive War*, pp. 86–87.

26. Augusta *Constitutionalist*, May 14, 1863; Raper, *Tenants of the Almighty*, p. 66; Rice and Williams, *History of Greene County, Georgia*, pp. 228–29;

Augusta *Weekly Chronicle and Sentinel*, October 16, 1861; Grave markers, John McKinley Howell and Emma Berrien Heard Howell, White Plains Cemetery, White Plains, Georgia.

27. A. B. Pickett to My Dear Cousin, June 24, 1864, Printup Papers, Perkins Library, Special Collections, Duke University.

28. Rawick, *The American Slave*, 12:108. Dosia said that her master, Samuel Davis, died during the war, but Samuel Davis actually lived until 1875. Mary Davis died in 1866, so almost certainly the events recalled occurred during the war. Samuel Davis and Mary A. Davis tombstone, Greensboro Cemetery, Greene County, Georgia.

29. Burr, *The Secret Eye*, pp. 226–27. Fox-Genovese, in *Within the Plantation Household*, presents a far more convincing picture of planter class women than does Clinton in *The Plantation Mistress*.

30. Faust, "Altars of Sacrifice," pp. 1200–1228; Augusta *Daily Chronicle and Sentinel*, March 11, April 1, 1863; Turnwold *Countryman*, March 18, 1862.

31. Raper, *Tenants of the Almighty*, p. 67; Burr, *The Secret Eye*, pp. 218, 243.

32. Johnny and Jodie to My Dear Pa, April 4, 1864, Printup Papers, Perkins Library, Special Collections, Duke University; Burr, *The Secret Eye*, p. 240.

33. M. E. Tidwell to George S. Tunnell, August 13, 1862, Tunnell Papers, GDAH.

34. Raper, *Tenants of the Almighty*, p. 64; The number of military-age males was determined from the 1860 Manuscript Census Returns, GDAH. Ages thirteen to forty-five were counted because the final Confederate Conscription Act of February 17, 1864, called up all men from the age of seventeen to fifty, and those individuals would have been thirteen to forty-five in 1860. See Beringer, Hattaway, Jones, and Still, *Why the South Lost the Civil War*, p. 453; List of Confederate Military Units from Greene County, Georgia, Confederate Military Units File, GDAH. The two new companies were Company D, Second Battalion, Georgia State Troops and Company E, Third Regiment, Georgia State Troops. Both units disbanded in April 1862, and most of the men then served in other units.

35. Shelton P. Sanford Papers, Woodruff Library, Special Collections, Emory University; Henderson, *Roster of the Confederate Soldiers of Georgia, 1861–1865*, 4:828–38; Raper, *Tenants of the Almighty*, p. 64.

36. Confederate Service Records, Phillip B. Robinson and Robert L. McWhorter, GDAH.

37. Henderson, *Roster of the Confederate Soldiers of Georgia, 1861–1865*, 5:743–55; Printup Papers, Perkins Library, Special Collections, Duke University.

38. List of Confederate Military Units from Greene County, Georgia, Confederate Military Units File, GDAH; compilation of sample done from service records in Henderson, *Roster of the Confederate Soldiers of Georgia, 1861–1865*, 1:457–66, 980–86, 4:828–38, 5:743–55.

39. Compilation of sample done from service records in Henderson, *Roster of the Confederate Soldiers of Georgia*, cited in Note 38 above.

40. Shelton P. Sanford Papers, Woodruff Library, Special Collections, Emory University.

41. Reed Journal, pp. 128–31, Reed Collection, Alabama Department of Archives. Reid changed the spelling of his name to "Reed" when he moved to Atlanta in 1882.

42. See Dean, "'We Will All Be Lost and Destroyed,'" pp. 138–53. The experience of these men in war perhaps explains something of the later organization and conduct of the Ku Klux Klan.

43. Reed Collection, Alabama Department of Archives; Rawick, *The American Slave*, 12:107–8.

44. For the changing nature of slavery in Georgia during the Civil War, see Mohr, *On the Threshold of Freedom*; Drago, "How Sherman's March through Georgia Affected the Slaves," pp. 361–75; and Escott, "The Context of Freedom," pp. 79–104.

45. Mohr, *On the Threshold of Freedom*, pp. 136–42; Grand Jury Presentments, Superior Court Proceedings, September 1863, Greene County Courthouse.

46. Linton Stephens to Alexander H. Stephens, September 6, 1863, quoted in Bryan, *Confederate Georgia*, p. 125; Waddell, *Biographical Sketch of Linton Stephens*, p. 263; Shivers, *The Land Between*, pp. 160–61; Augusta *Constitutionalist*, October 8, 1863; Milledgeville *Southern Recorder*, October 6, 1863.

47. *History of the Baptist Denomination in Georgia*, pp. 260–68; Mohr, *On the Threshold of Freedom*, pp. 247–56. Interestingly, Crawford did not see a contradiction between the status of slaves and their being brothers and sisters in Christ.

48. Population and Slave schedules, 1860 Manuscript Census Returns, GDAH; "Historical Data," Springfield Baptist Church Collection (private collection). Of the four church founders, only Jack Terrell can be identified. Terrell hired his own time from his master and traveled Greene County working as a blacksmith. See above, Chapter 2.

49. J. J. Printup to Daniel S. Printup, May 10, 1864, Printup Papers, Perkins Library, Special Collections, Duke University.

Chapter Six

1. Sherman, *Memoirs of General W. T. Sherman*, pp. 655–56.

2. Drago, "How Sherman's March through Georgia Affected the Slaves," p. 369. For Sherman's attitudes toward the slaves in Georgia, see Sherman, *Memoirs of General W. T. Sherman*, pp. 646–74, and Mohr, *On the Threshold of Freedom*, pp. 86–96.

3. Sherman, *Memoirs of General W. T. Sherman*, p. 657.

4. U.S. War Department, *The War of the Rebellion*, Ser. 1, vol. 44, pp. 866–73.

5. Ibid., pp. 269–71; Raper, *Tenants of the Almighty*, p. 70.

6. Paul Scott, "On the Road to the Sea," pp. 26–29.

7. Turnwold *Countryman*, November 29, December 6, 1864.

8. Rice and Williams, *History of Greene County, Georgia*, p. 425; Rawick, *The American Slave*, 12:109; Robertson, *The Diary of Dolly Lunt Burge*, pp. 101–8.

9. Rawick, *The American Slave*, 12:54, 13:101; Turnwold *Countryman*, December 6, 1864, January 10, 1865.

10. Paul Scott, "On the Road to the Sea," pp. 26–29; Turnwold *Countryman*, December 6, 13, 20, 1864.

11. Turnwold *Countryman*, December 6, 13, 20, 1864, January 10, 24, 1865; The U.S. War Department, *The War of the Rebellion*, series 1, vol. 44, pp. 269–71.

12. Turnwold *Countryman*, February 7, May 30, 1865.

13. Augusta *Daily Chronicle and Sentinel*, January 10, March 22, April 25, 1865.

14. Raper, *Tenants of the Almighty*, pp. 72, 73.

15. Rawick, *The American Slave*, 12:55, 101, 13:262.

16. William C. Davis, *Jefferson Davis, the Man and His Hour*, pp. 630–35; Rice and Williams, *History of Greene County, Georgia*, pp. 164, 435; Eliza Frances Andrews, *The War-Time Journal of a Georgia Girl, 1864–1865*, pp. 226, 254–55, 262, 263. Concrete information about events in Greene County during this crucial period is scarce, and most accounts, especially Rice and Williams's, consist of rumors and racist speculations. Military records in the National Archives in Washington, D.C. (RG 393) mention nothing of events during May 1865 in Greene County.

17. 175 N.Y. Vol. Regimental Order Book, June 7, 26, August 24, September 22, 1865. Records of the United States Army Continental Command, Record Group 393, National Archives, Washington D.C. Hereafter cited as RG 393, NA.

18. 175 N.Y. Vol. Description Book, Order Book Company A, Company B, Company C, Consolidated Morning Report and Letter Book, July 5, 1864–December 8, 1865, RG 393, NA.

19. 175 N.Y. Vol. Regimental Order Book, June 16, August 24, 30, 1865, RG 393, NA.

20. Rawick, *The American Slave*, 12:55, 112, 13:101.

21. Eliza Frances Andrews, *War-Time Journal of a Georgia Girl, 1864–1865*, p. 252; Cotterrell, "Jurisprudence and the Sociology of Law," pp. 26, 27; Bertrand Russell, *Power*, p. 38.

22. Augusta *Daily Chronicle and Sentinel*, May 27, 1865. Eugene Genovese brilliantly portrays the paternalistic relationship of master and slave in his *Roll, Jordan, Roll*. Roark, in *Masters without Slaves*, pp. 111–55, provides an overview of this transition period. Foner, in *Free Soil, Free Labor, Free Men*, pp. 11–74, paints an excellent picture of free labor assumptions and beliefs, as well as free labor politicians' critique of the slave South.

23. Augusta *Daily Chronicle and Sentinel*, May 28, 1865; John Bryant to Emma Bryant, May 29, 1865, Bryant Papers, Perkins Library, Special Collections, Duke University.

24. Rawick, *The American Slave*, 12:55.

25. Augusta *Daily Chronicle and Sentinel,* June 11, 1865; James Oakes, "A Failure of Vision," pp. 66–67; McFeely, *Yankee Stepfather.*

26. Turnwold *Countryman,* May 23, 30, June 13, 1865.

27. Roark, *Masters without Slaves,* pp. 94–95.

28. Burton, in "The Rise and Fall of Afro-American Town Life," convincingly explains why freedpeople were drawn to the towns.

29. Sidney Andrews, *The South Since the War,* pp. 352–53.

30. Raper, *Tenants of the Almighty,* p. 72.

31. Ibid., pp. 369–70.

32. Rawick, *The American Slave,* 12:55. Isaiah Green's stepfather probably suffered from epilepsy.

33. County Court Proceedings, July and September Terms, 1866, Greene County Courthouse.

34. Currie-McDaniel, *Carpetbagger of Conscience,* pp. 51–53; Augusta *Daily Chronicle and Sentinel,* May 21, June 1, 1865.

35. Avery, *The History of the State of Georgia from 1850 to 1881,* p. 343.

36. Augusta *Colored American,* December 30, 1865, January 6, 1866; *Proceedings of the Freedmen's Convention of Georgia, Assembled at Augusta, January 10, 1866,* pp. 3–7. Hereafter cited as *Proceedings, January 1866.* Charles Martin had been the slave of Dr. Floyd Martin of Penfield; Abram Colby, the son of planter John Colby, had lived independently as a barber since his father's death in 1850, though at law he was a slave.

37. Cimbala, "The 'Talisman Power,'" pp. 153–71; Conway, *The Reconstruction of Georgia,* pp. 76–78; Bentley, *A History of the Freedmen's Bureau,* p. 129.

38. Cimbala, "The 'Talisman Power,'" pp. 153–71; Bentley, *A History of the Freedmen's Bureau,* pp. 84, 129; Davis Tillson to Gov. Jenkins, February 3, 1866, Georgia Governors' Incoming Correspondence, GDAH.

39. *Proceedings, January 1866,* pp. 9–14. Over time, General Tillson's views changed, and he became convinced that white conservatives bore more responsibility for the problems of free labor than the freedmen. This change came too late, however, to materially help the freedpeople, for Tillson left the bureau soon after.

40. *Proceedings, January 1866,* p. 11.

41. Ibid., pp. 11, 15–17.

42. Ibid., pp. 18–20, 28–30, 32, 36. The freedmen clearly spoke in terms of an egalitarian constitution, using what Donald G. Nieman calls "the language of liberation." See Nieman, "The Language of Liberation," pp. 67–90. The Georgia Equal Rights Association was apparently a completely independent organization with no ties to the American Equal Rights Association formed in 1866 by women's rights advocates and abolitionists. The GERA never advocated equal rights or the vote for women; they focused on equal rights for black men.

43. *Proceedings, January 1866,* pp. 18–20.

44. Georgia, *Ga. Code,* 1867, pp. 14–15, 331–35.

45. See Georgia General Assembly, *Acts of the General Assembly of the State of Georgia,* 1865–66 and 1866. Hereafter cited as *Georgia Laws.*

46. Georgia General Assembly, *Georgia Laws*, 1865–66, pp. 64–71, 153–54, 234–36, 239–41.

47. Willis Willingham to D. Tillson, January 22, 1866, F. J. Robinson to D. Tillson, February 4, 1866, Records of the Assistant Commissioner for the State of Georgia, Bureau of Refugees, Freedmen, and Abandoned Lands, 1865–1869, Microfilm Publication M-798, National Archives. Hereafter cited as BRFAL-Ga.

48. Augusta *Weekly Chronicle and Sentinel*, May 2, 1866; Willis Willingham to D. Tillson, January 22, 1866, F. J. Robinson to D. Tillson, February 4, 1866, Jonathan T. Dawson to Assistant Commissioner, February 23, 1866, BRFAL-Ga.

49. Jonathan T. Dawson to Assistant Commissioner, February 23, 1866, Gen. Tillson to Bvt. Major Gen. Brannon, March 5, 1866, BRFAL-Ga; Raper, *Tenants of the Almighty*, pp. 77–79; James Davison to Capt. W. W. Deane, Woodville, Ga., June 29, 1866, BRFAL-Ga. See also Edward L. Ayers, *Vengeance and Justice*, p. 153. There are no records explaining exactly how the strike was resolved; presumably, freedpeople and landowners worked out compromise arrangements individually, and those arrangements varied.

50. R. H. Gladding to Gov. Bullock, November 29, 1869, Georgia Governors' Papers, GDAH; *Convention of Georgia Equal Rights and Educational Association*, p. 8. See Chapter 2 for more information on Abram Colby's life.

51. Abramham Colby to Mr. G. L. Eberhart, March 1, 1866, Greensboro Labor Contracts, Entry 886, Records of the Bureau of Refugees, Freedmen, and Abandoned Lands, Records Group 105, National Archives. Hereafter cited as RG 105, NA.

52. Drago, *Black Politicians and Reconstruction in Georgia*, p. 26.

53. Cimbala, "The 'Talisman Power,'" p. 169; Heard Papers, Perkins Library, Special Collections, Duke University; Confederate Military Units File, GDAH; County Court Minutes, June Term, 1866, Greene County Courthouse.

54. County Court Minutes, June–December Terms, 1866, Greene County Courthouse. The county court held a term every month, beginning in June 1866.

55. County Court Minutes, June–December Terms, 1866, Greene County Courthouse; Quinney, "The Ideology of Law," pp. 39–71.

56. Abram Colby et al. to Davis Tillson, August 3, 1866, BRFAL-Ga.

57. Bentley, *A History of the Freedmen's Bureau*, pp. 129, 157; Joseph Williams et al. to Col. C. C. Sibley, June 17, 1867, BRFAL-Ga.

58. Augusta *Weekly Chronicle and Sentinel*, May 30, July 4, September 3, 1866.

Chapter Seven

1. Reed Collection, Alabama Department of Archives. When Reid moved to Atlanta in 1882 he changed the spelling of his name to "Reed."

2. Augusta *Daily Chronicle and Sentinel*, November 1, 17, December 13, 1865.

3. Superior Court Proceedings, September Term, 1866, Greene County

Courthouse; Columbus Heard to John D. Wzlu, July 13, 1866, Heard Papers, Perkins Library, Special Collections, Duke University.

4. *Proceedings, January 1866*, p. 17; *KKK Testimony*, 1:701; McFeely, *Yankee Stepfather*, pp. 149–65. See Chapter 6 for a discussion of contracts, courts, and the failure of the Freedmen's Bureau. The Georgia Equal Rights Association was not formally aligned with the American Equal Rights Association, which promoted both black civil rights and women's voting rights.

5. Augusta *Weekly Chronicle and Sentinel*, May 2, 1866, May 16, 1867.

6. For discussions of the freedpeople's desire for independence, see Flynn, *White Land, Black Labor*, pp. 57–83. See also Foner, *Nothing But Freedom*; Lanza, *Agrarianism and Reconstruction Politics*, pp. 72–94; Litwack, *Been in the Storm so Long*; and Magdol, *A Right to the Land*.

7. Conway, *The Reconstruction of Georgia*, p. 78; Cimbala, "The 'Talisman Power,'" p. 171; Greensboro and Crawfordville, Georgia, Letters Sent, April 31 [sic], 1867–April 30, 1868, Entry 845, and Greensboro, Georgia, Letters Received, April 10, June 29, 1867, Entry 847; all in RG 105, NA.

8. Joseph Williams et al. to Col. C. C. Sibley, June 17, 1867, BRFAL-Ga.; Woodville, Georgia, Letters Sent and Received, September 18, 30, 1867, January 6, February 24, July 27, 1868, Entry 1059, RG 105, NA.

9. Woodville, Georgia, Letters Sent and Received, September 8, October 17, 1867, Entry 1059, and John H. Sullivan to Lt. H. Cathey, June 1, 1868, Greensboro, Georgia, Letters Sent, Entry 845, both in RG 105, NA.

10. John H. Sullivan to Lt. H. Cathey, June 1, 3, 4, 10, 22, 1868, Greensboro, Georgia, Letters Sent, Entry 845, RG 105, NA.

11. Oaks, "A Failure of Vision," pp. 66–76; McFeely, *Yankee Stepfather*, pp. 288–328.

12. Stanley, "Beggars Can't Be Choosers," pp. 1265–93.

13. *Proceedings of the Convention of Georgia Equal Rights and Educational Association*.

14. Georgia General Assembly, *Georgia Senate Journal*, 1866, p. 71, and *Georgia House Journal*, 1866, pp. 68–70; Conway, *The Reconstruction of Georgia*, p. 142; Coleman, *A History of Georgia*, pp. 210–11.

15. Cobb, *An Inquiry into the Law of Slavery*; Fields, "Ideology and Race in American History"; Wallerstein, *The Capitalist World Economy*, pp. 165–230; *Herald*, July 6, August 10, 1867.

16. *Herald*, August 24, 1867; Augusta *Loyal Georgian*, August 24, 1867.

17. *Herald*, August 24, September 7, 1867.

18. *Herald*, July 20, October 12, 1867.

19. Conway, *The Reconstruction of Georgia*, p. 148; *Herald*, July 20, October 12, November 2, 1867. As there were only 93,457 black men registered to vote in Georgia, at least 12,953 of the 95,214 registered white voters must have taken part in the election.

20. *Herald*, November 9, 16, December 14, 1867; Population schedule, 1860 Manuscript Census Returns, GDAH; Isaac A. Hall to Prov. Gov. Ruger, June 3, 1868, Governor's Incoming Correspondence, GDAH.

21. *Herald,* December 14, 1867.

22. *Herald,* February 27, 1868.

23. Ibid.; Wills, *A Battle from the Start,* p. 336; Deaton, "Violent Redemption," pp. 10–12, 26.

24. Reed, "What I Know of the Ku Klux Klan," *Uncle Remus Home Magazine,* January 1908, pp. 24–26.

25. Reed, "What I Know of the Ku Klux Klan," *Uncle Remus Home Magazine,* January 1908, pp. 24–26, April 1908, p. 19; *KKK Testimony,* 1:696, 697. See Trelease, *White Terror,* for a detailed account of Klan methods. John C. Reed believed his work in the Klan was far more important and meaningful than his service during the Civil War. See Reed, *The Brother's War,* for a detailed discussion of his beliefs.

26. Reed, "What I Know of the Ku Klux Klan," *Uncle Remus Home Magazine,* January 1908, pp. 24–26; *KKK Testimony,* 1:696–97; *Herald,* March 28, October 22, 1868.

27. *KKK Testimony,* 1:696–97; *Herald,* March 28, October 22, 1868. William H. Branch, whose father, John Branch, was known as the meanest slave owner in Greene County, also fit the profile, except that William had lost an arm during the war. A one-armed man commanding the Klan would have been far too easy to identify, so Branch probably had little active connection with the Klan.

28. Thaddeus Brockett Rice Collection, GDAH; Rice and Williams, *History of Greene County, Georgia,* p. 428; *Herald,* October 8, 1868. Rice's list of Klansmen may have been fabricated, but revealingly, it included all of the members of militia district Democratic Club committees in Greene County; see *Herald,* July 16, 1868. The Democratic Club seems to have been the public wing of the Ku Klux Klan, and like the Klan, was organized by militia district in Georgia.

29. Population and Slave schedules, 1860 Manuscript Census Returns, GDAH; *Herald,* March 26, May 14, 1868; Atlanta *Weekly New Era,* January 20, 1870.

30. Population and Slave schedules, 1860 Manuscript Census Returns, GDAH; St. Clair–Abrams, *Manual and Biographic Register of the State of Georgia, 1871–72,* pp. 22–23; Georgia General Assembly, *Georgia's General Assembly of 1880–81,* pp. 77–80. See Chapter 3 for a fuller discussion of Robert L. McWhorter's background.

31. St. Clair–Abrams, *Manual and Biographic Register of the State of Georgia, 1871–72,* pp. 22–23; *Herald,* March 26, May 14, 1868.

32. St. Clair–Abrams, *Manual and Biographic Register of the State of Georgia, 1871–72,* pp. 22–23; Georgia General Assembly, *Georgia's General Assembly of 1880–81,* pp. 77–80; *Herald,* March 26, May 14, 1868. The full text of the 1868 Georgia Constitution can be found in *Ga. Code,* 1873.

33. *Herald,* April 2, 23, 30, May 14, 1868; Deaton, "Violent Redemption," p. 33; Conway, *The Reconstruction of Georgia,* pp. 160–61.

34. Superior Court Proceedings, September Term, 1868, Greene County Courthouse; *KKK Testimony,* 1:696; Ragsdale, *Mercer University,* pp. 316–17; *Herald,* May 14, 1868.

35. *Georgia House Journal*, 1868, pp. 7–13.

36. *Georgia House Journal*, 1868, pp. 7–13, 49–52, 93, 201, 218.

37. *Herald*, August 27, 1868; Drago, *Black Politicians and Reconstruction in Georgia*, p. 49; *Georgia House Journal*, 1868, p. 224.

38. Redkey, *Respect Black*, pp. 15, 27; Currie-McDaniel, *Carpetbagger of Conscience*, p. 95.

39. *Herald*, September 17, 1868; Drago, *Black Politicians and Reconstruction in Georgia*, p. 53.

40. *Herald*, August 26, 1868.

41. "Philip Baldwin Robinson," in *History of the Baptist Denomination in Georgia*, pp. 451–52. In 1992, jurors' ideological assumptions still greatly controlled the actions of courts, as demonstrated by the police brutality case involving Rodney King in California.

42. Alfred H. Terry to Sherman, June 20, 1870, quoted in Drago, *Black Politicians and Reconstruction in Georgia*, p. 96.

43. Superior Court Proceedings, September Term, 1869, and District Court Proceedings, 19th Senatorial District, 1868–71, both in the Greene County Courthouse. See also Superior Court Proceedings for 1868, 1869, 1870, 1871, and 1872 for cases involving black people. Interestingly, Miles W. Lewis seemed to be the attorney of choice for Greene County's freedpeople.

44. Bartley, *The Creation of Modern Georgia*, p. 62; Joe McWhorter to John J. Knox, November 1, 1868, John H. Sullivan to J. H. Cathey, October 29, 1868, Governors' Incoming Correspondence, GDAH; *Herald*, September 17, October 22, 29, 1868.

45. Superior Court Proceedings, March and September Terms, 1868, March Term, 1869, Greene County Courthouse; U.S. Congress, *The Condition of Affairs in Georgia: Statement of Hon. Nelson Tift to the Reconstruction Committee of the House of Representatives, Washington, February 18, 1869*, p. 138; Sullivan to Lt. Cathey, October 31, 1868, Greensboro, Georgia, Letters Sent, Entry 845, RG 105, NA; *KKK Testimony*, 1:698–99.

46. Deaton, "Violent Redemption," pp. 38–40; *Herald*, November 5, 1868. See Reed, "What I Know of the Ku Klux Klan," January 1908, for an account of how the Klan controlled the polls in Oglethorpe County and prevented black voters from casting ballots there.

47. *Herald*, December 3, 1868; John H. Sullivan to J. H. Cathey, October 29, 1868, Governors' Incoming Correspondence, GDAH.

Chapter Eight

1. R. C. Anthony to Frank Gallagher, October 12, 1868, Governors' Incoming Correspondence, GDAH.

2. D. A. Newsom to R. B. Bullock, July 24, 1869; D. A. Newsom to Rufus Bullock, August 27, 1869, Governor's Incoming Correspondence, GDAH.

3. Lumpkin, *The Making of a Southerner*, pp. 86–92.

4. *KKK Testimony*, 1:797–800; John Sullivan to E. A. Ware, April 13, 1868, Greensboro, Georgia, Letters Sent, Entry 845, RG 105, NA; Rawick, *The American Slave*, 13:102.

5. Rawick, *The American Slave*, 12:54, 262, 13:102. Isaiah Greene explained that the money came from a mail wagon that had been covered by the mud of the creek. Greene County, however, abounds with legends about the lost Confederate treasury, which was last seen in Washington, Georgia. Many people believe that Confederate soldiers buried much of the money along the Oconee River in Greene County. Mr. E. H. Armor of Greensboro told me a variation of Isaiah Greene's story that involved freedmen finding part of the buried Confederate treasury. Perhaps this story helps explain the Klan's diligent punishment of Isaiah Greene's uncle and others who found the money. If such treasure was buried along the Oconee, today it would lie under the waters of Lake Oconee.

6. Abram Colby to R. B. Bullock, August 23, 1869, Governors' Incoming Correspondence, GDAH.

7. R. H. Gladding to R. B. Bullock, September 22, 1869, Governors' Incoming Correspondence, GDAH; Lumpkin, *The Making of a Southerner*, pp. 85–86.

8. *KKK Testimony*, 2:1111–19.

9. Ibid., 1111–13; *Herald*, September 16, November 4, 1869; Shivers, *The Land Between*, pp. 180–81; Affidavit of Jordan Williams, August 25, 1869, Governors' Incoming Correspondence, GDAH.

10. *KKK Testimony*, 1:696–705.

11. Ibid., 2:1113, 1114. Most probably Colby's brother Chapman met Hoyt's patrol.

12. D. A. Newsom to R. B. Bullock, September 13, 1869, D. A. Newsom and W. H. McWhorter to Rufus Bullock, September 22, 1869, Governors' Incoming Correspondence, GDAH; *KKK Testimony*, 1:697, 698, 2:1113, 1114; Atlanta *Daily New Era*, December 30, 1870.

13. Georgia Executive Records, Proclamation of November 29, 1869, GDAH; *KKK Testimony*, 1:697–99; Superior Court Proceedings, September Term, 1870, Greene County Courthouse.

14. Bartley, *The Creation of Modern Georgia*, pp. 66–69; Coleman, *A History of Georgia*, p. 214; Alfred H. Terry to Sherman, June 20, 1870, quoted in Drago, *Black Politicians and Reconstruction in Georgia*, p. 97; *KKK Testimony*, 1:700. Drago's marvelous *Black Politicians and Reconstruction in Georgia* gives a thorough account of the problems Georgia's black politicians faced in the legislature.

15. *KKK Testimony*, 1:703–5.

16. *Herald*, August 31, November 17, December 8, 1870; Currie-McDaniel, *Carpetbagger of Conscience*, pp. 97–117; Atlanta *Daily New Era*, November 8, 1870.

17. *Herald*, November 17, 24, 1870. William McWhorter, an ex-slave, gave a chilling account of Joe McWhorter's treatment of his slaves. See Chapter 2, and Rawick, *The American Slave*, 13:91–103.

18. *Herald*, November 17, December 1, 8, 1870.

19. Ibid., December 8, 1870.

20. Ibid., December 8, 15, 1870; Atlanta *Daily New Era*, December 27, 1870.

21. *KKK Testimony*, 1:697–98.

22. Ibid., 1:697–99; Superior Court Proceedings, March Term, 1871, Greene County Courthouse; Atlanta *Daily New Era*, December 30, 1870.

23. *Atlanta Constitution*, January 13, 1872; Coleman, *A History of Georgia*, pp. 215–16; *Savannah Morning News*, August 28, 1872. Bullock was later arrested, brought to Georgia, and put on trial for corruption. He was acquitted and later became a successful businessman in Atlanta. See Duncan, *Entrepreneur for Equality*, pp. 135–47.

24. *Herald*, January 18, November 7, 1872; Atlanta *Constitution*, November 7, 1872.

25. *Herald*, January 18, November 7, 1872; Atlanta *Constitution*, November 7, 1872. Ironically, Clayton had served as assistant secretary of the treasury under President James Buchanan, a Democrat. The Grant administration later rewarded Phillip Clayton with the ambassadorship to Peru, where he died of disease in 1877. Clayton Papers, Perkins Library, Special Collections, Duke University.

26. *KKK Testimony*, 1:697–701. Raper, in *Preface to Peasantry*, pp. 281–99, found that black people in Greene County had little faith in the "white folks' courts." The author's conversations with many black citizens in 1990 and 1991 revealed that this distrust of the "white" legal system continues today.

27. Superior Court Proceedings, March and September Terms, 1868–70, Greene County Courthouse; John W. T. Catching to Gov. James M. Smith, June 3, 1872, Governors' Incoming Correspondence, GDAH.

28. *Herald*, June 25, August 13, September 10, 1874; Rawick, *The American Slave*, 12:55–56.

29. *Herald*, September 10, 1874, John H. Sullivan to James M. Smith, August 3, 1872, Governors' Incoming Correspondence, GDAH.

30. *Herald*, October 8, 15, 1874; Augusta *Daily Chronicle and Sentinel*, December 3, 1874. L. B. Willis was Richard Willis's son.

31. *Herald*, October 8, 15, 1874.

32. Lumpkin, *The Making of a Southerner*, p. 80; *Herald*, October 8, 15, 1874.

33. *Herald*, November 12, 1874.

34. Ibid.; Augusta *Daily Chronicle and Sentinel*, November 10, 1874.

35. *Herald*, November 12, 19, 26, December 3, 1874; Augusta *Daily Chronicle and Sentinel*, November 10, 13, 18, 1874; Atlanta *Constitution*, November 10, 1874.

36. *Herald*, October 29, November 4, 18, 1875. Grand Jury Presentments, Superior Court Proceedings, Adjourned September Term, 1875, Greene County Courthouse.

37. *Georgia House Journal*, 1876, pp. 46, 53, 200, 210; *Georgia Senate Journal*, 1876, p. 345; *Georgia Laws*, January 1876, pp. 276–78; *Herald*, March 16, 1876.

38. Grand Jury Presentments, Superior Court Proceedings, March Term, 1876, Greene County Courthouse; Population and Slave schedules, 1860 Manuscript

Census Returns, and Population schedule, 1870 Manuscript Census Returns, all in GDAH; *Herald*, May 29, 1873, February 14, 1875; Printup Papers, Perkins Library, Special Collections, Duke University. Copelan's name was sometimes spelled "Copeland."

39. *Herald*, September 1, 8, 1876.

40. *Herald*, September 8, 15, 22, October 6, 1876.

41. *Herald*, October 6, 13, 1876. It is conceivable that fraud made such a lop-sided victory possible, but the general course of events and the lack of black voters' allegations of fraud make this possibility unlikely. Many black voters simply chose the safe course.

42. *Herald*, November 10, 1876, December 8, 1877.

Chapter Nine

1. For discussions of the effects of community dependency on national and international market economies, see Andre Gunder Frank, "The Development of Underdevelopment," pp. 3–17; Wallerstein, *The Capitalist World Economy*, pp. 49–94; Roxborough, *Theories of Underdevelopment*; and Charles Sellers, *The Market Revolution*.

2. Raper, *Tenants of the Almighty*, pp. 78–79; *Synopsis of Letters and Reports, Jan. 1866–March 1869*, BRFAL-Ga. Jaynes, in *Branches Without Roots*, argues that the freedpeople would have preferred cash wages.

3. *KKK Testimony*, 1:701.

4. Du Bois, *Black Reconstruction in America, 1860–1880*, pp. 197–98.

5. Jaynes, *Branches Without Roots*, pp. 16–23.

6. Bode and Ginter, *Farm Tenancy and the Census in Antebellum Georgia*, p. 128; see Rose, *Rehearsal for Reconstruction*, especially pp. 224–25.

7. *Herald*, October 29, November 5, 12, 1868.

8. *Herald*, February 16, April 13, 1871.

9. District Court Proceedings, 19th Senatorial District, 1869–71, Greene County Courthouse. Most white conservatives heartily disliked the district court, not because Judge McWhorter proved lenient, but because the Constitution of 1868 created it. In 1872 the district court became inactive, and in 1877, a new state constitution abolished the court. In 1873 special legislation created a second county court in Greene County, with Philip B. Robinson as judge.

10. *Herald*, July 15, September 16, 1869. In 1871 landowners again threatened to find immigrant replacements, this time Swedes. Again, this effort proved unsuccessful. See the *Herald*, July 20, 1871.

11. *Herald*, March 17, 1870, January 26, February 9, 16, August 24, 1871.

12. *Herald*, May 19, 1870.

13. *Herald*, May 19, June 23, September 15, 1870.

14. Georgia Department of Agriculture, Janes, *Fourth Annual Report of the Commissioner of Agriculture of the State of Georgia, 1877*, pp. 73–74, and *Handbook of the State of Georgia*, p. 151. Glymph, in "Freedpeople and Ex-Masters," pp. 48–72, argues that landowners sought and gladly accepted sharecropping

arrangements, which were preferable to paying cash wages. In Greene County and across the state of Georgia this clearly was not the case.

15. Ransom and Sutch, *One Kind of Freedom*, pp. 56–105; Population schedules, 1860 and 1870 Manuscript Census Returns, GDAH; Woodman, "Postbellum Social Change and Its Effects on Marketing the South's Cotton Crop," pp. 215–30.

16. Georgia General Assembly, *Georgia Laws*, 1866, p. 141; Ransom and Sutch, *One Kind of Freedom*, pp. 44–45, 125, 164.

17. See Burton, "The Rise and Fall of Afro-American Town Life," pp. 152–92.

18. Athens *Southern Cultivator* 31 (August 1873), pp. 286–87; Georgia General Assembly, *Georgia Laws*, 1866, p. 141, 1871–72, p. 71; *Benjamin Davis v. T. B. Meyers*, 41 Ga. 95 (1870). For a concise listing of common law rights of tenancy see Burby, *Real Property*, pp. 147–50.

19. *Davis v. Meyers*, 41 Ga. 95 (1870); *Taliaferro v. Pry*, 41 Ga. 622 (1871); *Harrell v. Fagan*, 43 Ga. 339 (1871); *Tift v. Newsom*, 44 Ga. 600 (1871); *Appling v. Odom*, 46, Ga. 583 (1872).

20. *Appling v. Odom*, 46 Ga. 583, 584 (1872); Georgia Supreme Court Case File A-5780, GDAH.

21. *Appling v. Odom*, 46 Ga. 583, 584 (1872). This case involving a little more than $200 worth of cotton moved through the courts quickly, suggesting the participants knew that more than the money was at stake. Nothing indicates that this was a sort of test case, but for the preceding two years the Georgia Supreme Court had seemed very activist in regard to landlord/tenant law.

22. Woodman, in "Post–Civil War Southern Agriculture and the Law," pp. 319–37, provides an excellent analysis of the creation of legal distinctions between sharecroppers and tenants. Winters, in "Postbellum Reorganization of Southern Agriculture," pp. 1–19, points out that sharecropping continued to be a form of tenancy in Tennessee throughout the nineteenth century. Despite this fact, landowners had no more difficulty controlling their tenants than landowners in states that distinguished sharecropping from tenancy, which puts into question the actual importance of cases like *Appling v. Odom*. Impressionistic evidence, particularly from the Athens *Southern Cultivator*, suggests that contemporaries thought the distinction between sharecroppers and tenants crucially important.

23. *Appling v. Odom*, 46 Ga. 584 (1872).

24. Grice, *The Georgia Bench and Bar*, 1:180, 272, 342, 364.

25. Georgia General Assembly, *Georgia Laws*, November and December 1871, pp. 288–98, 1872, pp. 42–43, 1873, pp. 35–36; *Ga. Code*, 1867, pp. 523–24; *Herald*, January 22, 1874. In 1873 the legislature amended the law to increase the County Court's jurisdiction in contracts cases involving up to $200. See Georgia General Assembly, *Georgia Laws*, 1873, pp. 35–36.

26. Georgia General Assembly, *Georgia Laws*, 1871, p. 292; *Herald*, January 22, 1874; County Court Minutes, 1874, Greene County Courthouse. Unfortunately, the file containing the actual contracts cannot be found, so the count only includes contracts mentioned in the minutes.

27. *Herald*, February 19, 1874, January 14, 1875, January 6, 13, 1876; County Court Minutes, 1874, Greene County Courthouse.

28. *Herald*, May 27, 1875.

29. Woodman, *King Cotton and His Retainers*, pp. 30–71, 132–38.

30. Population schedule, 1860 Manuscript Census Returns, GDAH. Many factors remained in operation long after the war, but the nature of their business changed dramatically. See Woodman, *King Cotton and His Retainers*, pp. 254–94. Ransom and Sutch, in *One Kind of Freedom*, pp. 52–53, argue that emancipation did not eliminate any southern wealth, it merely transferred that wealth to the freed slaves. Their argument, while perhaps theoretically correct, fails to recognize that for purposes of credit transactions, the wealth represented by slaves vanished. Emancipation also eliminated much of the capital reinvested by planters during the profitable antebellum years. For a devastating critique of Ransom and Sutch's argument, see Jaynes, *Branches Without Roots*, pp. 33–53.

31. C. Mildred Thompson, *Reconstruction in Georgia*, pp. 110–12; Wayne, *The Reshaping of Plantation Society*, pp. 161–63; Bryant, "A Dangerous Venture," pp. 26–34. Greene County Grantor-Grantee Index Books SS, TT, UU; Deed and Mortgage Books, 1866–85, and Superior Court Proceedings, 1866–85, both in Greene County Courthouse; Fields, "The Advent of Capitalist Agriculture," p. 87. The New England Mortgage Co. was very active in Greene County during the early 1880s, providing mortgages to smaller farmers throughout the county. For examples of failures to sell land at any price, see the sheriff's sale reports in the *Herald*, June 1, 1876, July 6, 1876, August 4, 1876.

32. Milledgeville *Southern Recorder*, February 12, 1866.

33. *The Savannah Daily News and Herald*, November 24, 1866; Georgia General Assembly, *House Journal*, 1866, pp. 154–55, 171, 319, 416; Georgia General Assembly, *Senate Journal*, 1866, pp. 351, 372, 416, 438, 439; Georgia General Assembly, *Georgia Laws*, 1866, p. 141.

34. Woodman, *King Cotton and his Retainers*, pp. 246–314; Ransom and Sutch, *One Kind of Freedom*, p. 125; Crop Lien Contracts, 1871, 1877, 1881, Henry T. Lewis Papers, Collection of Toombs DuBose Lewis, Watkinsville, Georgia, GDAH.

35. Wayne, in *The Reshaping of Plantation Society*, pp. 150–96, gives an excellent account of this process as it occurred in the old plantation districts of Mississippi and Louisiana.

36. *Herald*, January 30, May 12, 1870.

37. Agriculture schedules, 1850, 1860, 1870, 1880 Manuscript Census Returns, GDAH. The 1870 census may well have undercounted population and agricultural production in Greene County, but assuming equal errors across the 1870 Agriculture schedule, the ratio of corn to cotton should be sound.

38. Agriculture schedules, 1850, 1860, 1870, 1880 Manuscript Census Returns, GDAH. A "bushel equivalent of corn" reflects the food value of Greene County's total food production as reported to the U.S. Census Bureau. This value as well as subsistence surplus and shortfalls were calculated using the method in Ransom and Sutch, *One Kind of Freedom*, pp. 244–53.

39. Georgia Department of Agriculture, *Third Annual Report of the Commissioner of Agriculture of the State of Georgia for the year 1876*, pp. 49–56; Doster, "The Georgia Railroad and Banking Company in the Reconstruction Era," p. 11; Taylor, "From the Ashes," p. 93. The Greene Line was an early example of a "pooling" agreement between several railroads.

40. Georgia Department of Agriculture, *Third Annual Report of the Commissioner of Agriculture of the State of Georgia for the year 1876*, pp. 49–56. Income was calculated using an estimate of 15,000 inhabitants in Greene County in 1875. Other than cotton, Greene County produced little that could be sold for cash. By 1874 all cotton mills in Greene County had ceased operation, so the cotton shipped out represents closely the total production of the county.

41. Georgia Department of Agriculture, Janes, *Annual Report of Thomas P. Janes, Commissioner of Agriculture, 1875*, pp. 53–54; Georgia Department of Agriculture, Janes, *Third Annual Report of the Commissioner of Agriculture of the State of Georgia for the year 1876*, pp. 49–56. Janes's estimates of credit costs were conservative. He found that almost 80 percent of the 300 landowning farmers he surveyed in 1875 bought their supplies on credit, but he did not consider the credit costs to Georgia's growing numbers of tenants and sharecroppers.

42. Population schedule, 1880 Manuscript Census Returns, GDAH; *Herald*, August 6, 1879, August 11, 1881; Greene County Tax Digest, 1880, GDAH. Freedpeople may indeed have been wealthier in 1880 than they had been as slaves, but less than $6 per capita wealth could hardly provide for the acquisition of land or other capital investment.

43. Fields, "The Advent of Capitalist Agriculture," and Woodman, "The Reconstruction of the Cotton Plantation in the New South," pp. 73–119.

44. See Chapter 5 for the effects of the Civil War on Greene County's agricultural economy. Burke Davis, in *Sherman's March*, recounts numerous anecdotes of the Federal soldiers' reaction to the agricultural richness of Georgia's eastern cotton belt; see especially pp. 41–44.

45. Georgia Department of Agriculture, Janes, *Annual Report of Thomas P. Janes, Commissioner of Agriculture, 1875*, pp. 9–10; Athens *Southern Cultivator* 24 (November 1866), p. 257. For examples of calls for diversification see the *Southern Cultivator* 24 (January 1866), pp. 5–6; 25 (April 1867), pp. 126–27.

46. *Herald*, January 29, 1874, October 21, 1875, November 27, 1873.

47. *Herald*, November 27, 1873, March 26, 1874.

48. *Herald*, November 27, 1873.

49. Coulter, "Scull Shoals," pp. 33–63; Stover, "Northern Financial Interests in Southern Railroads, 1865–1900," pp. 205–20; Wallerstein, in *The Modern World-System*, pp. 147–239, presents a useful theoretical perspective for understanding different regions' roles in the world economy.

Chapter Ten

1. Rice and Williams, *History of Greene County, Georgia*, pp. 357, 360–61.

2. Georgia Department of Agriculture, Janes, *Manual of Georgia*, p. 71; Rice and Williams, *History of Greene County, Georgia*, pp. 356–61.

3. Population schedule, 1850 Manuscript Census Returns, GDAH; Charles A. Davis, Sr., and William S. Davis tombstones, Greensboro Cemetery, Greene County, Georgia; Greenesboro *Weekly Gazette*, December 14, 1859.

4. Greenesboro *Planters' Weekly*, October 10, 1860; Population, Slave, and Agriculture schedules, 1860 Manuscript Census Returns, GDAH.

5. Henderson, *Roster of the Confederate Soldiers of Georgia, 1861–1865*, 1:982; Superior Court Proceedings, 1866–68, Greene County Courthouse; Charles A. Davis Jr. Papers, Greene County Historical Society Museum. The few fortunes made in middle Georgia during the immediate postwar period seem generally to have come out of similar hardnosed business practices. David Dickson dominated Hancock County through similar methods; see Bryant, "Race, Class, and Law in Bourbon Georgia," p. 230.

6. *Herald*, February 16, 1871; Population schedule, 1870 Manuscript Census Returns, GDAH.

7. Charles A. Davis Jr. Papers, Greene County Historical Society Museum; *Herald*, September 15, 29, October 6, 1870, June 15, October 26, 1871, May 29, 1873, January 1, June 25, 1874. The extent of Davis's involvement in the various firms that leased the big store cannot be determined.

8. *Herald*, February 9, October 12, 1871, June 25, 1874.

9. *Herald*, January 4, 1872, January 7, 1875; Rice and Williams, *History of Greene County, Georgia*, 268–70; James Michael Russell, *Atlanta, 1847–1890*, pp. 118–28. Russell claims that Atlanta's business territory extended for a 200-mile radius by 1873, see p. 120.

10. Rice and Williams, *History of Greene County, Georgia*, pp. 216–17; *Herald*, December 5, 1872.

11. Dowell, *A History of Mercer University, 1833–1953*, pp. 109, 114, 117; H. H. Tucker to Col. R. L. Hunter, May 20, 1868, Governors' Incoming Correspondence, GDAH.

12. Dowell, *A History of Mercer University, 1833–1953*, pp. 126–35.

13. Ibid., pp. 174, 186–200. Professor Shelton P. Sanford moved to Macon with Mercer University, where he continued to teach mathematics and produced several successful textbooks. In 1891, after fifty-two years at Mercer, Sanford retired from teaching. His son, Charles V. Sanford, survived the Civil War and fittingly became a successful merchant in Conyers, Georgia. Charles's son, Steadman V. Sanford, rose to become president of the University of Georgia, then the first chancellor of the university system of Georgia. Sanford Stadium at the University of Georgia is named in his honor.

14. *Herald*, March 20, 1873, August 25, October 13, 1876.

15. Coulter, "Scull Shoals," pp. 45–51.

16. *Herald,* December 9, 1875; Woodman, *King Cotton and His Retainers,* p. 326; Ayers, *The Promise of the New South,* p. 64.

17. Population and Slave schedules, 1860 Manuscript Census Returns, Population schedule, 1870 Manuscript Census Returns, GDAH; Rice and Williams, *History of Greene County, Georgia,* p. 283.

18. Northen, *Men of Mark in Georgia,* 4: 153–56. When James B. Hart died in 1875, his plantation carried $10,000 of debt. Because of their new businesses, his sons were soon able to pay the debt and save the farm.

19. Northen, *Men of Mark in Georgia,* 7: 397–403; Florie Carter Smith, *The History of Oglethorpe County, Georgia,* pp. 167–68; *Biographical Souvenir of the States of Georgia and Florida,* pp. 555–57.

20. Florie Carter Smith, *The History of Oglethorpe County, Georgia,* pp. 167–68; *Herald,* April 27, 1882.

21. Georgia General Assembly, *Georgia's General Assembly, 1880–81,* p. 291; Park Family File, GDAH; Park Mill Collection, Greene County Historical Society Museum.

22. Henry T. Lewis Papers, Collection of Toombs DuBose Lewis, Watkinsville, Georgia; Boyd, *A Family History,* pp. 310–25.

23. Northen, *Men of Mark in Georgia,* 3:182–85; "The Last Will and Testament of Thomas P. Janes," Will Book H, 137–44, Greene County Courthouse; Greensboro *Herald Journal,* March 16, 1888.

24. Mildred P. Sanford Poullain to Mary Jane Sanford Monfort, September 17, 1875, Poullain Family Collection, and Thomas Noel Poullain File, both in Greene County Historical Society Museum; "Last Will and Testament of Thomas Noel Poullain," Will Book H, 163–66, Greene County Courthouse. T. B. Rice argues that through leases and family connections Poullain controlled 278 slaves. See Rice and Williams, *History of Greene County, Georgia,* p. 312.

25. Rice and Williams, *History of Greene County, Georgia,* pp. 121, 149.

26. Superior Court Proceedings, March and September Terms, 1859, 1860, 1861, 1883, 1884, 1885, Greene County Courthouse; Alexander, "Railway Management," p. 153. Divorce cases before the court also increased dramatically. From 1859 through 1861, divorce cases were rare, making up only less than 2 percent of the superior court's business. During 1883 through 1885, divorce cases made up 17 percent of all cases before the superior court. The laws for divorce had not changed; thus each divorce case had to be tried twice. Though 17 percent of all cases heard by the court were divorce cases, if the two trials for each divorce are combined and counted as one case, then about 9 percent of all civil cases involved divorce, still a remarkable increase from the prewar norm. Other types of civil suits, including trespass and personal injury, occurred with about the same frequency in both samples.

27. Ayers, *Vengeance and Justice,* pp. 141–265. E. P. Thompson, in *Whigs and Hunters,* presents an excellent account of a similar legal transformation in eighteenth-century England.

28. *Herald,* June 13, 1884. The Greene County grand jury investigated

conditions among both county and state convicts leased by Powell and Daven-port and found the situation to be appropriate for punishment of the criminals. Grand Jury Presentments, March and September Terms, 1881, March Term, 1882, Greene County Courthouse.

29. *Herald*, August 1, 1884. While on the Georgia Supreme Court during the 1890s, Lewis continued to argue that lynching was an unavoidable, democratic expression of the popular will. A pamphlet of Lewis's views on this subject from an address to the Georgia Bar Association circulated in the late 1890s. See Lewis, "Is Lynch Law Due to Defects in the Criminal Law, or Its Administration," 14–20.

30. Grand Jury Presentments, Superior Court Proceedings, March Terms, 1876, 1880, March, September Terms, 1884, Greene County Courthouse; Population schedules, 1870, 1880 Manuscript Census Returns, GDAH; See also analysis in Chapter 3 and Appendix. John B. Y. Warner almost certainly hailed from the same family as H. G. Warner of the *Rochester Courier*, who had objected to Frederick Douglass's daughter Rosetta attending the same school as his children in 1849. See McFeely, *Frederick Douglass*, p. 161.

31. *Herald*, June 27, 1878, September 5, 1884, August 7, 1885.

32. *Herald*, November 28, 1872. From 1875 through 1887, attorney Columbus Heard owned the *Herald* and hired young, progressive lawyers to edit the paper. These included Edward L. Lewis, Henry T. Lewis, and Edward Young, who were in the first decade of their careers.

33. Contract of E. F. M. Calloway with his workers, February 28, 1866, Greensboro, Georgia, Labor Contracts, Entry 886, RG 105, NA.

34. Agriculture schedule, 1860 Manuscript Census Returns, GDAH. Unfortunately, because of inadequate distinctions made by the assistant marshal taking the 1860 census in Greene County, it is impossible to determine exactly which households should be considered part of the Grey Lands districts. These are estimates based on an informed reading of the manuscript source, and exact calculations of cotton production, subsistence production, and farm size are impossible.

35. *Georgia State Gazetteer, Business and Planters Directory, 1881–1882*, pp. 156–57; Raper, *Tenants of the Almighty*, pp. 112–13.

36. Population and Slave schedules, 1860 Manuscript Census Returns, GDAH; Raper, *Tenants of the Almighty*, pp. 113–16; *Georgia State Gazetteer, Business and Planters Directory, 1886–87*, pp. 158, 377–78.

37. Georgia Department of Agriculture, Janes, *First Annual Report of the Commissioner of Agriculture, 1874*, p. 8; Raper, *Tenants of the Almighty*, p. 113; Population schedule, 1870, 1880 Manuscript Census Returns, GDAH.

38. Raper, *Tenants of the Almighty*, pp. 365, 372; James Michael Russell, *Atlanta, 1847–1890*, pp. 146–68. Some freedpeople came to own land through kinship ties with white families. See Schultz, "Interracial Kinship Ties and the Emergence of a Rural Black Middle Class," pp. 141–72, for an account of this process in neighboring Hancock County. Greene County's population continued to decline between 1890 and 1900 and then leveled off until 1920. Between

1920 and 1930 Greene County's population declined by one-third, and almost half the black inhabitants left the county. See Raper, *Tenants of the Almighty*, p. 365.

39. Raper, *Tenants of the Almighty*, pp. 119–29; *Herald*, December 8, 13, 1877, June 27, 1878, July 4, 1878, September 5, 1884, March 30, 1888.

Epilogue

1. *Herald*, March 26, 1874.

2. Carson, Luker, and Russell, *Called to Serve, January 1929–June 1951*, 1:1–26.

3. Genesis 27:1–46, 32:1–32, 33:1–20.

ᕉᕽ Bibliography ᕽᕉ

Manuscripts

Alabama Department of Archives, Montgomery, Alabama
   John Calvin Reed Collection
Atlanta Historical Society Archives, Atlanta, Georgia
   Charles Alfred Davis Collection
   John Marion Graham Papers
   Peter Northen Papers
Georgia Department of Archives and History, Atlanta, Georgia
   Governors' Correspondence and Governors' Incoming Correspondence
      Joseph E. Brown, 1860–65
      Rufus B. Bullock, 1868–71
      Alfred H. Colquitt, 1877–82
      Charles J. Jenkins, 1865–68
      James Johnson, 1865
      General Thomas H. Ruger, 1868
      James M. Smith, 1872–77
   Manuscripts Section
      Black Studies Papers
      Joseph E. Brown Collection
      Edmondson Family Farm Records
      Ku Klux Klan Collection
      Archibald Thomas MacIntyre Family Papers
      Minnie McWhorter Collection
      Arthur Raper Collection
      Reconstruction File
      Thaddeus Brockett Rice Collection
      George Heard Tunnell Papers
   State and County Records
      Confederate Service Records
      Georgia Executive Department Commissions
      Georgia Executive Records
      Greene County, Confederate Military Units File
      Greene County Loose Records, 1831–1900
      Greene County Tax Digests
   Other Records
      Janes Family File
      McWhorter Family File

Manuscript Census Returns, Greene County, Georgia, 1850, 1860, 1870,
1880
Park Family File
Penfield Baptist Church Papers, 1839–85
Supreme Court Case Files, 1870, 1872
Greene County Courthouse, Greensboro, Georgia
County Court Minutes, 1866–68, 1872–85
Deed and Mortgage Books
District Court Proceedings, 19th Senatorial District, 1868–71
Grantor-Grantee Index Books, SS, TT, UU
Inferior Court Minutes, 1848–68
Inferior Court Records
Loose Court Papers, 1808–1900
Superior Court Minutes, 1849–88
Superior Court Proceedings, 1855–88
Will Books
Greene County Historical Society Museum, Greensboro, Georgia
Civil War Collection
Conference Minutes of Bethesda Baptist Church, August 1817–December
1865, transcribed by Vivian Toole Cates
Charles A. Davis Jr. Papers
Greensboro First Baptist Church History
Old Homes in Greensboro and Greene County Collection
Park Mill Collection
Thomas Noel Poullain File
Poullain Family Collection
Hargrett Library, University of Georgia Libraries, Athens, Georgia
David Crenshaw Barrow Papers
Patrick Hues Mell Collection
Shepherd Greene Pryor Collection
National Archives, Washington, D.C.
Records of the Assistant Commissioner for the State of Georgia, Bureau of
Refugees, Freedmen, and Abandoned Lands, Microfilm Publication
M-798
Records of the Bureau of Refugees, Freedmen, and Abandoned Lands,
Record Group 105
Records of the U.S. Army Continental Command, Record Group 393
Perkins Library, Special Collections, Duke University, Durham, North Carolina
John Emory Bryant Papers
Martha "Mattie" Harper Clayton Papers
Columbus Heard Papers
Daniel S. Printup Papers
George S. Rives Papers
James R. Sanders Papers

Vincent Sanford Papers
E. Steadman Papers
Private Collections
   Henry T. Lewis Papers, Collection of Toombs DuBose Lewis, Watkinsville,
      Georgia
   Hugh Graham Lewis Papers, Private Collection, Greensboro, Georgia
   Springfield Baptist Church Papers, Collection of Mrs. Willie Patience
      Brown, Greensboro, Georgia
   Dr. Albert Henley Weyer Diary, Collection of E. H. Armor, Greensboro,
      Georgia
Southern Historical Collection, University of North Carolina, Chapel Hill,
   North Carolina
   Charles Haynes Andrews Papers
   Alexander R. Lawton Papers
   Arthur Raper Collection
   Wayside Home, Union Point, Georgia, Register, 1862–64
Woodruff Library, Special Collections, Emory University, Atlanta, Georgia
   George Foster Pierce Papers
   Shelton Palmer Sanford Papers

Newspapers

Athens *Southern Banner*, 1849
Athens *Southern Cultivator*, 1858–82
Atlanta *Constitution*, 1870–76
Atlanta *Daily Intelligencer*, 1870
Atlanta *Daily Sun*, 1872
Atlanta *Weekly New Era*, 1868–71
Atlanta *True Georgian*, 1870
Augusta *Colored American*, 1865–66
Augusta *Constitutionalist*, 1861–65
Augusta *Daily Chronicle and Sentinel*, 1849–76
Augusta *Loyal Georgian*, 1866–68
Augusta *Weekly Chronicle and Sentinel*, 1860–68
Greenesboro *Herald*, 1867–87
Greenesboro *Herald Journal*, 1887–90
Greenesboro Home Journal, 1877–84
Greenesboro *Planters' Weekly*, 1860–61
Greenesboro *Weekly Gazette*, 1859–60
Milledgeville *Southern Recorder*, 1863
Penfield *Temperance Banner*, 1853–55
The Savannah Daily News and Herald, 1866
Savannah Morning News, 1860–72
Turnwold *Countryman*, 1861–65

Government Publications

Georgia. Candler, Allen D., comp. *Confederate Records of the State of Georgia.* 6 vols. Atlanta, 1906–11.

——. *The Code of the State of Georgia.* Atlanta, 1845, 1861, 1867, 1873, 1882.

——. St. Clair–Abrams. *Manual and Biographic Register of the State of Georgia, 1871–72.* Atlanta, 1972.

Georgia Comptroller General. *Annual Report.* Milledgeville and Atlanta, 1862, 1873–80.

Georgia Department of Agriculture. Henderson, J. T. *The Commonwealth of Georgia: The Country; The People; The Productions.* Atlanta, 1885.

——. Henderson, J. T. *Manual on Cattle.* Atlanta, 1880.

——. Janes, Thomas P. *First Annual Report of the Commissioner of Agriculture, 1874.* Atlanta, 1874.

——. Janes, Thomas P. *Annual Report of Thomas P. Janes, Commissioner of Agriculture, 1875.* Atlanta, 1875.

——. Janes, Thomas P. *Third Annual Report of the Commissioner of Agriculture of the State of Georgia for the year 1876.* Atlanta, 1877.

——. Janes, Thomas P. *Fourth Annual Report of the Commissioner of Agriculture of the State of Georgia, 1877.* Atlanta, 1878.

——. Janes, Thomas P. *Fifth Annual Report of the Commissioner of Agriculture, 1878.* Atlanta, 1879.

——. Janes, Thomas P. *Handbook of the State of Georgia.* Atlanta, 1876.

——. Janes, Thomas P. *Manual of Georgia.* Atlanta, 1878.

Georgia General Assembly. *Acts of the General Assembly of the State of Georgia.* Milledgeville and Atlanta, 1865–86.

——. *Georgia's General Assembly, 1880–81.* Atlanta, 1882.

——. *Journal of the House of Representatives of the State of Georgia.* Milledgeville and Atlanta, 1851–86.

——. *Journal of the Senate of the State of Georgia.* Milledgeville and Atlanta, 1853–86.

Georgia Supreme Court. *Georgia Reports.* Milledgeville and Atlanta, 1858–85.

United States. *American State Papers, Indian Affairs.* 2 vols. Washington, 1832.

U.S. Census Bureau. *Aggregate Amount of Each Description of Persons within the United States of America, 1810.* Washington, 1811.

——. *Agriculture of the United States in 1860.* Washington, 1864.

——. *Appendix of the Seventh Cesnus of the United States, 1850.* Washington, 1853.

——. *Census for 1820.* Washington, 1821.

——. *Compendium of the Ninth Census.* Washington, 1872.

——. *Compendium of the Tenth Census, 1880, Part I.* Washington, 1883.

——. *Manufactures of the United States in 1860.* Washington, 1865.

——. *Population of the United States in 1860.* Washington, 1864.

——. *Report on the Cotton Production of the State of Georgia, 1880.* Washington, 1883.

———. *Report on the Production of Agriculture in the United States, Tenth Census.* Washington, 1883.

———. *Seventh Census of the United States, 1850.* Washington, 1853.

———. *Statistics of the Population of the United States, Ninth Census.* Washington, 1872.

———. *Statistics of the Population of the United States, Tenth Census.* Washington, 1883.

———. *Statistics of the United States in 1860.* Washington, 1866.

———. *Statistics of the Wealth and Industry of the United States, Ninth Census.* Washington, 1872.

———. *Tenth Census of the United States, 1880: Report on the Cotton Production of the United States.* Washington, 1883.

U.S. Congress. *Condition of Affairs in Georgia.* Washington, 1868, 1869.

———. *Condition of Affairs in Georgia: Statement of Hon. Nelson Tift to the Reconstruction Committee of the House of Representatives, Washington, February 18, 1869.* Washington, 1869.

———. *Report of the Joint Committee on Reconstruction.* Washington, 1866.

———. *Report of the Joint Select Committee to Inquire into the Condition of Affairs in the Late Insurrectionary States: Georgia.* 2 vols. Washington, 1872.

U.S. War Department. *The War of the Rebellion: A Compilation of the Official Records of the Union and Confederate Armies.* Series 1, 128 vols. Washington, 1880–1901.

Published Primary Sources

Alexander, E. P. "Railway Management." In *The American Railway: Its Construction, Development, Management, and Appliance,* 148–77. New York, 1889.

Andrews, Eliza Frances. *The War-Time Journal of a Georgia Girl, 1864–1865.* Edited by Spencer B. King. Macon, Ga., 1960.

Andrews, Garnett. *Reminiscences of an Old Georgia Lawyer.* Atlanta, 1870.

Andrews, Sidney. *The South since the War.* Boston, 1866.

Barrow, David C., Jr. "A Georgia Plantation." *Scribner's Monthly,* March 1881, 830–36.

Cobb, Thomas R. R. *An Inquiry into the Law of Slavery in the United States of America.* Philadelphia, 1858.

Convention of the Georgia Equal Rights and Educational Association, Macon, Georgia, October 30, 1866. Augusta, 1866.

Dennett, John Richard. *The South as It Is: 1865–1866.* Edited by Henry M. Christman. New York, 1965.

Georgia State Gazetteer, Business and Planters Directory, 1881–82, 1886–87. Savannah, Ga., 1882, 1887.

Harley, Timothy. *Southward Ho! Notes of a Tour to and through Georgia in the Winter of 1885–1886.* London, 1886.

Kennaway, Sir John H. *On Sherman's Track, or The South after the War*. London, 1867.

Proceedings of the Freedmen's Convention of Georgia, Assembled at Augusta, January 10, 1866. Augusta, Ga., 1866.

Rawick, George P., ed. *The American Slave: A Composite Autobiography, Georgia Narratives*. Series 2, vols. 12–13. Westport, Conn., 1972.

Rawick, George P., Jan Hillegas, and Ken Lawrence, eds. *The American Slave: A Composite Autobiography, Georgia Narratives*. Supplement series 1, vols. 3–4. Westport, Conn., 1977.

Reed, John C. "What I Know of the Ku Klux Klan." *Uncle Remus Home Magazine*, January–October 1908.

Sherman, William Tecumseh. *Memoirs of General W. T. Sherman*. 1875. Reprint, New York, 1990.

Somers, Robert. *The Southern States since the War*. London, 1871.

Stearns, Charles. *The Black Man of the South and the Rebels*. New York, 1872.

Transactions of the Southern Central Agricultural Society. Macon, Ga., 1852.

Trowbridge, J. T. *The South: A Tour of Its Battlefields and Ruined Cities, A Journey through the Desolated States and Talks with the People*. Hartford, Conn., 1866.

Turner, Henry M. *The Barbarous Decision of the United States Supreme Court Declaring the Civil Rights Act Unconstitutional*. Atlanta, 1893.

White, George. *Statistics of the State of Georgia*. Savannah, Ga., 1849.

Secondary Sources

Ambrose, Stephen E. "Cotton Prices and Costs: A Suggestion." *Georgia Historical Quarterly* 48 (March 1964): 78–80.

Anderson, Eric, and Alfred A. Moss Jr. *The Facts of Reconstruction: Essays in Honor of John Hope Franklin*. Baton Rouge, La., 1991.

Angell, Stephen Ward. *Bishop Henry McNeal Turner and African-American Religion in the South*. Knoxville, Tenn., 1992.

Appleby, Joyce. *Capitalism and a New Social Order: The Republican Vision of the 1790s*. New York, 1984.

Avery, I. W. *The History of the State of Georgia from 1850 to 1881*. New York, 1881.

Ayers, Edward L. *The Promise of the New South: Life after Reconstruction*. New York, 1992.

———. *Vengeance and Justice: Crime and Punishment in the Nineteenth-Century American South*. New York, 1984.

Bartley, Numan V. *The Creation of Modern Georgia*. Athens, Ga., 1983.

———. "In Search of the New South: Southern Politics after Reconstruction." *Reviews in American History* 10 (December 1982): 150–63.

Beck, John J. "Building the New South: A Revolution from Above in a Piedmont County." *Journal of Southern History* 53 (August 1987): 441–70.

Beirne, Piers, and Richard Quinney, eds. *Marxism and Law*. New York, 1982.

Bender, Thomas. *Community and Social Change in America*. Baltimore, 1978.

Bensel, Richard Franklin. *Yankee Leviathan: The Origins of Central State Authority in America, 1859-1877*. New York, 1990.

Bentley, George R. *A History of the Freedmen's Bureau*. Philadelphia, 1955.

Beringer, Richard E., Herman Hattaway, Archer Jones, and William N. Still Jr., eds. *Why the South Lost the Civil War*. Athens, Ga., 1986.

Billings, Dwight B. *Planters and the Making of a "New South": Class, Politics, and Development in North Carolina, 1865-1900*. Chapel Hill, N.C., 1979.

Blassingame, John W. *The Slave Community: Plantation Life in the Antebellum South*. New York, 1979.

Bode, Frederick A., and Donald E. Ginter. *Farm Tenancy and the Census in Antebellum Georgia*. Athens, Ga., 1986.

Bodenhamer, David J., and James W. Ely Jr., eds. *Ambivalent Legacy: A Legal History of the South*. Jackson, Miss., 1984.

Bonner, James C. "Profile of a Late Ante-Bellum Community." *The American Historical Review* 44 (July 1944): 663-80.

Boyd, John Wright. *A Family History: Wright-Lewis-Moore and Connected Families*. Atlanta, 1964.

Brundage, W. Fitzhugh. *Lynching in the New South: Georgia and Virginia, 1880-1930*. Urbana, Ill., 1993.

———. "Mob Violence, North and South, 1865-1940." *Georgia Historical Quarterly* 75 (Winter 1991): 748-70.

Bryan, Thomas Conn. *Confederate Georgia*. Athens, Ga., 1953.

Bryant, Jonathan M. "A Dangerous Venture: Three Legal Changes in Postbellum Georgia." Master's thesis, University of Georgia, 1987.

———. "My Soul An't Yours, Mas'r: The Records of the African Church at Penfield, 1848-1863." *Georgia Historical Quarterly* 75 (Summer 1991): 401-12.

———. "Race, Class, and Law in Bourbon Georgia: The Case of David Dickson's Will." *Georgia Historical Quarterly* 71 (Summer 1987): 226-42.

———. "We Have No Chance of Justice before the Courts: The Freedmen's Struggle for Power in Greene County, Georgia, 1865-1874." In *Georgia in Black and White: Explorations in the Race Relations of a Southern State, 1865-1950*, edited by John C. Inscoe, 13-37. Athens, Ga., 1994.

Burby, William E. *Real Property*. St. Paul, Minn., 1965.

Burr, Virginia Ingraham, ed. *The Secret Eye: The Journal of Ella Gertrude Clanton Thomas, 1848-1889*. Chapel Hill, N.C., 1990.

Burton, Orville Vernon. *In My Father's House Are Many Mansions: Family and Community in Edgefield, South Carolina*. Chapel Hill, N.C., 1986.

———. "The Rise and Fall of Afro-American Town Life: Town and Country in Reconstruction Edgefield, South Carolina." In *Toward a New South: Studies in Post-Civil War Southern Communities*, edited by Orville Vernon Burton and Robert C. McMath, 152-92. Westport, Conn., 1982.

Burton, Orville Burton, and Robert C. McMath Jr., eds. *Class, Conflict, and Consensus: Antebellum Southern Community Studies*. Westport, Conn., 1982.

———. *Toward a New South: Studies in Post–Civil War Southern Communities.* Westport, Conn., 1982.

Campbell, J. H. *Georgia Baptists: Historical and Biographical.* Macon, Ga., 1874.

Carlton, David L. *Mill and Town in South Carolina, 1880–1920.* Baton Rouge, La., 1982.

———. "The Revolution from Above: The National Market and the Beginnings of Industrialization in North Carolina." *Journal of American History* 77 (September 1990): 445–75.

Carson, Clayborne, Ralph E. Lucker, and Penny A. Russell, eds. *Called to Serve, January 1929–June 1951.* Vol. 1 of *The Papers of Martin Luther King, Jr.* Berkeley, 1992.

Cashin, Edward J. *The King's Ranger: Thomas Brown and the American Revolution on the Southern Frontier.* Athens, Ga., 1989

Cashin, Joan E. "The Structure of Antebellum Planter Families: 'The Ties that Bound us Was Strong.'" *Journal of Southern History* 56 (February 1990): 55–70.

Cason, Roberta F. "The Loyal League in Georgia." *Georgia Historical Quarterly* 20 (June 1936): 125–53.

Cassity, Michael. *Defending a Way of Life: An American Community in the Nineteenth Century.* Albany, N.Y., 1989.

Chandler, Alfred D., Jr. *The Visible Hand: The Managerial Revolution in American Business.* Cambridge, Mass., 1977.

Channing, Steven A. *Crisis of Fear: Secession in South Carolina.* New York, 1970.

Chaplin, Joyce E. "Creating a Cotton South in Georgia and South Carolina, 1760–1815." *Journal of Southern History* 57 (May 1991): 171–200.

Cimbala, Paul A. "The Freedmen's Bureau, the Freedmen, and Sherman's Grant in Reconstruction Georgia, 1865–1867." *Journal of Southern History* 55 (November 1989): 597–632.

———. "On the Front Line of Freedom: Freedmen's Bureau Officers and Agents in Reconstruction Georgia." *Georgia Historical Quarterly* 76 (Fall 1992): 577–611.

———. "The 'Talisman Power': Davis Tillson, the Freedmen's Bureau, and Free Labor in Reconstruction Georgia, 1865–1866." *Civil War History* 28 (June 1982): 153–71.

———. "The Terms of Freedom: The Freedmen's Bureau and the Reconstruction of Georgia, 1865–1870." Ph.D. diss., Emory University, 1983.

Clark, Christopher. *The Roots of Rural Capitalism: Western Massachusetts, 1780–1860.* Ithaca, N.Y., 1990.

Clinton, Catherine. *The Plantation Mistress: Women's World in the Old South.* New York, 1982.

Cobb, James C. "Beyond Planters and Industrialists: A New Perspective on the New South." *Journal of Southern History* 54 (February 1988): 45–68.

———. "Making Sense of Southern Economic History." *Georgia Historical Quarterly* 71 (Spring 1987): 53–74.

———. *The Most Southern Place on Earth: The Mississippi Delta and the Roots of Regional Identity*. New York, 1992.

Cockcroft, James D., André Gunder Frank, and Dale L. Johnson, eds. *Dependence and Underdevelopment: Latin America's Political Economy*. New York, 1972.

Cohen, William. *At Freedom's Edge: Black Mobility and the Southern White Quest for Racial Control, 1861–1915*. Baton Rouge, La., 1991.

———. "Negro Involuntary Servitude in the South, 1865–1940: A Preliminary Analysis." *Journal of Southern History* 42 (February 1976): 31–60.

Coleman, Kenneth, ed. *A History of Georgia*. Athens, Ga., 1977.

Collins, Bruce W. "Governor Joseph E. Brown, Economic Issues, and Georgia's Road to Secession, 1857–1859." *Georgia Historical Quarterly* 71 (Summer 1987): 189–225.

Conway, Alan. *The Reconstruction of Georgia*. Minneapolis, Minn., 1966.

Cotterrell, Roger. "Jurisprudence and the Sociology of Law." In *The Sociology of Law*, edited by William M. Evans, 22–36. New York, 1980.

———. *The Politics of Jurisprudence: A Critical Introduction to Legal Philosophy*. London, 1989.

———. *The Sociology of Law: An Introduction*. London, 1984.

Coulter, E. Merton. "Cudjo Fye's Insurrection." *Georgia Historical Quarterly* 38 (September 1954): 213–25.

———. *James Monroe Smith, Georgia Planter: Before Death and After*. Athens, 1961.

———. "The Movement for Agricultural Reorganization in the Cotton South during the Civil War." *Agricultural History* 1 (January 1927): 1–15.

———. "The Politics of Dividing a Georgia County: Oconee from Clarke." *Georgia Historical Quarterly* 57 (Winter 1973): 475–92.

———. "Scull Shoals: An Extinct Georgia Manufacturing and Farming Community." *Georgia Historical Quarterly* 48 (March 1964): 33–63.

———. *The South during Reconstruction, 1865–1877*. Baton Rouge, La., 1947.

Cowdrey, Albert E. *This Land, This South: An Environmental History*. Lexington, Ky., 1983.

Crawford, George B. "Cotton, Land, and Sustenance: Toward the Limits of Abundance in Late Antebellum Georgia." *Georgia Historical Quarterly* 72 (Summer 1988): 215–47.

Crowe, Charles, ed. *The Age of Civil War and Reconstruction, 1830–1900: A Book of Interpretive Essays*. Homewood, Ill., 1975.

Cumming, Mary G. *Georgia Railroad and Banking Company, 1833–1945*. Augusta, Ga., 1945.

Currie-McDaniel, Ruth. "Black Power in Georgia: William A. Pledger and the Takeover of the Republican Party." *Georgia Historical Quarterly* 62 (Fall 1978): 225–38.

———. *Carpetbagger of Conscience: A Biography of John Emory Bryant*. Athens, Ga., 1987.

Curtin, Philip D. *The Rise and Fall of the Plantation Complex: Essays in Atlantic History*. New York, 1990.

Custer, Lawrence B. "The Good Time Is Coming: The Nineteenth-Century Legal Education of Enoch Faw." *Georgia State Bar Journal* 27 (August 1990): 31–40.

Dahl, Robert A. *Who Governs?: Democracy and Power in an American City*. New Haven, Conn., 1961.

Darnton, Robert. *The Great Cat Massacre and Other Episodes in French Cultural History*. New York, 1984.

Davis, Burke. *Sherman's March*. New York, 1980.

Davis, Harold E. "Henry Grady, the Atlanta *Constitution*, and the Politics of Farming in the 1880s." *Georgia Historical Quarterly* 71 (Winter 1987): 571–600.

Davis, William C. *Jefferson Davis, the Man and His Hour: A Biography*. New York, 1991.

Dean, Eric T. " 'We Will All Be Lost and Destroyed': Post-Traumatic Stress Disorder and the Civil War." *Civil War History* 37 (June 1991): 138–53.

Deaton, Stanley Kenneth. "Violent Redemption: The Democratic Party and the Ku Klux Klan in Georgia, 1868–1871." Master's thesis, University of Georgia, 1988.

Debo, Angie. *The Road to Disappearance: A History of the Creek Indians*. Norman, Okla., 1941.

Doster, James F. "The Georgia Railroad and Banking Company in the Reconstruction Era." *Georgia Historical Quarterly* 48 (March 1964): 1–32.

Douglass, Frederick. *My Bondage and My Freedom*. 1855. Reprint, New York, 1969.

Dowell, Spright. *A History of Mercer University, 1833–1953*. Macon, Ga., 1958.

Doyle, Don H. *New Men, New Cities, New South: Atlanta, Nashville, Charleston, Mobile, 1860–1910*. Chapel Hill, N.C., 1990.

Drago, Edmund L. *Black Politicians and Reconstruction in Georgia: A Splendid Failure*. Baton Rouge, La., 1982.

———. "Georgia's First Black Voter Registrars During Reconstruction." *Georgia Historical Quarterly* 78 (Winter 1994): 760–93.

———. "How Sherman's March through Georgia Affected the Slaves." *Georgia Historical Quarterly* 57 (Fall 1973): 361–75.

Du Bois, W. E. B. *Black Reconstruction in America, 1860–1880*. New York, 1935.

———. *The Souls of Black Folk*. 1903. Reprint, New York, 1989.

Duncan, Russell. *Entrepreneur for Equality: Governor Rufus Bullock, Commerce, and Race in Post–Civil War Georgia*. Athens, Ga., 1994.

———. *Freedom's Shore: Tunis Campbell and the Georgia Freedmen*. Athens, Ga., 1986.

Eckert, Ralph Lowell. *John Brown Gordon: Soldier, Southerner, American.* Baton Rouge, La., 1989.

Edwards, Laura F. "The Politics of Manhood and Womanhood: Reconstruction in Granville County, North Carolina." Ph.D. dissertation, University of North Carolina at Chapel Hill, 1991.

Ehrlich, Eugen. *Fundamental Principles of the Sociology of Law.* Translated by W. L. Moll. New York, 1962.

Escott, Paul D. "The Context of Freedom: Georgia's Slaves during the Civil War." *Georgia Historical Quarterly* 58 (Spring 1974): 79–104.

Eskew, Glenn T. "Black Elitism and the Failure of Paternalism in Postbellum Georgia: The Case of Bishop Lucius Henry Holsey." *Journal of Southern History* 58 (November 1992): 637–66.

Faragher, John Mack. *Sugar Creek: Life on the Illinois Prairie.* New Haven, Conn., 1986.

Faulkner, William. *The Hamlet: A Novel of the Snopes Family.* New York, 1991.

Faust, Drew Gilpin. "Altars of Sacrifice: Confederate Women and the Narratives of War." *Journal of American History* 76 (March 1990): 1200–1228.

———. *The Creation of Confederate Nationalism: Ideology and Identity in the Civil War South.* Baton Rouge, La., 1988.

Fields, Barbara Jeanne. "The Advent of Capitalist Agriculture: The New South in a Bourgeois World." In *Essays on the Postbellum Southern Economy,* edited by Thavolia Glymph and John J. Kushma, 48–72. College Station, Tex., 1985.

———. "Ideology and Race in American History." In *Region, Race, and Reconstruction: Essays in Honor of C. Vann Woodward,* edited by J. Morgan Kousser and James M. McPherson, 143–77. New York, 1982.

———. "The Nineteenth-Century American South: History and Theory." *Plantation Society* 2 (April 1983): 7–27.

———. "Slavery, Race, and Ideology in the United States of America." *New Left Review* 181 (1990): 95–118.

Finkelman, Paul. *An Imperfect Union: Slavery, Federalism, and Comity.* Chapel Hill, N.C., 1981.

Fishlow, Albert. *American Railroads and the Transformation of the Antebellum Economy.* Cambridge, Mass., 1965.

Fite, Gilbert C. *Cotton Fields No More: Southern Agriculture, 1865–1980.* Lexington, Ky., 1984.

Fitzgerald, Michael W. "Radical Republicanism and the White Yeomanry during Alabama Reconstruction, 1865–1868." *Journal of Southern History* 54 (November 1988): 565–96.

———. "'To Give Our Votes to the Party': Black Political Agitation and Agricultural Change in Alabama, 1865–1870." *Journal of American History* 76 (September 1989): 489–505.

Flanigan, Daniel. "Criminal Procedure in Slave Trials in the Antebellum South." *Journal of Southern History* 40 (November 1977): 537–64.

Flynn, Charles L., Jr. *White Land, Black Labor: Caste and Class in Late Nineteenth-Century Georgia*. Baton Rouge, La., 1983.

Fogel, Robert William. *Railroads and American Economic Growth: Essays in Econometric History*. Baltimore, 1964.

Fogel, Robert William, and Stanley Engerman. *Time on the Cross: The Economics of American Negro Slavery*. New York, 1974.

Foner, Eric. *Free Soil, Free Labor, Free Men: The Ideology of the Republican Party before the Civil War*. New York, 1970.

——. *Nothing but Freedom: Emancipation and Its Legacy*. Baton Rouge, La., 1983.

——. *Politics and Ideology in the Age of the Civil War*. New York, 1980.

——. *Reconstruction: America's Unfinished Revolution, 1863–1877*. New York, 1988.

Ford, Lacy K. *Origins of Southern Radicalism: The South Carolina Upcountry, 1800–1860*. New York, 1988.

——. "Rednecks and Merchants: Economic Development and Social Tensions in the South Carolina Upcountry, 1865–1900." *Journal of American History* 71 (September 1984): 294–318.

Forgacs, David. *An Antonio Gramsci Reader: Selected Writings, 1916–1935*. New York, 1988.

Formwalt, Lee W. "Antebellum Planter Persistence: Southwest Georgia—A Case Study." *Plantation Society* 1 (October 1981): 410–29.

——. "The Camilla Massacre of 1868: Racial Violence as Political Propaganda." *Georgia Historical Quarterly* 71 (Fall 1987): 399–425.

Fox-Genovese, Elizabeth. *Within the Plantation Household: Black and White Women of the Old South*. Chapel Hill, N.C., 1988.

Fox-Genovese, Elizabeth, and Eugene D. Genovese. *Fruits of Merchant Capital: Slavery and Bourgeois Property in the Rise and Expansion of Capitalism*. New York, 1983.

Frank, André Gunder. "The Development of Underdevelopment." In *Dependence and Underdevelopment: Latin America's Political Economy*, edited by James D. Cockcroft, André Gunder Frank, and Dale L. Johnson, 3–17. New York, 1972.

Frank, John Paul. *Lincoln as a Lawyer*. Urbana, Ill., 1961.

Freehling, William W., and Craig M. Simpson, eds. *Secession Debated: Georgia's Showdown in 1860*. New York, 1992.

Friedman, Jean E. *The Enclosed Garden: Women and Community in the Evangelical South, 1830–1900*. Chapel Hill, N.C., 1985.

Friedman, Lawrence M. *A History of American Law*. New York, 1973.

——. "Opening the Time Capsule: A Progress Report on Studies of Courts over Time." *Law and Society Review* 24 (April 1990): 229–40.

Galbraith, John Kenneth. *The Anatomy of Power*. Boston, 1983.

Garrison, Ellen Barrier. "Old South or New?: Georgia and the Constitution of 1877." Ph.D. diss., Stanford University, 1981.

Geertz, Clifford. *The Interpretation of Cultures*. New York, 1973.

Genovese, Eugene D. *The Political Economy of Slavery: Studies in the Economy and Society of the Slave South.* Middletown, Conn., 1989.

——. *Roll, Jordan, Roll: The World the Slaves Made.* New York, 1976.

——. *The Southern Tradition: The Achievement and Limitations of an American Conservatism.* Cambridge, Mass., 1994.

Gerber, Rudolph J. "Of Lawyers and Lawsuits." *National Forum* 71 (Fall 1991): 31–35.

Gillette, William. *Retreat from Reconstruction, 1869–1879.* Baton Rouge, La., 1979.

Gitlin, Todd. "Postmodernism." *Dissent,* Winter 1989, 100–108.

Glymph, Thavolia. "Freedpeople and Ex-Masters: Shaping a New Order in the Postbellum South, 1865–1868." In *Essays on the Postbellum Southern Economy,* edited by Thavolia Glymph and John J. Kushma, 48–72. College Station, Tex., 1985.

Glymph, Thavolia, and John J. Kushma, eds. *Essays on the Postbellum Southern Economy.* College Station, Tex., 1985.

Goetchius, Henry R. "Litigation in Georgia during the Reconstruction Period." *Proceedings of the Fourteenth Annual Session of the Georgia Bar Association.* Atlanta, 1898.

Goodrich, Peter. "Law and Language: An Historical and Critical Introduction." *Journal of Law and Society* 11 (Spring 1984): 173–206.

Grice, Warren. *The Georgia Bench and Bar: The Development of Georgia's Judicial System.* 2 vols. Macon, Ga., 1931.

Griffin, Richard W. "The Textile Industry in Greene County, Georgia, before 1860." *Georgia Historical Quarterly* 48 (March 1964): 81–84.

Gutman, Herbert G. *The Black Family in Slavery and Freedom, 1750 to 1925.* New York, 1976.

Habermas, Jürgen. *Reason and Rationalization of Society.* Vol. 1 of *Communicative Action.* Boston, 1984.

Hahn, Steven. "Class and State in Postemancipation Societies: Southern Planters in Comparative Perspective." *American Historical Review* 95 (February 1990): 75–98.

——. "A Response: Common Cents or Historical Sense?." *Journal of Southern History* 59 (May 1993): 243–58.

——. *The Roots of Southern Populism: Yeomen Farmers and the Transformation of the Georgia Upcountry, 1850–1890.* New York, 1983.

Hall, Kermit L. *The Magic Mirror: Law in American History.* New York, 1989.

——, ed. *Race Relations and the Law.* New York, 1987.

Hall, Kermit L., and James W. Ely Jr., eds. *An Uncertain Tradition: Constitutionalism and the History of the South.* Athens, Ga., 1989.

Harris, J. William. "The Organization of Work on a Yeoman Slaveholder's Farm." *Agricultural History* 64 (Winter 1990): 39–52.

——. *Plain Folk and Gentry in a Slave Society: White Liberty and Black Slavery in Augusta's Hinterlands.* Middletown, Conn., 1985.

————. "Portrait of a Small Slaveholder: The Journal of Benton Miller." *Georgia Historical Quarterly* 74 (Spring 1990): 1–19.

Hart, John Fraser. "The Role of the Plantation in Southern Agriculture." *Proceedings: Tall Timbers Ecology and Management Conference* 16 (February 1979): 1–19.

Henderson, Lillian. *Roster of the Confederate Soldiers of Georgia, 1861–1865.* 6 vols. Hapeville, Ga., 1960.

Hindus, Michael Stephen. "Black Justice under White Law: Criminal Prosecution of Blacks in Antebellum South Carolina." *Journal of American History* 63 (December 1976): 575–99.

————. *Prison and Plantation: Crime, Justice, and Authority in Massachusetts and South Carolina, 1767–1878.* Chapel Hill, N.C., 1980.

Hirst, Paul. *On Law and Ideology.* Atlantic Highlands, N.J., 1979.

History of the Baptist Denomination in Georgia. Atlanta, 1976.

Hobsbawm, E. J. *The Age of Capital, 1848–1875.* New York, 1979.

————. *The Age of Empire, 1875–1914.* New York, 1987.

Hobson, Wayne K. "The American Legal Profession and the Organizational Society, 1870–1930." Ph.D. diss., California State University, Fullerton, 1986.

Hodler, Thomas W., and Howard A. Schretter. *The Atlas of Georgia.* Athens, Ga., 1986.

Holifield, E. Brooks. *The Gentlemen Theologians: American Theology in Southern Culture, 1795–1860.* Durham, N.C., 1978.

Holmes, William F. "Moonshining and Collective Violence: Georgia, 1889–1895." *Journal of American History* 67 (December 1980): 589–611.

Holt, Sharon Ann. "Making Freedom Pay: Freedpeople Working for Themselves, North Carolina, 1865–1900." *Journal of Southern History* 60 (May 1994): 229–62.

Horwitz, Morton J. *The Transformation of American Law, 1780–1860.* Cambridge, Mass., 1977.

————. *The Transformation of American Law, 1870–1960: The Crisis of Legal Orthodoxy.* New York, 1992.

Huffman, Frank Jackson, Jr. "Old South, New South: Continuity and Change in a Georgia County, 1850–1880." Ph.D. diss., Yale University, 1974.

Hunter, Floyd. *Community Power Structures.* Chapel Hill, N.C., 1953.

Hurst, James Willard. *The Growth of American Law: The Law Makers.* Madison, Wis., 1950.

————. *Law and the Conditions of Freedom in the Nineteenth-Century United States.* Madison, Wis., 1956.

Hyman, Michael R. "Taxation, Public Policy, and Political Dissent: Yeoman Disaffection in the Post-Reconstruction Lower South." *Journal of Southern History* 55 (February 1989): 49–76.

Inscoe, John C., ed. *Georgia in Black and White: Explorations in the Race Relations of a Southern State, 1865–1950.* Athens, Ga., 1994.

Irwin, James R. "Farmers and Laborers: A Note on Black Occupations in the Postbellum South." *Agricultural History* 64 (Winter 1990): 53–60.

Jaynes, Gerald David. *Branches without Roots: Genesis of the Black Working Class in the American South, 1862–1882.* New York, 1986.

Jenkins, William Sumner. *Pro-Slavery Thought in the Old South.* Chapel Hill, N.C., 1935.

Johnson, Michael P. *Toward a Patriarchal Republic: The Secession of Georgia.* Baton Rouge, La., 1977.

Jones, Charles C., Jr., and Salem Dutcher. *Memorial History of Augusta, Georgia.* Syracuse, N.Y., 1890.

Kairys, David, ed. *The Politics of Law: A Progressive Critique.* New York, 1982.

Kantor, Shawn Everett, and J. Morgan Kousser. "Common Sense or Commonwealth?: The Fence Law and Institutional Change in the Postbellum South." *Journal of Southern History* 59 (May 1993): 201–42.

Kelman, Mark. *A Guide to Critical Legal Studies.* Cambridge, Mass., 1987.

Kenzer, Robert C. *Kinship and Neighborhood in a Southern Community: Orange County, North Carolina, 1849–1881.* Knoxville, Tenn., 1987.

King, Spencer B. *Sound of Drums.* Macon, Ga., 1984.

Kirby, Jack Temple. "The Southern Exodus, 1910–1960: A Primer for Historians." *Journal of Southern History* 49 (November 1983): 585–600.

Klein, Herbert S. *African Slavery in Latin America and the Caribbean.* New York, 1986.

Kousser, J. Morgan, and James M. McPherson, eds. *Region, Race, and Reconstruction: Essays in Honor of C. Vann Woodward.* New York, 1982.

Kutler, Stanley I. *Judicial Power and Reconstruction Politics.* Chicago, 1968.

Lanza, Michael L. *Agrarianism and Reconstruction Politics: The Southern Homestead Act.* Baton Rouge, La., 1990.

Lears, T. J. Jackson. "The Concept of Cultural Hegemony: Problems and Possibilities." *American Historical Review* 90 (June 1985): 567–93.

Levinson, Sanford. "On Critical Legal Studies." *Dissent,* Summer 1989, 360–65.

Lewis, Henry T. "Is Lynch Law Due to Defects in the Criminal Law, or Its Administration," *Proceedings of the Fourteenth Annual Session of the Georgia Bar Association.* Atlanta, 1898.

Link, William A. *The Paradox of Southern Progressivism, 1880–1930.* Chapel Hill, N.C., 1992.

Litwack, Leon F. *Been in the Storm So Long: The Aftermath of Slavery.* New York, 1979.

Lloyd, Christopher. "The Methodologies of Social History: A Critical Survey and Defense of Structurism." *History and Theory* 30 (May 1991): 180–219.

Lumpkin, Katharine Du Pre. *The Making of a Southerner.* New York, 1947.

Luraghi, Raimondo. *The Rise and Fall of the Plantation South.* New York, 1978.

McCloskey, Donald N. "History, Differential Equations, and the Problem of Narration." *History and Theory* 30 (February 1991): 21–36.

McFeely, William S. *Frederick Douglass.* New York, 1991.

——. *Grant: A Biography*. New York, 1981.

——. *Yankee Stepfather: General O. O. Howard and the Freedmen*. New York, 1968.

McGuire, Peter S. "The Railroads of Georgia, 1860–1880." *Georgia Historical Quarterly* 16 (September 1932): 179–213.

McKenzie, Robert Tracy. "Freedmen and the Soil in the Upper South: The Reorganization of Tennessee Agriculture, 1865–1880." *Journal of Southern History* 59 (February 1993): 63–82.

McKinney, John C., and Edgar T. Thompson, *The South in Continuity and Change*. Durham, N.C., 1965.

McPherson, James M. *Battle Cry of Freedom: The Era of the Civil War*. New York, 1988.

Magdol, Edward A. *A Right to the Land: Essays on the Freedmen's Community*. Westport, Conn., 1977.

Malone, Ann Patton. "Piney Woods Farmers of South Georgia, 1850–1900: Jeffersonian Yeomen in an Age of Expanding Commercialism." *Agricultural History* 60 (Fall 1986): 51–84.

Mandle, Jay R. "The Plantation Economy Mode of Production in the Postbellum South." *Plantation Society* 2 (May 1989): 279–94.

Marable, Manning. "The Politics of Black Land Tenure, 1877–1915." *Agricultural History* 53 (January 1979): 142–52.

Matthews, John M. "Negro Republicans in the Reconstruction of Georgia." *Georgia Historical Quarterly* 60 (Summer 1976): 145–64.

Milovanovic, Dragan. *A Primer in the Sociology of Law*. New York, 1988.

Mohr, Clarence L. *On the Threshold of Freedom: Masters and Slaves in Civil War Georgia*. Athens, Ga., 1986.

Montgomery, Horace. *Cracker Parties*. Baton Rouge, La., 1950.

Moore, Barrington, Jr. *Social Origins of Dictatorship and Democracy: Lord and Peasant in the Making of the Modern World*. Boston, 1966.

Moore, James Tice. "Redeemers Reconsidered: Change and Continuity in the Democratic South, 1870–1900." *Journal of Southern History* 44 (August 1978): 357–78.

Moore, Winfred B., Jr., and Joseph F. Tripp. *Looking South: Chapters in the Story of an American Region*. New York, 1989.

Morris, Christopher. *Becoming Southern: The Evolution of a Way of Life, Warren County and Vicksburg, Mississippi, 1770–1880*. New York, 1995.

Morrison, Toni. *Beloved: A Novel*. New York, 1987

Munger, Frank. "Trial Courts and Social Change: The Evolution of a Field of Study." *Law and Society Review* 24 (April 1990): 217–26.

Newby, I. A. *Plain Folk in the New South: Social Change and Cultural Persistence, 1880–1915*. Baton Rouge, La., 1989.

Nieman, Donald G. "The Language of Liberation: African-Americans and Equalitarian Constitutionalism, 1830–1950." In *The Constitution, Law, and American Life: Critical Aspects of the Nineteenth-Century Experience*, edited by Donald G. Nieman, 67–90. Athens, Ga., 1992.

———. *Promises to Keep: African-Americans and the Constitutional Order, 1776 to the Present.* New York, 1991.

———. *To Set the Law in Motion: The Freedmen's Bureau and the Legal Rights of Blacks, 1865–1868.* Millwood, N.Y., 1979.

———, ed. *The Constitution, Law, and American Life: Critical Aspects of the Nineteenth-Century Experience.* Athens, Ga., 1992.

———. *The Day of the Jubilee: The Civil War Experience of Black Southerners.* New York, 1994.

Norman, Andrew P. "Telling It Like It Was: Historical Narratives on Their Own Terms." *History and Theory* 30 (May 1991): 119–35.

Northen, William J. *Men of Mark in Georgia.* 9 vols. Atlanta, 1907–12.

Oakes, James. "A Failure of Vision: The Collapse of the Freedmen's Bureau Courts." *Civil War History* 25 (March 1979): 66–76.

———. *Slavery and Freedom: An Interpretation of the Old South.* New York, 1990.

Oates, Stephen B. *To Purge the Land with Blood: A Biography of John Brown.* New York, 1970.

O'Brien, Gail Williams. *The Legal Fraternity and the Making of a New South Community, 1848–1882.* Athens, Ga., 1986.

Orser, Charles F., Jr. *The Material Basis of the Postbellum Tenant Plantation: Historical Archaeology in the South Carolina Piedmont.* Athens, Ga., 1988.

Otto, John Solomon. "Southern 'Plain Folk' Agriculture: A Reconsideration." *Plantation Society* 2 (April 1983): 29–36.

Oubre, Claude F. *Forty Acres and a Mule: The Freedmen's Bureau and Black Land Ownership.* Baton Rouge, La., 1978.

Owens, Harry P., and James J. Cooke, eds. *The Old South in the Crucible of War.* Jackson, Miss., 1983.

Owsley, Frank L. *Plain Folk of the Old South.* Baton Rouge, La., 1949.

Paludan, Phillip Shaw. *A People's Contest: The Union and the Civil War, 1861–1865.* New York, 1988.

Perman, Michael. *The Road to Redemption: Southern Politics, 1869–1879.* Chapel Hill, N.C., 1984.

Phillips, Ulrich B. *American Negro Slavery: A Survey of the Supply, Employment and Control of Negro Labor as Determined by the Plantation Regime.* 1918. Reprint, Baton Rouge, La., 1990.

———. *Georgia and State Rights.* Macon, Ga., 1984.

———. *A History of Transportation in the Eastern Cotton Belt to 1860.* New York, 1908.

———. *Life and Labor in the Old South.* Boston, 1929.

Polanyi, Karl. *The Great Transformation: The Political and Economic Origins of Our Time.* Boston, 1944.

Poster, Mark. "Foucault and History." *Social Research* 49 (Summer 1982): 116–42.

Quinney, Richard. "The Ideology of Law: Notes for a Radical Alternative to Legal Oppression." In *The Sociology of Law: A Conflict Perspective*, edited by Charles F. Reasons and Robert M. Rich, 39–71. Toronto, 1978.

Rable, George C. *But There Was No Peace: The Role of Violence in the Politics of Reconstruction*. Athens, Ga., 1984.

———. *Civil Wars: Women and the Crisis of Southern Nationalism*. Urbana, Ill., 1989.

Ragsdale, B. D. *Mercer University*. Vol. 1 of *Story of Georgia's Baptists*. Atlanta, 1932.

Range, Willard. *A Century of Georgia Agriculture, 1850–1950*. Athens, Ga., 1954.

Ransom, Roger L., and Richard Sutch. "Capitalists without Capital: The Burden of Slavery and the Impact of Reconstruction." *Agricultural History* 63 (Fall 1988): 133–60.

———. *One Kind of Freedom: The Economic Consequences of Emancipation*. New York, 1977.

Raper, Arthur F. *Preface to Peasantry*. Chapel Hill, N.C., 1936.

———. *Tenants of the Almighty*. New York, 1943.

Rapport, Sara. "The Freedmen's Bureau as a Legal Agent for Black Men and Women in Georgia: 1865–1868." *Georgia Historical Quarterly* 73 (Spring 1989): 26–53.

Reasons, Charles E., and Robert M. Rich, eds. *The Sociology of Law: A Conflict Perspective*. Toronto, 1978.

Redkey, Edwin S., ed. *Respect Black: The Writings and Speeches of Henry Mc-Neal Turner*. New York, 1971.

Reed, John C. *The Brother's War*. New York, 1906.

Reidy, Joseph P. *From Slavery to Agrarian Capitalism in the Cotton Plantation South: Central Georgia, 1800–1880*. Chapel Hill, N.C., 1992.

———. "Masters and Slaves, Planters and Freedmen: The Transition from Slavery to Freedom in Central Georgia, 1820–1880." Ph.D. diss., Northern Illinois University, 1982.

Reisch, George A. "Chaos, History, and Narrative." *History and Theory* 30 (February 1991): 1–20.

Rice, Thaddeus Brockett, and Carolyn White Williams. *History of Greene County, Georgia*. Spartanburg, S.C., 1961.

Richardson, Joe M. *Christian Reconstruction: The American Missionary Association and Southern Blacks, 1861–1890*. Athens, Ga., 1986.

Roark, James L. *Masters without Slaves: Southern Planters in the Civil War and Reconstruction*. New York, 1977.

Roberts, Derrell. "Joseph E. Brown and the Convict Lease System." *Georgia Historical Quarterly* 44 (June 1960): 399–410.

———. "Joseph E. Brown and His Georgia Mines." *Georgia Historical Quarterly* 52 (September 1968): 284–92.

Robertson, James I., Jr., ed. *The Diary of Dolly Lunt Burge*. Athens, Ga., 1962.

Rose, Willie Lee. *Rehearsal for Reconstruction: The Port Royal Experiment*. New York, 1964.

Rothenberg, Winifred Barr. *From Market-Places to a Market Economy: The Transformation of Rural Massachusetts, 1750–1850*. Chicago, 1992.

Roxborough, Ian. *Theories of Underdevelopment*. Atlantic Highlands, N.J., 1979.

Royster, Charles. *The Destructive War: William Tecumseh Sherman, Stonewall Jackson, and the Americans*. New York, 1991.

Ruggles, Steven, and Russell R. Menard. "A Public Use Sample of the 1880 U.S. Census of Population." *Historical Methods* 23 (Summer 1990): 104–15.

Russ, William A., Jr. "Radical Disfranchisement in Georgia, 1867–71." *Georgia Historical Quarterly* 19 (September 1935): 175–209.

Russell, Bertrand. *Power: The Role of Man's Will to Power in the World's Economic and Political Affairs*. New York, 1938.

Russell, James Michael. *Atlanta, 1847–1890: City Building in the Old South and the New*. Baton Rouge, La., 1988.

Rutman, Darrett B., and Anita H. Rutman. *Small Worlds, Large Questions: Explorations in Early American Social History, 1600–1850*. Charlottesville, Va., 1994.

Sampford, Charles. *The Disorder of Law: A Critique of Legal Theory*. London, 1989.

Sasson, Anne Showstak. *Approaches to Gramsci*. London, 1982.

Saye, Albert Berry. *A Constitutional History of Georgia, 1732–1945*. Athens, Ga., 1948.

Schafer, Judith Kelleher. *Slavery, the Civil Law, and the Supreme Court of Louisiana*. Baton Rouge, La., 1994.

Scheiber, Harry N. "Instrumentalism and Property Rights: A Reconsideration of American 'Styles of Judicial Reasoning' in the Nineteenth Century." *Wisconsin Law Review*, no. 1 (1975): 1–18.

Schott, Thomas E. *Alexander H. Stephens of Georgia: A Biography*. Baton Rouge, La., 1988.

Schultz, Mark R. "Interracial Kinship Ties and the Emergence of a Rural Black Middle Class: Hancock County, Georgia, 1865–1920." In *Georgia in Black and White: Explorations in the Race Relations of a Southern State, 1865–1950*, edited by John C. Inscoe, 141–72. Athens, Ga., 1994.

Schweikart, Larry. "Southern Banks and Economic Growth in the Antebellum Period: A Reassessment." *Journal of Southern History* 53 (February 1987): 19–36.

Scott, Anne Firor. *The Southern Lady: From Pedestal to Politics, 1830–1930*. Chicago, 1970.

Scott, Carole E. "Coping with Inflation: Atlanta, 1860–1865." *Georgia Historical Quarterly* 69 (Winter 1985): 536–56.

Scott, Paul, ed. "On the Road to the Sea: Shannon's Scouts, Texas' Forgotten Thirty." *Civil War Times* 21 (January 1983): 26–29.

Sellers, Charles. *The Market Revolution: Jacksonian America, 1815–1846*. New York, 1991.

Sellers, Frank M., and Samuel E. Smith. *American Percussion Revolvers*. Ottawa, Ont., 1971.

Shaw, Barton C. *The Wool Hat Boys: Georgia's Populist Party*. Baton Rouge, La., 1984.

Shivers, Forrest. *The Land Between: A History of Hancock County, Georgia to 1940*. Spartanburg, S.C., 1990.

Shklar, Judith N. *Legalism: Law, Morals, and Political Trials*. Cambridge, Mass., 1964.

Shore, Laurence. *Southern Capitalists: The Ideological Leadership of an Elite, 1832–1885*. Chapel Hill, N.C., 1986.

Smith, Adam. *An Inquiry into the Nature and Causes of the Wealth of Nations*. New York, 1937.

Smith, Albert C. "Down Freedom's Road: The Contours of Race, Class, and Property Crime in Black Belt Georgia, 1866–1910." Ph.D. diss., University of Georgia, 1982.

———. "'Southern Violence' Reconsidered: Arson as Protest in Black-Belt Georgia, 1865–1910." *Journal of Southern History* 51 (November 1985): 527–64.

Smith, Florie Carter. *The History of Oglethorpe County, Georgia*. Washington, Ga., 1970.

Smith, Warren I. "The Farm Journal of John Horry Dent." *Georgia Historical Quarterly* 42 (March 1958): 44–53.

Speak, David M. *Living Law: The Transformation of American Jurisprudence in the Early Twentieth Century*. New York, 1987.

Stanley, Amy Dru. "Beggars Can't Be Choosers: Compulsion and Contract in Postbellum America." *Journal of American History* 78 (March 1992): 1265–93.

Starr, June, and Jane F. Collier, eds. *History and Power in the Study of Law: New Directions in Legal Anthropology*. Ithaca, N.Y., 1989.

Stover, John F. "Northern Financial Interests in Southern Railroads, 1865–1900." *Georgia Historical Quarterly* 39 (September 1955): 205–20.

Sugarman, David, ed. *Legality, Ideology, and the State*. London, 1983.

Taylor, A. Elizabeth. "The Abolition of the Convict Lease System in Georgia." *Georgia Historical Quarterly* 28 (September 1942): 273–87.

———. "The Origin and Development of the Convict Lease System in Georgia." *Georgia Historical Quarterly* 26 (June 1942): 113–28.

Taylor, Arthur Reed. "From the Ashes: Atlanta during Reconstruction, 1865–1876." Ph.D. diss., Emory University, 1973.

Thomas, Emory M. *The Confederate Nation, 1861–1865*. New York, 1979.

Thompson, C. Mildred. *Reconstruction in Georgia: Economic, Social, Political, 1865–1872*. New York, 1915.

Thompson, E. P. *The Making of the English Working Class*. New York, 1963.

———. *Whigs and Hunters: The Origins of the Black Act*. New York, 1975.

Tischendorf, Alfred. "British Enterprise in Georgia, 1865–1907." *Georgia Historical Quarterly* 42 (June 1958): 170–75.

Todd, Richard C. *Confederate Finance*. Athens, Ga., 1954.

Topolski, Jerzy. "Towards an Integrated Model of Historical Explanation." *History and Theory* 30 (October 1991): 324–38.

Touraine, Alain. "The Idea of Revolution." *Theory, Culture, and Society* 7 (June 1990): 121–42.

Trelease, Allen W. *White Terror: The Ku Klux Klan Conspiracy and Southern Reconstruction*. New York, 1971.

Tushnet, Mark. *The American Law of Slavery, 1820–1860: Considerations of Humanity and Interest*. Princeton, N.J., 1981.

Unger, Roberto Mangaberia. *The Critical Legal Studies Movement*. Cambridge, Mass., 1982.

Vinovskis, Maris A. "Have Social Historians Lost the Civil War?: Some Preliminary Demographic Speculations." *Journal of American History* 76 (June 1989): 34–58.

Waddell, James D. *Biographical Sketch of Linton Stephens*. Atlanta, 1877.

Wallenstein, Peter. "Prelude to Southern Progressivism: Social Policy in Bourbon Georgia." In *Developing Dixie: Modernization in a Traditional Society*, edited by Winfred B. Moore Jr., Joseph F. Tripp, and Lyon G. Tyler Jr., 137–48. New York, 1988.

Wallerstein, Immanuel. *The Capitalist World Economy*. New York, 1979.

———. "Culture as the Ideological Battleground of the Modern World-System." *Theory, Culture, and Society* 7 (June 1990): 31–55.

———. *Historical Capitalism*. London, 1983.

———. *The Modern World-System: Capitalist Agriculture and the Origins of the European World-Economy in the Sixteenth Century*. New York, 1975.

———. *The Modern World-System III: The Second Era of Great Expansion of the Capitalist World-Economy, 1730–1840*. New York, 1989.

Ward, Judson Clements, Jr. "Georgia under the Bourbon Democrats, 1872–1898." Ph.D. diss., University of North Carolina at Chapel Hill, 1947.

Watson, Alan. *Society and Legal Change*. Edinburgh, 1977.

Wayne, Michael. "An Old South Morality Play: Reconsidering the Social Underpinnings of the Proslavery Ideology." *Journal of American History* 77 (December 1990): 838–63.

———. *The Reshaping of Plantation Society: The Natchez District, 1860–1880*. Baton Rouge, La., 1983.

Weber, Max. *Law in Economy and Society*. Cambridge, Mass., 1954.

———. *The Protestant Ethic and the Spirit of Capitalism*. New York, 1958.

Wetherington, Mark V. *The New South Comes to Wiregrass Georgia, 1860–1910*. Knoxville, Tenn., 1994.

Wiebe, Robert H. *The Search for Order, 1877–1920*. New York, 1967.

Wiener, Jonathan M. "Class Structure and Economic Development in the American South, 1865–1955." *American Historical Review* 84 (October 1979): 970–1006.

———. *Social Origins of the New South: Alabama, 1860–1885*. Baton Rouge, La., 1978.

Wight, Willard E. "Negroes in the Georgia Legislature: The Case of F. H. Fyall of Macon County." *Georgia Historical Quarterly* 44 (January 1960): 85–97.

Williams, William Appleman. *The Contours of American History*. New York, 1988.

Williamson, Joel. *After Slavery: The Negro in South Carolina during Reconstruction, 1861–1877*. Chapel Hill, N.C., 1965.

Wills, Brian Steel. *A Battle from the Start: The Life of Nathan Bedford Forrest*. New York, 1992.

Winters, Donald L. "Postbellum Reorganization of Southern Agriculture: The Economics of Sharecropping in Tennessee." *Agricultural History* 62 (Winter 1988): 1–19.

Wood, Ellen Meiksins. "The Politics of Theory and the Concept of Class: E. P. Thompson and His Critics." *Studies in Political Economy* 9 (Fall 1982): 45–75.

Wood, Gordon S. *The Radicalism of the American Revolution*. New York, 1992.

Woodman, Harold D. "How New Was the New South?." *Agricultural History* 58 (Fall 1984): 529–45.

———. *King Cotton and His Retainers: Financing and Marketing the Cotton Crop of the South, 1800–1925*. Lexington, Ky., 1968.

———. *New South–New Law: The Legal Foundations of Credit and Labor Relations in the Postbellum Agricultural South*. Baton Rouge, La., 1995.

———. "Postbellum Social Change and Its Effects on Marketing the South's Cotton Crop." *Agricultural History* 56 (January 1982): 215–30.

———. "Post–Civil War Southern Agriculture and the Law." *Agricultural History* 53 (January 1979): 319–37.

———. "The Reconstruction of the Cotton Plantation in the New South." In *Essays on the Postbellum Southern Economy*, edited by Thavolia Glymph and John J. Kushma, 94–119. College Station, Tex., 1985.

———. "Sequel to Slavery: The New History Views the Postbellum South." *Journal of Southern History* 43 (November 1977): 523–54.

Woodward, C. Vann. "Bourbonism in Georgia." *North Carolina Historical Review* 16 (1939): 23–35.

———. *Origins of the New South, 1877–1913*. Baton Rouge, La., 1951.

———. *Reunion and Reaction: The Compromise of 1877 and the End of Reconstruction*. New York, 1966.

———. *The Strange Career of Jim Crow*. New York, 1974.

———. *Tom Watson: Agrarian Rebel*. Savannah, Ga., 1973.

Wooster, Ralph. "The Georgia Secession Convention." *Georgia Historical Quarterly* 40 (March 1956): 21–55.

———. *The People in Power: Courthouse and Statehouse in the Lower South, 1850–1860*. Knoxville, Tenn., 1969.

Wright, Gavin. *Old South, New South: Revolutions in the Southern Economy since the Civil War*. New York, 1986.

———. *The Political Economy of the Cotton South: Households, Markets, and Wealth in the Nineteenth Century*. New York, 1978.

Wrong, Dennis. *Power: Its Forms, Bases, and Uses.* Oxford, 1979.
Wyatt-Brown, Bertram. *Southern Honor: Ethics and Behavior in the Old South.* New York, 1982.
Wynne, Lewis Nicholas. *The Continuity of Cotton: Planter Politics in Georgia, 1865–1892.* Macon, Ga., 1986.

Index